2

Cashing Out @ Full Value

...A novel/guide for 'boomers' selling the family business...

By: Michael P. Gendron

3

Table of Contents

4

Preface

Selling the family business is an emotional experience, often completed on short notice and without effective preparation. Family owned and/or middle-market company executives, often inexperienced in preparing a company for sale, sell a company at a discount when compared to one 'prepared for sale.' It requires at least 1-2 years to effectively prepare a company for sale – having the right people, ingrained processes, and a history of well-executed plans creates value.

The sale value of a company is not built exclusively on past performance, but value represents the acquiring company's estimate of worth, based on the company's future performance. Past performance reinforces the credibility of future earnings, but well-developed and proven business processes implemented by a highly qualified organization, successfully executing a business plan will define future value for a buyer.

The business plan – preferably a 3+ year strategic plan – considers Company strengths and weaknesses, and the competitive and macro business environment. The plan will define measurable deliverables, timelines and executive responsibilities.

This book is a novel that recognizes the emotional challenges felt by an entrepreneur who approaches retirement, but has no plan to successfully transition the business. The book represents a collection of tactics used to improve company performance. Using the processes outlined in the book, companies have grown by 20% or more annually in competitive markets that grew at less than 5%. Calculate the impact on company selling price of such stellar growth and determine the return on your investment if you *'prep for sale'* and improve your business processes and organization.

Analytical templates that can be used in any business to improve their performance are included for reference. Preparing a company for sale is not window-dressing, or 'putting lipstick on a pig,' but rather it is improving processes that will increase company performance to match strategic priorities.

Let the journey begin.

November 7, 2013 - "Introspection"

*Find an expert
*Listen - don't talk
*Budgets
*Cash Flows

City office towers gouged tears in the low storm clouds dumping monsoon-like rain across the region. The heavy rain-sleet mix coated the office window and blurred the cityscape as wind gusts tossed deck furnishings asunder... a fitting day to contemplate tomorrow. Not just Saturday, but the rest of tomorrows... whatever that means.

Time...faster than the speed of light and it feels like it. Now, grey hair and an extra 18 pounds ... my knees throb every afternoon after walking the shop floor. Where has the time gone?

The Company's first sale – the same year Nixon resigned and Gerry Ford bumped his head on Marine-1. For the past 37 years, I've bet the family future on this business, and …well it's just not as exciting as a few years ago. Janice and I launched the business in the garage – a real Horatio Alger – when the twins were about 6 months old. … No money but filled with enthusiasm and naiveté… rose-colored glasses named after our stupidity. First year sales of $11,451.18 left no profit, but we had a business. Such fools we were, not to realize that we couldn't be successful, and in spite of ourselves, we kept serving customers. Desperately lean years occasionally tainted the banner expansion years across the US and eventually into international markets. Our secret to success… never really identified, except that we served customers well and cared for our employees. Quality standards – impeccable. Service – *numero-uno* by any measure. Maybe that's *all* it takes.

The employees – many who have been here for more than 20 years; some more than 30 years – often worked like indentured servants. Six day weeks… seven day weeks… holidays… I've lost count of the number of Christmas holidays we've worked together. Yes, we paid them double – maybe triple time - but they sacrificed to make this place successful. Janice and I attended their weddings… in some cases their children's weddings. I'm godfather to the casting cell manager - Jonny K's - son. Employees' parents and children's funerals were emotionally wrenching. Janice was especially sensitive to their grieving moments – far more emotional – very personal - than other required essential activities.

Our customers – just like family. How many times have we extended collection terms when a few of them were cash flow challenged? Sales calls were really social meetings – business trip write-offs - just to pick up the next product order. The unnecessary travel? …Just to share gossip, have a cocktail and dinner, and jokingly criticize their golf skills.

Vendors? They were there when we needed them. A handshake in the mid-west – no contracts required. My word was more meaningful than a contract. When we extended sales territory to a national footprint, things changed a bit. When we sold internationally, banks, attorneys, and CPA's involved. Not all bad but certainly more complex.

We bought an airplane - a Mooney - in 1994, and moved up to the King-air in 2004. Private planes may seem a luxury to some, but three cities in a day can't be done on commercial flights. And the price of commercial flights – gimme-a-break! It's nice to have the King-air available when Janice and I visit the grandkids. So far, more than 1,500 hours in the left-seat of the planes.

We actually started to feel successful when 'The Gipper' ran the country – hard to believe… 1981. Strange how these things stick in your head…

Now, 37 years later, sales are $29.5 million and we're making 10% pretax… not so bad. The twins are grown up and in their own *careers*… the business thrives, but for the past few years, I'm not having much fun, and there is nobody to take over. Our little Jenny is an RN and stay-at-home mom with our two granddaughters, and 'sonny boy' Jerrod has a thriving dental practice. And I've got a business with no one to take over.

Janice's brother, Robert, occupies an office down the hall – no more than ballast in this ship. Wish he were more productive, but he's family. We discovered years ago that our best advantage was to sequester him in a secluded office in the back of the building… let him digest every article in the Wall Street Journal, and not disrupt our business. His two children – Chip and Janelle - I guess they have the millennial entitlement attitude. The only thing they do quickly is fetching the coffee. Sure, I'm to blame since I allowed it, but peace in the family was most important.

Damn – I hate these dark, early winter afternoons.   My wealth – anchored to the business. I kept reinvesting to grow the business and haven't diversified much. The guys at the club continuously chide me about my wealth…they tell me I could easily sell the business for "ten-times EBITDA" – whatever the hell EBITDA is. They never tell me *who* will buy it for 10X – but they always tap me for the round of drinks. No matter, since I always recoup the drinks through the skins game. Better yet, if I buy a few rounds before the golf, I always have enough winnings after 11 holes to buy them all dinner.

Joseph – kind of a quiet guy - often repeats "Ten-times EBITDA" at the end of every round. Is he BS'ing me, or does he really know what he's talking about?

Through the rain distorted window, a sole flash of lightening brightened the dark sky… 1-one thousandth…2-one thousandth…3-one thousand… the thunderous boom rippled the coffee that was cooling in the 1989-Master's Tournament coffee cup. That lightning strike's about a half-mile away.

A gentle knock on the door announced Cynthia's entrance. She took over as CFO about 3 years ago, after more than 7 years in the finance organization. "Hey boss – I've got the November numbers. Shall we talk?"

This is the only way to run a business. She always has the results by the 20th of every month. Perfection. The summary is so simple – I know exactly where we stand every month… to the penny. "Let's talk Cynthia."

12

Jackson Manufacturing

	2013	2012
Sales	26,511,123.14	25,491,464.56
Cost of sales	12,455,242.22	12,122,496.29
Gross Profit	14,055,880.92	13,368,968.27
%	53%	52%
SG&A		
Sales	6,886,987.14	5,998,987.52
Admin	3,232,884.33	3,121,433.25
Other	1,454,837.38	1,885,984.30
Total	11,574,708.85	11,006,405.07
Pretax Profit	2,481,172.07	2,362,563.20
After Tax Profit	1,240,586.04	1,181,281.60
Cash	1,288,676.39	990,343.28
Accounts Receivable	8,748,670.64	6,372,866.14
Accounts Payable	5,286,589.24	5,782,225.34

She thoroughly discusses every line on the statements. "Sales up by about a million dollars – the West Coast customer…gross profit is up – the sales increase - and cash in the bank beats last year. Receivables up about

$2 million - the European customer is a bit late, as usual. No major issues boss. We'll get the money eventually... just takes a bit of time... maybe need to offer a discount for some minor things..."

Cynthia never hassles me about unnecessary budgets or strategy – great CFO - she tells me what I need to know, and she keeps the banks happy.

We must be paying 'Payables' a bit faster than earlier years, but Cynthia knows what she's doing.

"Great job, Cynthia. I'd be lost without you."

Heck, I don't even need to read all those banking documents anymore, since Cynthia and Keith take care of everything. "Sign here," works every time. I learned many years ago that Keith was *the man.* We started working with Keith when he passed the bar exam in 2001. His rates were low, and he was a bona fide, licensed attorney. ... Would have been foolish to pay exorbitant rates charged by a regional firm. I trust him. He would never lead me astray or allow me to get in a legal mess.

So, if I'm so comfortable with the business, why is it that each month I'm tempted to share the financials with Joseph – Mr. Know-It-All 10x EBITDA at the club - to get his insight? Why my uneasiness?

The club Board meeting is tomorrow... yes, I'll call Joseph and have a quick discussion.

Easing the mobile phone from his pocket, he punched up the *golf buds*, 'favorite # 6' – Joseph Dozier. "Hey Joseph, Don Janus here. You gonna' attend the Board meeting tomorrow?" …A brief pause…"Yeah, I'll be there - but I wanted to catch you for a few minutes after the meeting. … Wanted to talk about EBITDA and a few other financial things. You game? OK? Great – see you at 2:30."

Meeting set … now I've opened Pandora's box and will have to deal with *it*.

Don poured the temperate bitter coffee from his mug and decided to tour the factory. He enjoyed strolling the plant, feeling the rhythm of the business. At frequent stops, he touched the heavy machines to feel the pulsing power as titanium DG-4's were precision laser-cut, polished and assembled within the snakelike conveyor assembly line process. These Talus and Navicular replacement bones – "Knuckles" as we say informally - were the only FDA approved *bones* available on the market. The DG-1, 2, and 3 prototypes, developed over five years, were key to the success of the DG-4 approved 2006 – can it really be 6 years ago? The "Knuckles" segment was far too small for J&J when we launched a few years ago. Such great fortune that these two bones often failed in septuagenarian joggers, and that boomer population has exploded in the last 5 years.

As Don touched the keypad on the digital lathe, he mused about the feel of that light machine oil on his

fingertips. When times were tough that silky touch
soothed his anxiety better than a Valium. Walking the
plant floor among the pallets and mounded bins of raw
material and WIP satisfied his lust for tangible security…
substance … a feeling of wealth confirmed when he
could touch those *things* that they converted to product.

Don wandered through the plant reminiscing about so
many wonderful years.

November 9 2013 - Meet the Specialist

```
*Find an expert
*Listen - don't talk
*Budgets
*Cash Flows
```

On Saturday, Don awakened at 5:30 AM to drive to LA Fitness for his daily workout. Winter mornings, so dark and cold, made spring a welcome season – but spring arrives in a distant 21 weeks. He noticed the light dusting of fresh powder that would blow off the SUV once he accelerated. He powered down the passenger and driver side windows to see oncoming traffic, activated front and rear wipers to be startled by the rattling blades across the chunks of ice on the glass. Defrosters engaged, he would wait for a few minutes to melt the ice.

Stan Getz' mellow saxophone tunes warmed the car's interior despite the outside 4° wind chill. Don activated his iPhone and scanned 'city favorite' temperatures: Paris- 43°; Naples, Italy - 67°; Jacksonville, Fl - 64°. "So why am I living in Cincinnati, Oh?" he mused.

The uneventful drive on ice-covered roads surrendered his attention to distracted driving, and thoughts about 'tomorrow' – a frequent topic these days. The boredom of the 'fitness' workout had few distractions on a Saturday – not like a weekday when the facility was filled with hard-bodies in spandex, bouncing pony tails, and smiles as people prepared for the workday like gladiators readying for a competition.

The series of machines was a medieval gauntlet of stress, stretch and discomfort designed to make one live longer and healthier. Sure thing. But the Saturday, distraction free machine time allows for total focus on "What's next?" in my life's journey. Same thoughts... same conclusions. I really don't know what's next, but I need a way out.

After the workout and a series of routine weekend errands – groceries, dry cleaner, and a few hours of volunteer work at the homeless shelter - Don arrived at the Club for the Board meeting and confidential discussion with Joseph. After a well-managed board meeting, Joseph and Don adjourned to the pub.

Joseph was mild mannered, of modest stature, and wore round owlish titanium glasses, suitable for a contemplative thinker. His grey heather chamois cloth shirt and wide wale corduroys broadcast his conservative nature. I've known him for about 6 summers, since I seldom saw him in the off-season. However, our mutual board membership allowed a more in-depth understanding of his executive skills and manner.

The Club's enthusiastic waitress, Sandy, greeted and seated us, and asked for our order. Joseph and I had similar thoughts, and coincidentally each ordered an Irish coffee.

The steaming cups of java arrived quickly. "So, Joseph, we've known each other for about – what can it be – 6-7 years? I've watched you in the board meetings, and must say I like the way that you think. Surprisingly, I'm not sure what you do for a living…"

"Don, the past few years have been great working with you on the board. I've enjoyed all our conversations and I like your style. You cut through the nonsense and get to the pressing issues. Simply put, Don, I help people create personal wealth by improving their business."

Sandy served a small plate of complimentary oatmeal-raisin cookies, and asked if we needed anything else. "Thanks, Sandy, we're all right for now."

Joseph continued. "I've had a good career, primarily focused on finance. CPA and MBA … a few decades working in corporate America in a variety of industries and roles." He paused and sipped the steaming Irish coffee. "The last few years in corporate America, I was a trouble shooter. The CEO often asked me to review troubled divisions and recommend how we might extract value from an underperforming operation. …Many industries… a lot of functional breakage… you know, manufacturing, R&D, Sales & Marketing… This experience helped me to formulate a process to create wealth…capture value. Prior to the trouble-shooting, I always believed that value was historical earnings, but I quickly learned that value is determined by future cash flows. Historical performance – not just earnings, but cash flow – might be an indicator of worth, but *the thing* that people value is *future cash flow*. Historical cash flow and earnings are simply credibility – an indicator of the future if the right people and processes are in place.

Have you ever noticed that some high-flying companies reach a pinnacle of value, then the stock price tanks? Ever studied why they crash?"

"Joseph, tell me about cash flow. My CFO doesn't talk much about cash flow, but just tells me the monthly cash balance. Is that good or bad?"

"I like to talk about better and best when I talk about company performance, Don. It would be best to understand the Company cash flow, and compare results to the budgeted cash flows. When cash flow is equal to or better than budget, that's best. When cash flow is below expected, the CFO should be analyzing *why*."

"Budgets and budgeted cash flow?"

Joseph's furrowed brow showed concern. As he leaned back in the deep overstuffed leather chair, the leather-on-leather sound whispered of elegance. He sipped the Irish coffee, and gazed into the crackling fire. "Don, do you prepare annual budgets?"

"The CFO does… well, I look at a spreadsheet, Joseph. Cynthia just takes the current year results and adds somewhere between 3-5% to the numbers… depends on the economy. Sometimes we make it… sometimes we miss, but for the past few years, my income has gone up, and cash in the bank is solid. I've been happy. Is that good or bad?"

"Think better or best, Don." Joseph set his cup on the oak table and leaned forward. Looking Don in the eye, he asked, "When the year is better than the spreadsheet, do you understand why?"

Don fidgeted in the deep chair and the china cup rattled slightly on its saucer. For the past few years, Don's income increased, and cash in the bank was nearly $1.5 million. No bank debt… leased the King-air in 2004. Kept part of the family on the payroll… paid a comfortable salary to Janice. Joseph is beginning to irritate me.

"Joseph, we've done a hell of a job during the past decade. Just because we can't answer some of your questions doesn't mean we aren't good business people. We treat our customers well… we deliver quality product … we treat our employees well."

"Better or best, Don… better or best. Not having budgets and cash flow doesn't mean you aren't doing a good job. But it may mean that you can improve. Heck, you've brought the business from the garage to what $10-15 million annual revenue? Most people can't do that. Guaranteed! You've done a helluva job, Don."

Joseph sensed Don's defensiveness, but decided to gently probe some specifics. "Hey, you mentioned that you treat the customers well … deliver quality product … treat employees well. Here are a couple of questions to think about… When I think business, I like to talk about People, Product, Process, Plant and Market. 4 "P's" and an "M."

In quick, staccato sentences, Joseph smiled and launched some rapid-fire questions. "So, for example, what revenue increases from products introduced in the past 3 years? … Production quality OK? … Lose any major customers in the past year? Don, these are some of the questions I asked in my corporate role of *trouble-shooter.* Quite often answers to these questions would lead to improvements." Joseph was grateful that they were in the casual pub environment. Sipping an Irish coffee softened the harsh questions that would often be perceived as too aggressive in the office.

Don drew a deep breath and smiled, slid forward in the deep chair and gazed around the lounge to ensure no one was nearby and quietly, with a self-satisfied air, said, "$29 million, Joseph… $29 million annual …"

He had trumped Joseph's expectation, and thought this
was a perfect time to conclude the conversation.
"...Nuff shop-talk, Joseph. Heading to Naples anytime
soon?" Another 30 minutes of small talk, Don called for
the check and double tipped Sandy. She was a good
college kid who was always attentive to Don and his
guests.

On his drive home, Don started a mental punch-list of
questions... why not probe?
  ✓ Budgets
  ✓ Cash flow
  ✓ Customers lost
  ✓ Manufacturing stats
  ✓ New products

... Should be simple enough to get this info from
Cynthia...

November 11, 2013 - Awareness

> *The right information is key
> *Listen to the organization

Monday mornings were notoriously upbeat as Don anxiously anticipated the workweek. Unlocking the massive hand-hewn oak door on the shop reaffirmed the value of craftsmanship and quality materials. Don purchased the door from a proud shopkeeper in Logrono Spain, when walking the Camino de Santiago – a 2,000-year-old trek. The serendipitous meeting with the merchant started when Don spotted an elderly gentleman – Eduardo - polishing the solid brass door fixtures - from the elegantly cast hinges to the mirror-like finished latch. While neither was fluent in the other's language, the Spanglish conversation drifted among topics ranging from family values to skills necessary to create outstanding products. Don hijacked Eduardo to the neighboring *el restaurante* for a cold drink, *chorizo and Jamon Serrano con pan*. After consuming numerous sangria's, dining on a selection of tapas, and finishing with a double espresso, Don blurted, "I comprar di puerta." The puzzled look on the shopkeepers face quickly morphed into a smile… a brief negotiation, and Don bought the massive ancient door – el Puerto. Eight weeks later, the door was installed at the shop.

Morning optimism bubbled when he felt the weathered grain of the massive portal, recognizing the permanence of extraordinary craftsmanship, and that touch rekindled warm memories of a wonderful trip. Don mused, "I'd like to take a few months off to stroll other European regions… but can't do that and manage the business…"

He fired up the Keurig for a chill beating Barista Prima Italian Roast coffee to launch a new week. As the coffee maker whooshed and the nozzle drained steaming nectar into the 1997 Commemorative *Masters* cup from Augusta, Don jotted some 'to-do' notes in his Moleskine notebook. "Cynthia - budgets, cash flow; Stephen - customers lost; " - manufacturing stats; Allison - new products."

Once settled at his barren plate-glass desk, Don awakened the iMac to review recent emails and send some invitations…

"Cynthia – let's discuss budgets & cash flows… Wednesday afternoon OK – or what would you suggest?"

Checking off open items in his notebook, he sent similar notes to Stephen, JB and Allison.

While scanning his weekly sales report, he wondered how the recently launched supply kits were moving through the sales channel. These kits were R&D serendipity, identified when Stephen analyzed *knuckles* 'Other Consumables', and noticed that more than 75% of the hospitals and surgical centers ordered a consistent ration of similar supplies. Rather than sell the supply items individually, and chance a hospital out-of-stock, Stephen suggested selling a standard 'Supply Kit' to provide better customer service and avoid emergency shipments and stock-outs. … Would be nice to have those performance numbers.

Weekly sales totaled $427,000.55 and were below the average – 'wonder what's happening – what's order backlog like?'

He punched the "JB" button on the phone and sipped the Prima. "Morning JB. How was the weekend?" After a few minutes discussing the football scores, recent national events and the grandchildren, Don probed the manufacturing operations.

JB's summary was quick, efficient and on point. "Don, we had a decent week last week. Backorders are ok.

We cleared up the materials quality variance with the China supplier – took more time than it should have, but – well, I don't speak Chinese, and they often misunderstand English when it's to their advantage. Production was as expected – just a shade above average – and our customer service stats are holding strong. You'll be happy to hear that the WIP inventory is right up there so that we don't have any line stoppage. Great to have that stuff around – lets me sleep better at night."

JB's been with the Company for nearly 18 years and has never let me down. Purdue engineering grad... first job at Caterpillar for – what was it - 4 years and then joined us. He worked his way through the organization and settled into the VP Operations job about 3 years ago. Settled into – good choice of words. When he started with us, he was just a skinny kid – maybe weighed 170 pounds. Now weighs – guessing - nearly 280 pounds, can't pass a donut or desert, and smokes those dark 'Joya De Nicaragua' cigars that look like rotted hemp deck lines. ... Certainly not the picture of health.

"JB – I just sent you an email to get together this week to talk about production and customer service in a bit more depth. Bring some numbers with you. You know, things that are important --- things that focus on the pulse of the business. OK - see you Thursday at 2 PM."

The next several days of customer meetings and teleconferences with some major vendors were exhausting. At last, Wednesday afternoon to talk with

Cynthia about Budgets and Cash Flows. Cynthia's distinctive knock and staccato steps on the hardwood announced her arrival. Her long blond hair, stretched taught in a ponytail, bounced frivolously as she strode across the hardwoods. While she wasn't overly attractive, her exceptional poise and personal deportment boasted confidence. Cynthia wore a Douglas Gray tartan plaid skirt, snow-white starched shirt monogrammed on the left cuff, accessorized by matching Tiffany black onyx cufflinks, necklace and earrings. Her Ferragamo's clicked sharply with each step. A light scent of Chanel was in the air.

"Cash flows and Budgets, Boss? Not sure what you're looking for. Help me out." Always direct and to the point – confident or overconfident?

"I was talking with one of the club members over the weekend, and he mentioned that most companies our size use budgets … helps companies grow and become more profitable. I mentioned that we don't use budgets, since we believe that they are inflexible and restrictive. …Ever considered preparing more in-depth planning?"

Cynthia's frown and furrowed brow were a first response. "Detailed budgeting is a huge workload for me, Don, and I'm not sure to what benefit other than dozens of excel spreadsheets with thousands of numbers that all have to balance. We've done just fine for the past few years – why would we change things now?"

"OK Cynthia, I just wanted to check with you. I'm not convinced that we should, but this *Joe* seems to have a good handle on business and he was surprised that a Company our size didn't have budgets. Let's not change anything for now."

"Say, I noticed that sales were a bit light last week. How are the new kits selling?"

"Allison thinks the kits are going extremely well. Many customers have adopted the kits as a standard order – in fact some are set up for automatic reorders."

"Any specifics? How are they selling compared to what we expected? The California State hospital system is a major customer... have they adopted the product?"

"Overall we are doing great... many of the customers are extremely satisfied with the thinking behind the kit."

"... Guess that's it, Cynthia. I'll talk to you later..."

Cynthia quickly turned, strode out of the office perturbed at Don's challenges to her financial management skills. Sure he is the owner, but now he's considering grinding thousands of budget numbers built on pure speculation... checking on details of how a product launch is progressing? ... Hope he forgets this nonsense and just let's me do my job.

Don puzzled over the discussion, knowing that Cynthia is competent and trustworthy, and she is certainly self-confident, but we really didn't talk about any facts. I wonder how Sales thinks the new product launch is going?

Don printed the weekly sales report, picked up his Master's Cup and strolled down executive row to Stephen's office. The Sales VP has been selling FDA regulated products for more than 30 years. His unique ability to work with customers is based on his bio-medical undergrad degree, and an NYU MBA with a marketing concentration. He speaks their technical language. Despite his 50+ years, he was trim and extremely fit – at last count, 6 marathons and 2 recent Iron-man competitions. At 5'8," perhaps 175 pounds, bald pate surrounded by a graying halo, he was not an imposing figure, but when he entered a room he was a known presence. Impeccable grooming, custom tailored suits of fine Italian wools, and highly polished calfskins reflected his personality – precision, thoroughness and high quality.

"How's life Stephen?" After suitable small talk, Don focused on sales volumes and trends.

"So, Stephen, what do you think of the latest sales figures? Comfortable? Any issues?"

"It has been an interesting year, Don. Overall, not a bad year, but really not outstanding. We've been getting some pushback on the kitting project from some of the majors – California in particular is mad-as-hell about us – so they say 'you're loading my inventory'. I don't think the problem is insurmountable, but they need some TLC. I'll be flying out next week to meet with their Director of Medical Supplies. I've been trying to assemble some sales information for the past 2 weeks so that I have solid information to discuss with them. It's not an easy task since sales reporting is sparse… our systems are somewhat limiting as an analytical resource."

"I haven't heard of the systems issues. Talk to me."

"Cynthia knows better than I, but something about downloading the entire Y-T-D sales file, then a series of steps I don't have a clue about - *delimiting and parsing*, sorting by date, customer number and finally using an *alpha sort* to get the info we need. She can get the info for some of the majors, but easy analysis just can't be done on short notice."

"How are the kitting sales going overall? Meeting your expectations?"

"*Download, delimit, parse, alpha sort etc*. Don, as much as I'd like to tell you I know how the product is going, at best it's a guess. I'm guessing that we're doing OK, since there doesn't seem to be a huge inventory buildup on the floor."

Don strolled to the coffee machine craving something without caffeine, puzzling about why he hadn't heard of these issues before. Don's entrepreneurial spirit loathes bureaucracy and non-value-added investment and work.

Traditionally, data systems have been a necessary evil –
pure overhead that doesn't add value to the Company...
doesn't sell or deliver product ... just pure cost. As Don
watched the chamomile fill his cup, his hand
unconsciously moved to his face, index finger gently
rubbing his temple. He needed to talk with Joseph.

November 19, 2013 - Sale Considerations: Future Earnings

> *Future cash flow & earnings = value
> *Historical performance = credibility

Don stood and extended his hand to Joseph as he approached the corner table at Ruth's Chris. "Thanks for joining me, Joseph," as Don smiled and delivered a politician's handshake – left hand on Joseph's elbow as if friends for decades. Brief discussions about sports, the national economy, and the world subsided as Don asked the theme question for the night. "I'd like to talk about managing the business better... value concepts and some other things that I may not be totally familiar with. Do you mind spending some time over dinner?"

Don selected the corner table to avoid disruption from other guests, and the hectic flow of servers rushing to anticipate patrons' needs. Servers carefully filled the water glasses, provided dark napkins to minimize unwanted lint displays, and recommended specialties of the day. Although Don enjoyed the sizzling strip steak and steamed asparagus, he allowed Joseph to order and would follow his lead to properly pair a wine.

Since Joseph ordered the seared sea scallops, asparagus and three-cheese au gratin potatoes, Don selected the blackened salmon. Joseph agreed that the Sancerre 2012 Reserve Sauvignon Blanc was a good selection.

"Your questions about how we use budgets and reporting to manage our business were intriguing, Joseph. Would you mind sharing some information with me?"

Joseph's subtle smile showed comfort in the process. During the next three hours – including a second bottle of Sancerre and several espressos' – Joseph ambled through a mini-MBA. Joseph's Yoda-type personality was at ease with any questions that Don posed. Quite often he answered a question with a question. Joseph admitted that since he really didn't understand the business, it would be foolish to pontificate. A better approach was to probe Don's knowledge of the business.

They covered so many topics – ranging from organization development and succession planning to new product pipeline, and customer portfolio management. After an hour, Don wished he had recorded the conversation since he was becoming saturated with information.

As they discussed Company worth, Joseph explained that value is whatever someone is willing to pay. Don pressed for more details, referencing the frequent jibes of "10 times EBITDA." Joseph leaned back in his chair, a half-glass of Sancerre offered as if in a toast, smiled showing deep wrinkles at the corners of his eyes. "The phrase was bait mainly to get you to think about value."

"It's a simple metric, but only one measure of value, sometimes used as a benchmark to determine if a price is fair and reasonable. EBITDA multiples are really just a range of acceptable values, but unfortunately a single number is often quoted. Another measure of value might be price to book value.

These are all rough benchmarks, but the key to value is the future cash flow of the business being sold. ... The projected EBITDA, and the probability of actually achieving the earnings. I've seen some companies that have strategically invested in new product lines, have minimal earnings from the new lines, but based on their ability to successfully develop and launch products, sell for a higher company value... effectively a higher multiple. Some companies sell for a multiple of revenue."

While looking at a server, he raised his hand and gestured with his right hand while sounding out the words 'paper & pen'. He enthusiastically scratched out two hypothetical P&L's and asked Don which company was worth more… or since they had the same PBT in year 3, should they have identical value?

Millions $	A					B				
	History			Future		History			Future	
Year	1	2	3	4	5	1	2	3	4	5
Sales	25	25	26	27	30	19	23	26	27	30
Cost of Sales	12	12	13	14	14	9	11	13	14	14
SG&A	8	9	10	8	9	9	9	10	8	9
PBT	5	4	3	5	7	1	3	3	5	7

"Certainly Company B is worth more, because they've grown the profit from $1 million to $3 million in three years. Joseph challenged, "How that could happen?" Bouts of Q&A continued into the late evening. They discussed the functions such as manufacturing, R&D, Sales and Marketing, and how each could influence value. Sometimes Joseph challenged Don personally about the Jackson Manufacturing organization – quality, depth and 'headroom'. Making a gentle fist as if holding a handful of loose change, Joseph tapped his hand repeatedly on the table and leaning forward, he said, "I'll bet you haven't identified the top three processes in your company."

At times, it seemed somewhat confrontational, but each time Joseph sensed that he was cutting into delicate tissue, he smiled as if to say, "…you're not alone in this situation…'

By now, most guests finished their deserts and coffee, and abandoned us to our *business seminar*. The evening was a fascinating exploration of valuation principles and a crude "How to Sell Your Business for Dummies" session. Joseph's thrust and parry discussion technique often left Don uneasy, yet somehow his guidance through his constant reassurances got Don off the ledge.

When they finished, Don had two pages of Joseph's handwritten notes, scratched on butcher paper from the kitchen.

"Joseph, will you help us get ready for sale? Although we may never make the move, it seems best to hedge the future."

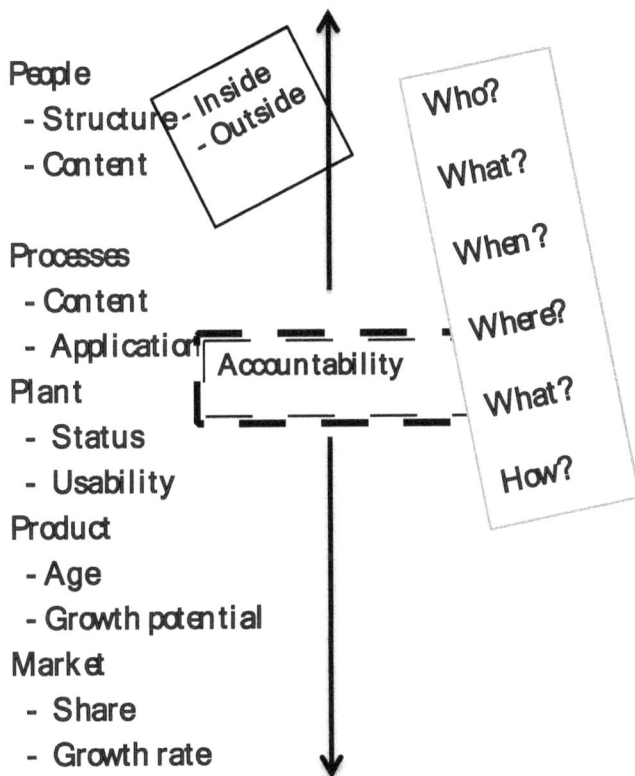

People
 - Structure
 - Content

- Inside
- Outside

Who?

What?

Processes
 - Content
 - Application

When?

Where?

Accountability

Plant
 - Status
 - Usability

What?

How?

Product
 - Age
 - Growth potential

Market
 - Share
 - Growth rate

December 17, 2013 - Specialist Meets CFO

CFO must:
▸Understand the business
▸Analyze the business
▸Provide accurate, timely
information to organization

Three weeks later, Joseph joined the monthly staff meeting as an interested observer. Don mentioned to the staff that Joseph might help the team rethink some business challenges during the next few months ... no specific agenda, but rather observe how we manage. Occasionally he would meet with each of them individually to talk about the business.

The monthly staff meetings, starting at roughly 8:30 AM on the 3rd Thursday after month end, were driven by the financial results. Allison frequently arrived late, always appearing rushed and always apologetic about her delay. Although no standard seating assignments, everyone took the same seat at each meeting. Surprisingly, when someone is absent his or her respective seat remains open. Although there is no fixed agenda, the queuing habitually begins with Cynthia leading the discussion, followed by manufacturing, sales/marketing, R&D, and human resources. The meeting usually drones on for 2-3.5 hours

Cynthia projected the brief first slide:

	2013	2012
	November	
Sales	29,544,144.23	28,407,830.99
Cost of sales	14,396,663.34	13,244,234.23
Gross Profit	15,147,480.89	15,163,596.76
%	*51%*	*53%*
SG&A		
Sales	6,956,455.23	6,723,423.23
Admin	3,878,766.23	3,777,833.23
Other	1,922,422.34	1,885,984.30
Total	12,757,643.80	12,387,240.76
Pretax Profit	2,389,837.09	2,776,356.00
After Tax Profit	1,194,918.55	1,388,178.00
Cash	998,354.44	990,343.28
Accounts Receivable	11,226,774.81	8,522,349.30
Accounts Payable	5,973,947.57	6,407,868.75

"On a year-to-date basis, we are off last year by..." as Cynthia's monotone discussed the numbers.

Cynthia's report verbalized the numbers on the screen with little additional information. Don squirmed in his seat while feverishly scratching notes on his legal pad. Occasionally he would question sales composition, major variances from prior year and what actually happened during the month. Customary answers followed – "We'll have to check on that Don." As Don probed each area – Sales, Manufacturing and R&D, answers were consistent – almost scripted.

Joseph and Don met at the coffee machine shortly after the meeting. "Is that a typical monthly meeting Don?"

"Quite so... three hours of frustration. Answers are vague, no in depth discussion about expectations or results and worst of all, we don't seem to get any actions out of the process. I'm sure not happy about the process, but don't know how to fix it. Suggestions, Joseph?"

"It seems that there is little accountability – perhaps based on the limited reporting and planning where you define expectations – perhaps because you don't have reasonable processes set up. ... Tough to tell at this point.

Don, you talked about possibly selling the business. Considering the monthly management meeting and management processes, what would a potential buyer observe? What would they be acquiring?"

Don was embarrassed and while his jaws tensed, he stared at the floor. He was unaccustomed to being the point of tough questions, and had no response. After a moment, not saying a word, he reached for an espresso K-cup, selected the 4-ounce cup size, and awaited the dark steaming elixir to stain the cup.

"Joseph, you don't shy from stating the facts. Suggestions?"

"I'd like to spend a couple of hours with each of your direct reports – my agenda? Simply have them tell me how they manage. After the discussion, I usually write up some notes, send them to the exec to be sure that we're on the same page, and I discuss alternatives that may improve the operation. Overall, 3-4 hours of their time, over a 5-day period. Non-intrusive on their schedule, but very informative. I'd like to start with Cynthia."

Two days later, Cynthia and Joseph met in the small, sparsely decorated conference room adorned only by the poster-sized photo of a rowing shell with the words 'teamwork'. The 4-foot round laminated table, dotted with dried coffee stains the shape of mugs, and 4 roller-based composite chairs were the only furnishings. The scent of Chanel filled the small conference room.

Cynthia was visibly tense while awaiting Joseph's arrival. Not knowing the extent of the discussion, she brought a stack of files covering the past 2 years financial results and bank records that created an informal defense barrier against Joseph's presence. Her left hand boasted a simple "Tiffany & Company" engraved platinum wedding band.

Joseph arrived, dressed in a blue blazer, gray pants and tassel loafers, French cuffs with gold Gordian knot cufflinks each accented with a single diamond. When working with larger companies, he may have worn a 3-piece dark suit, but he discovered that such formality intimidated the developing companies. He seated across from Cynthia, unconsciously guided by the stack of history.

During the initial banter, Cynthia mentioned that she was a backpacker, and recently completed walking the Camino de Santiago. While she did not appear to be an outdoorsperson, her brief stories confirmed her skills and experience. After brief introductions, Joseph asked, "How do you help Don manage the company."

As Cynthia described her role in the Company, her routines, and explained some of the Excel spreadsheet reporting selected from the stack of files, Joseph scratched notes on the conference room white-board.

After more than an hour, Cynthia was emotionally drained, not because the meeting was so intense, but because she felt so inadequate in her CFO role. In a brief 1.5 hours, she discovered an entirely new facet of financial management that she had never before understood... not accounting, but financial management. She no longer considered her role to be one of uninterested reporter who prepared 'the numbers', but rather perceived herself as an equal member of the executive team... an active participant – someone who contributed to the management process, and not just the lady scribe in the corner. Now the quandary – how to evolve into that new role without the experience?

Joseph understood her sense of failure and her desperate need for encouragement. Positive words nurtured her desire to excel and lead rather than simply observe. The challenge – highlighted on the whiteboard!

"And now, let's shift gears for a few minutes. Tell me about the Camino, Cynthia. I've never heard of it before."

She described the origin, history and grand scale of the Camino. Her enthusiasm was visible, and the pace of her description quickened.

"Physically, the most demanding effort that I've ever undertaken. Twenty-two days of intense exercise. The routine was simple – awaken at 6:30 each morning… eat breakfast … walk for 8 hours crossing broad plains… desert areas … the Pyrenees mountains… register at a hostel… shower and laundry… dinner and sleep until 6:30 AM the next day. Several days of intense rain – one day, temps reached 99°. Always alone – sometimes in the most desolate areas I've ever encountered – but never too far from a fellow pilgrim experiencing the same forlorn emotion – fellow peregrino's. Some days I felt an overpowering sense of desperation – inability to finish what I started - will the effort ever end. But then, around the next bend or over the next knoll, a hillside town appeared – white stucco houses capped with red-tiled roofs – civilization… restaurants and shelter for the night."

"So, just how do you prepare for such an adventure?'

Cynthia was now smiling, the furrowed brow and tension expelled by the thrill of the personal adventure … the forward posture aggressively leaning into the table disarmed and replaced by a warm smile… hands open and palms up as if welcoming a close friend.

"I guess the secret to success is to understand the challenge – the risks, opportunities, upsides and downsides to such an adventure. Know what is required – physical activity, financial resources, time – lay out a plan and begin. It was considerably more challenging since I didn't have any reservations, traveled alone, and I don't even speak Spanish."

"Sounds high-risk to me, Cynthia. More risk than I would ever take personally."

"Not so much, Joseph. When you prepare a detailed plan, understand the options along the way, you really just have to execute. Best of all, when the planning is done properly, you have a plan B, C, and D – just in case plan A is a bust. Really never out of control, but not 100% predictable… always within the control guidelines. Think of it like this," as she stretched to sketch out a quick diagram on the whiteboard:

46

```
─────────────────────  [ upside ]

- - - - - - - - - - - - -  [ target - time...$$ ... physical ]

─────────────────────→  [ downside ]
```

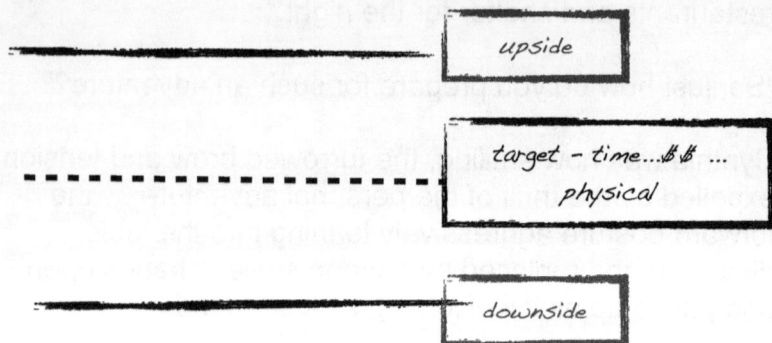

"Green's good... red's bad. My goal – whether time, spending, or effort – is represented by the dotted line...I expected to spend about $40/day... on the trail for about 25 days ... no more than 6-8 hours/day of exercise. Nothing to it. One thing for sure – I knew that I would finish the Camino before I left Spain. As far as spending – my budget was $50/day...downside was as much as $100/day... the 25 days couldn't be longer – too many commitments here in the states... the exercise of no more than 8 hours per day – if I needed more than 8 hours, I took the bus or train to the next town, since I knew that I must finish within 25 days. Plan A – B – C – D."

"Fascinating – seems like a lot of time for planning. And I can't imagine how difficult it was to manage all those parameters – money, destinations, time, effort etc. –

when you are dead-beat at the end of every day. You're a tougher person than I, Cynthia."

"Joseph, you give me far too much credit. Once you identify the right items, and have the right tools, measuring is pretty simple... not much effort. I used the iPhone throughout – time, distance, costs, reservations, and transit – everything I needed in a simple, well-thought-out activity. Minutes of effort per day to be sure that I met the goals..."

Joseph sensed the change in emotion... a warm spirit embraced the conference room. "Hey, Cynthia, you're the expert around here. Break some dishes willya? Think about our conversation, and sketch out what you think is important to run this Company – you know, financials and planning things. Nothing is off the table. Ask yourself, 'How can I help Don?' Hey, let's help the others as well – you know, help them run the Company. Don't be shy – ask some questions of Stephen, JB and Allison. ...Ya never know what can happen...

Can you think about this business like you did your Camino plan? Set some important parameters – not every number on the planet, but the important stuff – think through the upsides and downsides – plan A-B-C. Sort of like you did for the Camino?"

"Will do, Joseph... you made me nervous at first – unsure what to expect - but I think I understand where you're going. Can we get together next week – maybe Wednesday - same time and place? I'll try to pull some drafts together to talk about."

December 18, 2013 - Specialist Meets R&D

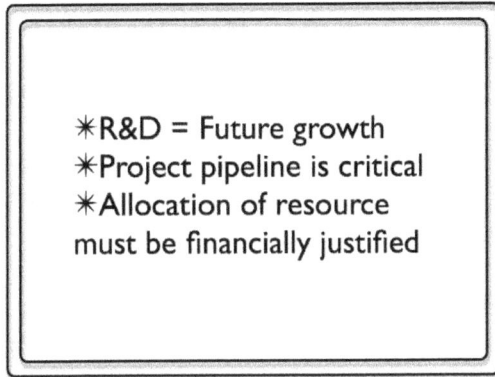

*R&D = Future growth
*Project pipeline is critical
*Allocation of resource
must be financially justified

The next day, Joseph saw Don adjusting the Coffee machine water supply line. "Hey Don, working on a new product design?"

"Sometimes engineers make things far too complicated. Simple design provides longer life, and a more reliable product. That's what we've tried to do with our *knuckles*."

"Great concept – simple and reliable design – probably frequently updated to reflect things like new materials, customer needs – things that you engineers know about. When was the last product release on your *knuckles*?"

Don gazed at the counter top and tapped his fingers on the surface for perhaps 30 seconds. He gently bit his lower lip, winced and said, "Too long ago… t-o-o long ago… must be 3 years anyway." Talking to himself in a whisper he said, "How can that be?" He wrapped his hands around the commemorative coffee cup, raised it taking a long sip and slowly walked toward his office.

Joseph knew he touched a delicate topic and quickly shifted to the coffee selection. "What kind of coffee do you suggest?"

Don did not hear the question. He walked as if in a deep meditative state – consumed by a critical question that he hadn't considered in years. How can our product development be so out-of-date?

After Don's response, Joseph decided to concentrate on R&D and new product development. Rather than the office environment, he thought a venue change to the local Olive Garden restaurant was best. The restaurant had quiet rooms with broad table set-ups that allowed for confidential discussion and sketching on a placemat.

Allison arrived for the noon lunch at about 12:15, consistent with her normal tardy performance.

Allison was a 50's something PhD in Bio-medical science. Her rimless eyeglasses, consistent with many scientific types, and glacier blue eyes were a perfect compliment to her makeup free porcelain complexion. No doubt her teen years' penchant for science and her inquisitive mind alerted her to the damage of ultraviolet A & B rays on fair-skinned blonds. And now, after many careful years, her youthful complexion was a minor contrast to her shoulder-length graying hair, pulled taught and wrapped in a bun. A navy blue Pea coat covered the simple cotton shirt, dark wool pants and black Clark's wedges. A gold chain and "Π" sign with a centered half-carat diamond stud was her only adornment.

Speaking as she rolled back the dark wood Captain's Chair to be seated, "Good morning, Joseph. How would you like to begin?"

A true scientific approach. No need to apologize for the late arrival… get to the facts, all the while with a lifeless dull expression and a monotone voice.

"Allison, thank you for meeting me for lunch. This is a great place for a business discussion – spacious, quiet and we can speak without too much concern of others overhearing the conversation. Have you dined here before?"

"Yes – they have excellent specials, and I agree with your assessment of quiet. How shall we begin? I understand that you don't ask specific questions, but rather ask, 'How do you run the business?'"

"That's right Alison… somewhat of a rambling discussion to hear about your management style and how you manage the R&D and new product development function."

The next 1.5 hours covered everything from her matronly lifestyle... to her love of animals and volunteer work ... to new product development. Initially Allison was very reluctant to discuss her life outside the business, but eventually shared her deep feeling of social responsibility and her favorite charity – the SPCA. Surprisingly, she was also an instrument rated private pilot, certified for flying single-engine, high-performance airplanes and the twin turboprop.

Her flying hobby started when Don purchased the Company's first airplane – the Mooney-201. After several trips with Don at the controls, she suggested that, in the best interest of the Company, she should become a pilot as a safety measure. Of course Don agreed, certainly as a safety measure alone. Besides, it was an excellent perk for a valued employee. During the past few years, as the Company upgraded to a turbo-prop, her ratings kept pace.

The hobby developed into volunteer piloting for the SPCA – relocating animals to distant shelters – and angel flights to assist less fortunate families' transit to distant medical treatment.

Her answer to the question of new product development was succinct and stoic. "We don't have any new product development. When planning starts and ends with the prior year's spending plus 3-5%, there is no room for development." Such an unemotional response from someone so well educated in a search for scientific development surprised Joseph.

Joseph challenged the budgeting process and discovered that for the past 5 years, there was no spending growth allowed beyond expected inflation. Typically, Cynthia and Don called a meeting in late December and delivered the annual budget to the management team. In the early years, the team often resisted the minimal spending increases and defended their challenge with discussion about activities that would improve the business. Cynthia and Don supported their sparse spending goals with a bastion of risk-averse logic …end of discussion at those annual meetings. After the first few years, the team no longer challenged the budget process and allowed their imaginations and enthusiasm to become dormant.

He pressed Allison about risk aversion and product development. At one point, in true scientific form, she declared, "Of course it is higher risk to avoid product development, but it's Don's Company. As long as the paychecks continue, and I can use the planes for my hobby, there is no point to challenge the boss. Get real, Joseph. We've tried for a decade!" At last the conversation had bottomed-out with a burst of emotion, highlighted by the exaggerated statement of 'a decade'. Now it was time to build.

Joseph squeezed the life out of a lemon wedge and watched the last drop of moisture mix with the

unsweetened iced tea. After a brief pause, he shifted
topics to Allison's hobbies – flying and the SPCA - and
turned the negative emotion to a more enjoyable tone.
He noticed an immediate change in Allison's body
language, no more aggressively leaning across the table
with a locked jaw and pulsing temple. She shared
several of her flying stories that demonstrated her
calculated risk-taking, thorough planning capabilities,
preparedness and precision execution. Stories of
landing in severe wind shear, mild icing conditions, and
losing the entire electrical system in IFR conditions
defined a steely personality that can deal with almost
any challenge.

As he guided the conversation and built on the positive
direction, he asked Allison, "If you had unlimited
resource, what would you do in this Company?"
The immediate metamorphosis from mindless drone that
executed as directed to a creative leader surprised
Joseph. Allison ordered an espresso, and asked the
server for paper and pen to begin to sketch out potential
development plans. Awaiting the coffee, her Sharpie's
swift movements on the place mat started to shape out
some interesting concepts. While she did not have
complete market information, she built conceptual
models for product line extensions, joint ventures with
other device manufacturers that complemented Jackson
Manufacturing's strengths and supplemented the
Company's weaknesses.

She enthusiastically scratched rough product designs,
circles with dollar signs and numbers, arrows linking

boxes, development costs and risk weighted returns. As she drafted an R&D organization chart, she identified critical missing skills and many question marks with exclamation points. She admitted her knowledge shortcomings, but other executive team members may have the answers. Forcefully, she stated, "If we don't have the answers, we should get them. The business is too important – to us and to the patients that we help - to let it atrophy – drift to non-existence." She capped the Sharpie, aligned it parallel with the final page of notes, and closed the conversation. After filling three placemats with notes, she rolled away from the table, arms resting on the dark wood armchair, smiled coyly and said, "Nobody's ever asked me for what I would do."

Astounding!

Subcontract:
Proprietary:

	Materials			Methods		
	Pure	60/40	80/20	Mcahined	Cast	Nano
Titanium						90%
Tantalum			90%			

Description	Design	Market		
		US	China (Millions $$)	Other
Youth	☐			
Male	☐		75	50
Female	☐	20	45	150
Women	☐	50	25	50
Men	☐	30	80	80
Obese	☐	75		

Trending to more.

Check out demographics

With her permission, he gathered the notes and asked how she would like to proceed.

"Strawberry cheesecake, of course."

As often happens, the first discussion with an executive at a new company is relatively mellow and uneventful, with little new information to leverage among the team members. As word about the process circulates within the executive teams, information and innovation becomes a torrent - a virtual flash flood of ideas - to improve the business. Of course, while many of the ideas have merit, implementation may be difficult due to limited resources. The key to the process is to engage the enthusiasm and creativity of the executives.

December 20, 2013 - Specialist Feedback to CEO

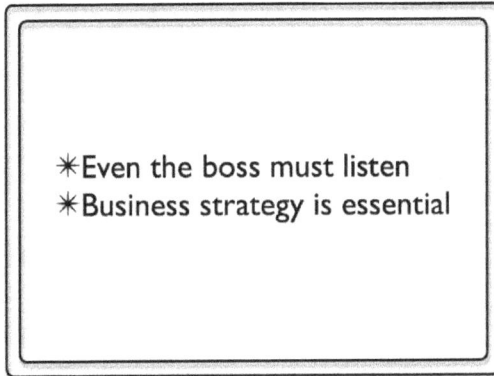

*Even the boss must listen
*Business strategy is essential

Joseph scheduled a progress update meeting with Don at the club, a neutral territory without the structured office atmosphere. The informality encouraged an open, creative discussion.

Sandy directed them to a quiet table next to the blazing fireplace overlooking the idle, frozen 18th green. As she filled the water goblets, she asked about drink orders.

Don ordered a Grey Goose martini – extra olives and only a whisper of vermouth - while Joseph ordered a Johnny Walker-Black on the rocks. The drinks arrived, a quick toast of "cheers", and both listened momentarily to the crackling fire. The light scent of burning apple wood and cocktail set a contemplative tone.

"Well, it's been a few weeks since we started this investigative journey, Joseph. How are things going?"

"Glad you chose the word 'journey' Don. And for sure, it is an uncharted journey. You're the Captain of the ship, and while we don't have a final destination defined, we both want to make progress. When we started this discussion, you were considering 'tomorrows' but weren't sure exactly what that meant. Have you given 'tomorrow' any thought?"

"This business has been my life for the past 30+ years. The ups and downs – euphoria to desperation – built a relationship. Janice and I have two children and they have a sibling called Jackson Manufacturing. Just as the kids must grow up and develop on their own, there is a time the business needs to do the same. 'When?' is the question.

Raising the kids – well success can be determined by their outcome. College educated, good citizens, independent, families of their own. In a business staying alive is one measure of success... performance compared to others in a peer group might be another. We've never been overly concerned about performance compared to others. We've always been able to earn a good living, pay our bills and take care of the employees. We've defined that as success."

Don toyed with the extra martini olives using the sabre shaped bamboo spike. Unconsciously, he avoided eye contact with Joseph. As a leader, he seldom lacked direction and a plan, and now he lacked a plan, and wasn't even sure of a destination.

"Joseph, a crossroads may be approaching – could be soon, could be later. I haven't been having as much fun during the past few years, but I haven't been aware of the lack of joy – I'm starting to recognize that I don't have 20 years ahead of me. My priorities are changing – I don't know how fast… and I really don't know where I'm going."

"Don, this is not an unusual position for a successful entrepreneur, after many years dedicated to a single purpose – build the business. I'm glad that you've taken some time to think about your tomorrow's.

The timing is perfect, since you still have some enthusiasm for the business. One of the things that we must do is preserve the value of your decades of effort. I can only guess that a considerable part of your wealth is tied up in the business. If that's the case, let's preserve the wealth – perhaps increase the wealth – and take some steps to give you options.

Not necessarily to sell the business, but to create the opportunity to sell if you want to enjoy some free time in your 'tomorrows'.

Some entrepreneurs wait too long and emotionally reach a point of no return. They allow the business to become an emotional burden – a poison that must be expelled immediately. They resent the commitment required."

Joseph nodded to Sandy who quickly arrived to take their order as she served a basket of fresh crusty dinner rolls. Sizzling steaks were in order – a carnivore's delight - with a bottle of Greg Norman Cabernet to complement the groomed fairway view.

Joseph knew that his silence was his next best step – just listen to the crackling fire until Don summoned the courage to proceed. Don selected a kalamata olive roll, split the roll and spread a generous layer of butter on half. While conversation seemed to be banned, Don unconsciously brushed the resulting breadcrumbs into three small piles – one representing the children, one for he and Janice, and the last mound to represent the business. His stare boring holes in the table, submissive, he said, "Talk to me Joseph."

"Preparation for sale doesn't mean you must sell, Don, but it will help you create options for this illiquid pool of wealth. Most times, 'prep for sale' will increase earnings and wealth, because you'll be examining the business as if you were an outside investor – perhaps a long-term investor such as a major corporation, or a new platform business for a private equity buyer.

In any case, you'll be strategizing how to improve wealth, which means more earnings and less investment.

A quick example. Increase your inventory turns by 1 – say from 4 turns per year to 5 – you just created a

61

million-and-a-half bucks cash flow. Good today, and
good for a potential investor."

"Yeah, but we need all the inventory we can get just to
protect the future, Joseph."

"Maybe not Don. Have you looked at your inventory
lately? Is it all usable, or do you have some – let's say
unrecognized – scrap on the floor?

Hey, let's not get into the specifics tonight, Don. Let's
think about how we may want to approach the challenge
– no long term obligations... no commitments, but let's
just call it an informal review of your operations."

"I'm not ready for a rigid commitment, but I do want to
hear more."

"Don, I've met with Cynthia and Allison so far. We spent
about 1-2 hours and – well, there's a lot of talent, and
some good ideas. I'd like to do the same with the other
executives – is that JB for Manufacturing/Operations
and Stephen for Sales & Marketing? Overall, in a matter
of a few more hours, I think we can frame out some
alternatives that will make you feel a lot better about the
business, and we may chart some enhancements that
will make everyone's careers better."

"Not sure how important Human Resources is, but
Margaret from Human Resources is on my staff. We
usually don't include her in our Executive Team
sessions where we talk about business decisions, since

she only takes care of HR matters. If you want to
include her, let's get on with this. I'd be crazy not to
invest a few more hours now to – as you say – capture
the value."

Don enjoyed this particular table near the heat and
dancing flames of the well-tended fire. The fire's warmth
and winter view of the 18th green always reminded him
of those sunny afternoons when he fleeced fellow
golfers who chose to bet against him on the round. Not
big money, but just enough to sting a bit.

He puzzled over why had he not considered Margaret
earlier in this process?

"Dessert Joseph?"

Joseph was extremely pleased with the discussion and
overall direction… needs to schedule meetings with JB,
Stephen and Margaret. It is interesting how Don views
Margaret and Human Resources as a function other
than a key part of the Executive Team.

December 21, 2013 - Specialist Meets Sales VP

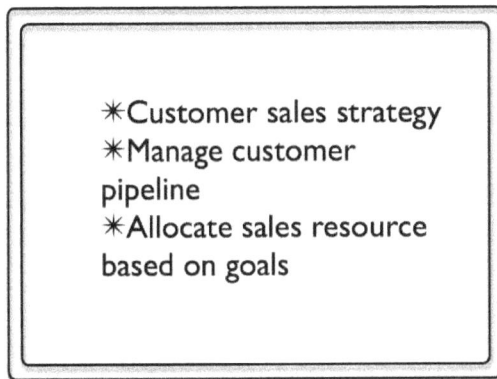

> *Customer sales strategy
> *Manage customer pipeline
> *Allocate sales resource based on goals

Stephen's schedule was exceptionally busy during the next few weeks, and the only time available for meeting was at the CVG Delta Skymiles Club. Joseph was creative, and purchased a refundable ticket to Chicago. The ticket plus his Homeland Security Global Entry pass allowed him to clear security for ready access to the Club.

Although Joseph had never met Stephen, Stephen was easily identified by his SBB monogrammed French cuff, Navy Blue Pinstripe, royal lavender tie, and highly polished dress oxfords. Don said, "Look for the magazine cover, and you've got Stephen." His trim stature and erect posture could have been that of an F-18 Naval aviator. His demeanor - precise, direct, and pragmatic.

"Hello Joseph – Stephen Bianchy – glad to meet you. Apologies for the location, but I have to visit several of our biggest clients in the next week, and I know how important these discussions are. I've made arrangements for a conference room and refreshments, or we could just be seated in the alcove overlooking the runways." Stephen gestured to an isolated quad of overstuffed leather chairs and glass coffee table.

"Informal works for me. Let's go with the quad. Hey, how do you arrange for refreshments? Clubs don't serve, do they?"

"Typically not, but I spend enough time in some of these clubs, treat the folks with respect, and tip heavily... they really just reciprocate when it's important. Good folks overall... tough job being in the service business.

As a heads-up, I talked with Allison and Cynthia to get an idea of what to expect. ... Seems like you just ask some general questions and have a good discussion about the business. Cynthia said that I might expect an assignment out of the discussion – not sure what she meant and she wouldn't elaborate."

Joseph enjoyed the description of the expected discussion, and also that Cynthia would allow Stephen's imagination to anticipate an assignment.

"So tell me a bit about yourself, Stephen. It is helpful to understand a person's background when we get started."

Stephen's immediate response was to get Joseph talking. "...Be glad to tell you about myself, but how about you first? Somehow you've convinced Don to open up a bit and I'd like to understand the magic you have to make that happen?"

After a brief bio discussion, Joseph reloaded the question for Stephen.

Stephen shared his background for about 10 minutes and described a person who was virtually self-made. He was the second oldest of 4 children, raised in a blue-collar household, in a blue collar Midwest neighborhood, and the first in the family to finish college. In his first semester, he majored in Liberal Arts and was sleepwalking to a 4.0 GPA. Since he was personally financing his education, he shifted to Bioengineering to improve his immediate marketability upon graduation.

Unafraid to work and desperate for tuition money, he worked 3 part-time jobs and started a small service company while attending full-time university. Johnson & Johnson recruited him from the university upon graduation, and subsequently paid for his MBA. He acknowledged these critical career development stages – big-company discipline coupled with an MBA was the perfect career platform. After 7 years with J&J, he moved to St. Jude Medical for early advancement to Director-level, responsible for Mid-west marketing.

"Well Stephen, I can't imagine a better foundation for a successful career. What brought you to Jackson Manufacturing?"

A uniformed attendant with an artificial smile delivered a small plastic tray of refreshments – 2 Pepsi's; 2 Heinekens; a selection of Kalamata olives; a dish of trail mix; 4 plastic wrapped cheddar cheese servings with saltine packets and 2 apples. Truly a balanced traveler's diet...

While many executives are tense when the discussion starts, Stephen smiled and reclined deeply into the stuffing, crossing his legs comfortably at the ankles.

He stretched for a Pepsi and started discussing *the business.* Jackson Manufacturing lured him from the big company environment, appealing to his penchant for challenge, results, and personal responsibility. "Don described the open VP's role as one requiring vision, calculated risk taking, and accountability. He offered a qualified self-starter the opportunity to flourish in an entrepreneurial environment that would help grow the Company."

Joseph interrupted, "… and did Don deliver?"

Spilling some trail mix into his palm, Stephen replied, "My career has been ok, and when you consider the overall life-style flexibility allowed, I'm ok with things."

"I notice that you didn't answer my question – atypical for you isn't it?"

"Look Joseph, we both know that everything promised sometimes doesn't work out. On balance, it's ok. I've had the opportunity to earn a good living, and because of a somewhat relaxed approach to performance, I've had the opportunity to develop some unusual hobbies. It's not everywhere that will allow a person to train for an Iron-man competition and several marathons."

"So you've had a great well-rounded lifestyle. Here we are in 2013 – we're all a bit older … you know the Company and customers well… you know that Don is a boomer. If you could do anything you wanted – no constraints – would you do anything differently today?"

"Loaded question, Joseph," as he speared several olives using the plastic sabers. Delaying his response, he toyed with the cheese and saltines like a 4 year old."

"What do you want me to say? That the Company could do better? Of course we can, but that creates a 'two-fer' conflict. Fight the battle for change within the Company, and then fight the competitors for market presence. I learned that some battles aren't worth the effort. The Company's doing ok, I get a monthly paycheck, and if we reach our targets, Don is extremely generous with bonus bucks. It's not so bad"

"Does that mean you're sort of a *low-t* participant in this venture? Seems counter-intuitive given your competitive nature. ... Not easy to compete in marathons, and – I'm thinking that you are the only person I've ever met that competes in an iron-man event."

"Let's play this out, Stephen. Let's say you're in your early 50's – you've got a comfortable nest egg, but you aren't *rich*. You're a bit bored in your professional life, so you've substituted physical challenge for career challenge. Am I close?"

Joseph has played this script many times. There are two endings to this soap opera – a Greek tragedy where the hero figuratively ends his career quietly spiraling into complacency and non-performance, or a Disney flick where the super hero conquers all challenges and lives happily ever after. Intuition suggests that Stephen is a Disney character who can thrive in any challenge.

"For the right opportunity at Jackson, I'd trade a few marathons and an Iron-man – but I said the *right* opportunity, correct?"

"Ok- rock 'n roll, Stephen. Describe the *right* opportunity."

Stephen adhered to the Disney story line, and now was driving for empowerment to fulfill his lust for challenge.

The open Heineken bottle perspired pooling condensation on the plastic tray. Stephen pinched several napkins from the table, wiped the excess moisture from a bottle, siphoned a third of the bottle as if playing beer-pong. "Joseph, can I assume that what we discuss is just between us… won't go any further unless we 'clear' the issues." Stephen had little downside to share some creative ideas, since if Joseph repeated the information and Don was offended, Stephen could smooth things over. The upside, if Joseph leaked the information to Don, is that Don would actually change how we run the business. Stephen had used this baiting technique before to good advantage.

He slipped a folio from the side pocket of his burnished leather, mahogany tone coach bag. The silk-covered folio opened to three labeled sections – BS; bs; Gold. Stephen noticed Joseph's curious look when he spotted the labels.

"BS is for Brain Storming. I've generated some of my best ideas when on a two-hour – no-interruptions flight. 'bs' is my way to vent…and yes, it means bullshit. When I'm furious about something, rather than write a caustic email or have an emotional rant on a phone call, I write a brief note about the circumstances in my 'bs' file. And Gold? Those are the action items I concentrate on to make the year's bonus, and build next year's pipeline."

This treasured folio, with a Waterman fountain pen
tightly looped in the center crease, bulged at the 'bs'
section, while 'BS' and 'Gold' were athletically trim.
Stephen leafed through the 'BS' section and selected
two pages from the half-dozen Crane 100% cotton
sheets. Each page had two main headings printed in
block letters, followed by carefully written script in
Sapphire Blue ink – almost calligraphy – of several bullet
points. 'STRENGTHS, WEAKNESSES,
OPPORTUNITIES, THREATS' headings were printed in
capital letters, and represented Stephen's business
SWOT analysis for Jackson Manufacturing.

Jackson Manufacturing

STRENGTHS	WEAKNESSES
•Manufacturing - exotic metals	•Regulatory - Europe
•FDA relationships	•University contacts - International
•University contacts - US	•Sales representation - offshore
•Key customer relationships - research institutions	•Information systems
•Key vendor relationships - coating industry	

71

Jackson Manufacturing

OPPORTUNITIES	THREATS
• International sales: Europe; China • JV's - European companies that want US ops • Nanotechnology materials	• Competitors: J&J; Stryker Medical • Foreign competitors • Increased regulation • Financial resources • Don's future... company future

Stephen cleaned a section of the table and proudly aligned the two pages side-by-side. "Some of my ideas."

Allowing Joseph to scan the pages, Stephen drained the Heineken bottle, and gestured to Joseph as if to ask, "Do you want the last Heineken?"

"Please do, Stephen. I'm just trying to absorb your Brain Storming. Obviously you take great care with these pages – not a haphazard effort."

Given the pride displayed in the presentation, Joseph knew he would be unable to take the pages with him.

He flipped his reporter's 3x5 Moleskine open, jotted a few quick notes, and began to probe behind the scripted words to validate the depth of analysis. Stephen demonstrated his analytic capabilities in all facets of the business – from regulatory to manufacturing - to competitive conditions and opportunities.

His talent was unappreciated – worse yet, completely unknown to Don.

"Hey, talk to me about some of those 'bs' sheets. Anything you're particularly PO'd about?"

Spinning the portfolio aligning to Joseph's view, Stephen said, "Go ahead, flip through my notes." These pages, while on Crane's finest, were not as carefully scripted. In addition to the occasional rant about airline service, narrow poorly padded seats, and excess charges for 'full-size person' legroom and baggage, there were monthly notations about unavailable customer information, and frequent notes about the dearth of new products. These pages, desperate for good housekeeping, included numerous unintelligible scrawls, coffee and food stains, various writing styles scratched with instruments that ranged from fine fountain pens to colored sharpies or cheap blotchy ballpoints. These were emotional outbursts rather than carefully crafted notes.

Joseph poked at several lines double-boxed for emphasis or perhaps to display frustration and asked, "Can you talk to me about customer information?"

Clearly, customer information was a major frustration for Stephen, since a series of exclamation points frequently chased these notations across the page. Somewhat sheepishly, Stephen talked about incomplete customer information and the sorry state of data systems. Despite Cynthia's inability to provide information, he defended her role since he believed their data system was originally developed in the 18th century – if not before. He suggested that Cynthia's predecessor was a shaved-head, hopsack-clothed monk who scribed manually with a quill pen on parchment paper.

When customers challenged order pricing, delivery status or future product availability, Stephen was defenseless and embarrassingly unable to respond with other than milquetoast babble – transparent to customers that Jackson had little real information. Thank goodness they had great products – but oh, such limited product lines.

When Joseph baited Stephen with a 'new products' question, Stephen scowled, immediately stood erect like a Vatican Swiss guard, turned and paced to the rest room. Returning in a few minutes, he merely said, "We need some new products. Desperately. 'Nuff said."

His flight announcement triggered a packing exercise. Carefully returning 'BS' to it's hallowed home and stuffing 'bs' in it's assigned sleeve, closing the silk folio, he said, "Next time, maybe we'll get a chance to do some 'Gold' mining. Cheers." He turned and in double-time march, he descended the two flights of stairs to the main floor, and trotted the length of the terminal to Gate 29.

December 22 - Specialist Meets VP Manufacturing

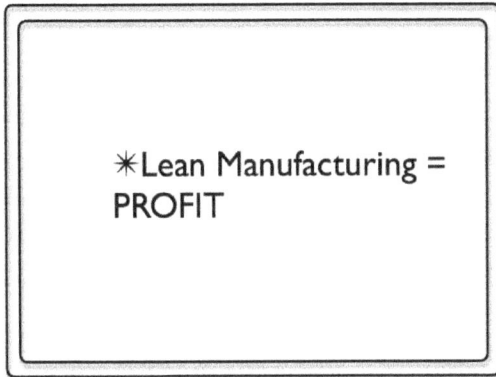

＊Lean Manufacturing =
PROFIT

JB was scheduled next, but rather than wait for Joseph's request, he emailed Joseph asking to meet on Tuesday at the factory. "See you at 9 AM – my office."

Joseph arrived promptly at 9 AM. Knowing that JB was less formal than the others and wanting to avoid any culture clash, he decided to dress down, wearing a beige cable-knit sweater, corduroys and penny loafers.

JB's office was a museum of manufacturing artifacts displayed on ascending rows of narrow floor to ceiling shelves affixed to any wall without windows. Dusty machined metal pieces adorned each shelf, some neatly

arranged while others apparently randomly distributed.
His heavy wooden desk was stacked with vendor
catalogs, invoices awaiting approval, and an in-box
overflowing with a hodgepodge of unopened envelopes,
envelopes that looked like they were opened with a
chain saw, and single and stapled pages scattered
throughout the stack.

Despite the facility 'no smoking' regulation, two large
ceramic ashtrays with dark rope-like stubs leased open
space on the crowded desk surface. The credenza
behind his time-distressed leather captain's chair
displayed a portable Honeywell Commercial Grade
Hepa air filter.

JB was an overweight, somewhat unkempt individual
who could easily star in an over-the-road trucking
commercial where censors frequently bleeped the
dialogue. Don was proud of how JB developed within
the Company. Don also tolerated JB's rough side,
considering the results of continued profitability and
negligible stock outs.

JB immediately tried to hijack the conversation by
boasting of his major accomplishments, while reaching
for the hand-wrapped Nicaraguan and Bic lighter.
Joseph disrupted the smoking plan, "Buy me a coffee,
JB?"

While walking to the coffee area, Joseph's small talk
unobtrusively aligned the ground-rules for their meeting.
"I know how busy you are JB, and I would just like to

understand the highlights of how you manage the business. It's obvious from your bookshelves that you've accomplished a lot during the past years. I can only say well done! So tell me about how you manage... how you run meetings, what kind of reporting you get, and your planning processes."

When they returned to the office, JB described his informal management style and his disdain for big-business practices. Earlier in his career, while at Caterpillar, he was stranded in an engineering function in which he had little influence on product development or manufacturing quality, despite his recent Engineering degree from Purdue. The 4-year stint at Caterpillar confirmed his dislike for big business and wasteful overhead.

He coveted a role in an entrepreneurial firm like Jackson – few layers of management, minimal interference from *those who just didn't get it*, minimal written procedures that, at best, only interfere with improved performance. During his early years with Jackson, his ability to get things done impressed Don, who mentored JB throughout his career.

JB was so distracted by his enthusiastic discussion that he neglected to light up the rolled Nicaraguan.

Joseph invited JB to, "... show me around. I'd like to see your factory."

JB beamed, plucked 2 pairs of safety glasses from the top drawer of his desk, and started to the door. He offered the unopened wrapped goggles to Joseph, saying, "I think that you'll really enjoy seeing how we make money around this place."

The facility tour matched the materials flow from raw materials - receiving and inspection - through all manufacturing steps to final inspection. Occasionally JB would highlight areas of particular importance, and frequently boast about how the abundance of inventory – from raw stock throughout the entire work-in- process area, and at final inspection – provided a 92% customer order performance. Joseph observed, "So you are ok with an 8% failure rate?"

Joseph recognized faults, if the factory were viewed as a lean business. While the factory had proper signage and floor layouts, he noticed that bins of product were often 'outside the lines' requiring forklifts to dodge the occasionally damaged containers. Bins of parts scattered among the machining areas were inconsistently filled, ranging from overflowing to a single part in a pallet-sized container.

Parts, sometimes coated with a heavy layer of protective dust, appeared to be archaeological discoveries rather than usable components. JB explained that occasionally he had excess parts that would be used, '... in the near term... but nothing major to be concerned about...'

An area in the back of the factory resembled a police crime scene; all taped off with 3 inch wide, bright yellow 'CAUTION' tape. Machines in this desolate area were in various stages of disrepair – some mere skeletons as their critical components were previously extracted for use in their healthier cousins on the manufacturing floor. JB referred to this area as his spare parts shop.

Machines on the manufacturing floor were asset tagged, and most included 'PM' tickets, indicating preventive maintenance cycle times and compliance. PM compliance seemed to stop in late 2010. JB defended the timing by saying that 2010 was, "...the year of the big downturn. All non-essential work was deferred until a better year." Apparently the better year had not arrived.

As they strolled the manufacturing floor, JB frequently shouted out a, "Hey!" to employees, and addressed them by name. He seemed to be well liked and respected, and was proud of the relationships that he had with the employees. "These guys have pulled us through some tough times during the past few years. They've cancelled vacations, worked holidays and 12 hour days to pull us through."

"JB, how many new products have you manufactured in the past few years?"

"We've really concentrated our energy in producing THE best products in the marketplace. New products – well that's Allison's game, not mine. But when I think about it, I guess that we really haven't had many new products in the past few years."

"Do you have much training for the folks on the floor?"

"Whenever we get a new machine, we make sure that the employees are properly trained. We also have open meetings so that the associates can ask questions whenever they need information."

"And I noticed that several of the employees weren't wearing safety goggles. Any thoughts?"

"The guys have said that the glasses distort their vision, and they can't get the tolerances right when wearing the safety glasses. We confirmed that when they wear the goggles scrap goes up, so we *wink* at the eye protection requirement to keep production up. We haven't had an accident in nearly 18 months, and for those departments where we rigidly enforce all the regulations, it has been nearly 5 years."

"How's the data system work for you?"

"Honestly, it isn't very effective. We get by, using it to record product releases to finished goods, but the rest of the accounting stuff isn't worth the effort. Years ago, we changed the production flow, and we were never able to change the system. Something about we didn't have the software maintenance upgrade necessary to change computer parameters. We get by just fine without the system... we're flexible and make things work."

"JB, what would you change if you could do anything you want to make the business run better?"

"Nothing. Why change when we can meet the customer needs at 92%? Seems like a waste of money to me."

Joseph understood the desperate need for improved systems and full integration into the shop floor operations. "Any thoughts about putting a new system in... maybe adopting some of the latest 'lean business' techniques?"

"Don's been reluctant to invest in data systems. And I guess we haven't invested much time in some of the newer management techniques since we've been getting by without them."

They had arrived at JB's office and concluded their discussion. "See you at the next management meeting JB. Thanks for the information and tour."

January 2, 2014 - Specialist Meets VP of Human Resources

> *Effective HR management = Success
> *Define org structure & policies; hire right for success

Salt and pepper-haired Margaret was a well groomed, trim 50-something executive dressed in a Diamond Jacquard jacket with a powder blue oxford shirt. Her efficient graduated bob hairstyle and artificially whitened smile reinforced her need to be viewed as a business professional and executive.

Don hired Margaret after meeting her at a Human Resources seminar discussing "The Need for Human Resource (HR) Professionals in any Business", since People costs were generally the largest single line item in any business. Shortly thereafter, Margaret joined the executive team as Manager – Human Resources.

Although she did not have a degree, her 2.5 years of college included some courses in Organization Management. Early in her career, she managed the HR operations in several small privately held companies, concentrating on tactical activities such as governmental compliance reporting, payroll operations, and control reporting for vacations, holidays and sick days.

As proof of her value, Don earlier noted that there had been no major HR issues since she joined the team. However, since Don considered her to be an HR tactician, he seldom included her in the business decision-making meetings.

Margaret's office was simple elegance. Her desk was neatly arranged with thin layers of correspondence in the stacked wooden In/Out boxes. A Waterford crystal commemorative clock from a previous employer nested between the stapler and In-box. A yellow legal pad was centered on a chocolate brown leather desk pad. A matching Mont Blanc roller ball and mechanical pencil, neatly stored in an unadorned, brown leather 2-pen pouch, aligned with the legal pad.

Her bookshelves prominently displayed several of Peter Drucker's management tomes, in addition to "Human Resource Management – 13th Edition," and "The Fundamentals of Human Resource Management." Several human resources journals fanned across her locked wooden file cabinet.

84

Although a lonely replica Picasso line drawing of wildlife was centered on the wall, there were no personal items such as a model sailboat, family pictures or vacation photos from exotic locations. The office – professionally sterile – or was it the ultimate HR feng shui?

Although Joseph arrived as scheduled, he opened with "Good afternoon, Margaret. Is this a good time for you?" as a professional courtesy. Margaret greeted Joseph with a firm handshake and pleasant yet unsmiling face.

"Good to meet you Joseph. I have been anticipating our discussion." Her glacier blue eyes appeared nervous as if staring over the edge of a safety fence along the Grand Canyon. She seldom smiled, indicating some insecurity with her position, knowing that a stoic appearance might be perceived as more authoritative.

"So what are your expectations today, Margaret?"

"The jungle drums say you just want to hear how we run our business. Correct?"

During the next hour Joseph's warm smile and easy demeanor coaxed Margaret to share her routines and observations about the business. While she was recently promoted to Director of HR, her skills and experience would only support a Manager's title. During the past few years, she implemented a rudimentary performance appraisal system focused exclusively on sales and earnings, limited to Director level and above.

She also ensured that other employees' compensation level was routinely compared to peers within a 50-mile radius.

"Margaret, have you ever considered career development programs for the broad employee base?"

"That would be great, Joseph, except Don believes that employees are responsible for their own development. We'll train them for the specific job they are doing, but career growth is a personal responsibility. Many area companies don't offer development training, so we are with the average."

"So is it fair to say that Don wants to be just an *average* Company?"

Margaret's jaw tightened and her eyes narrowed indicating her displeasure with the term *average*.

Although her tactical performance for HR compliance and reporting seemed flawless, her depth of knowledge for effective Human Resources management seemed limited.

As they explored strategic Human Resource topics such as succession planning, executive compensation, Company-wide bonus plans, phantom stock and options, employee reviews and alignment with Company goals, she became more self-conscious as if naked in crowded restaurant. Joseph detected her uneasiness and shared anecdotes from other assignments to calm her anxiety. It was customary to find such gaps in complex Human Resources management issues in middle market companies.

To further ease her concerns, he focused on her apparent flawless record in all areas of compliance with Federal, State and local regulations, and impeccable record keeping related to vacations and holidays. As an HR confidant who never disclosed her sources, she was an invaluable source for Don about attitudes and concerns within the Company.

After an hour's discussion, she shared some personal insight about her life-style, hobbies, and work-life balance. As an amateur chef, she enjoyed exploring ethnic and regional cuisine from around the globe. Winter meals were based on various hoof, fin and fowl delights with wine marinades and simple sauces as part of multi-course dinners she prepared for herself and partner. Summer season shifted to rubs and marinades while grilling over hardwood embers, or smoking over mesquite, apple or cherry hardwoods.

At the conclusion of their meeting, Margaret selected the rollerball and posted some notes on her legal pad. For emphasis, the term *average* was printed in capital letters, followed by three exclamation points and double-boxed with heavy lines. Joseph couldn't determine if anger or frustration drove the notations.

Joseph
11/25/13

✓ *Succession planning*
✓ *Exec Compensation*
✓ *All-employee bonus*
✓ *Phantom stock*
✓ *Reviews*
✓ *Alignment*

AVERAGE!!!

Joseph made a mental note of her list, unsure of her next steps.

January 3, 2014 - Specialist Challenges
CEO/Owner

Satisfied that the initial executive meetings awakened their creative spirit and developed some personal angst, Joseph characterized the business as typical middle market... very successful entrepreneur who excelled in a technical specialty, created a profitable niche, employed those he was comfortable with, delivered excellent customer service, and made a decent living.

As a successful boomer, Don was now searching for the next steps, unclear what to do, and how to do it, all the while his wealth and retirement handcuffed to the business. While he still felt energized by the business, the energy reserves and enthusiasm to launch another major expansion didn't exist. There was no vision for the year 2040, since he knew he wouldn't be running the business. Don was uncomfortable not knowing the next steps for the first time in his life.

Joseph scheduled a breakfast meeting with Don to provide an update.

"Don, you have an exceptional team that has helped you become successful. They know the business' tactical requirements, and seem to consistently deliver for you... your customers and your vendors. ...According to JB, 92% of the time.

And you are very generous with each team member."

Somewhat embarrassed, Don acknowledged their strong performance and simply said, "We've been through some interesting times, and I'm proud of what we have done. Good folks all the way around."

"So what's next, Don?"

Don's eyes shifted to the table, as he nervously fidgeted with the table accessories– first rearranging the salt and pepper shakers ... then stacking and restacking the Blackberry Jelly, Orange Marmalade and Strawberry Jam, first by flavor, then alternating flavors. ... Never looking up.

"Joseph, the emperor has no clothes. I don't know what's next and it bothers me." After a brief pause and almost in a whisper, " ... bothers me a lot..."

"My money is tied up in the business, and the family isn't interested in managing the Company. I don't get excited about the Company the way I used to – not that I don't like it – enjoy it - but it's just not the same. Other things have become more important to me – I like to travel... want to see the grandkids more... spend time just enjoying a quiet sunset dinner with Janice. Heck, some days I'd just like to call home and tell Janice, 'Pack a bag and meet me at the plane – we're going to Boston for some fresh seafood."

His eyes met Joseph's and submissively said, "I just don't know what's next, Joseph."

Joseph had seen this emotional purge many times before. An executive accustomed to being in control, and who was no longer driving forward, like being caught in an eddy in a raging river ... directionless... expending energy but going nowhere.

Enthusiastically, Joseph said, "OK, Don. Let's make some magic. This is a very typical situation for baby-boomers. You've been a hard driver for decades – always knowing what's next, and now – well, an adventure that you've never encountered. There is no magic to what happens next. Simply put – set up the business as if you are going to sell the operation. During the process, you never execute any decisions that will require you to sell, unless you're ready to move on. But you manage the business to grow ... to thrive ... to have some legs for the next owner." Joseph leaned forward, his hands casually around the table setting ... somewhat of an open stance. "You've got a situation with some upside ... or some downside ... depending what decisions you make.

"Tell me about your new product development pipeline, Don"

"Bare naked... zilch... no focus in the past few years."

"Is that good or bad?

"As they say, 'sure ain't good!'"

"So what do we do about that?"

"Develop some new products."

"Big or little? Let's explore. Can you afford to put a million bucks up for a 5 year development cycle?"

"I can afford it, but I'm not ready to risk it or commit to a 5-year cycle."

"So you've just made a decision."

Joseph fired questions as if he had an endless supply, all the while leaning forward confident in this process. "Why are you successful, Don?"

"We have a helluva manufacturing process. Always meet customer requirements… great engineers on staff."

"So a core strength is manufacturing capability, with highly talented engineers. Have you asked the engineers to develop any new products lately?"

Don was startled speechless by the question's directness. Quickly ratcheting through the last 6 months activity and communications with the engineering group, he desperately tried to think of when he last asked for new products. The sad truth – he couldn't recall any such request. Once again, he stared at the table.

"Don't beat yourself up, Don. It happens when you don't have a strategy that drives the entire organization. For the past – oh, perhaps, few years – you've been a tactical master – meet or exceed the customers' needs. That's been your mantra. It is not life or death, but do you think – do you want to change that tactical orientation?"

"Not knowing for sure what that means, probably yes. I'm saying that I know I want product development and growth, but I'm not sure how to get there."

"I've had some excellent meetings with your staff. You've got some organization and operational gaps that might need to be filled, and you'll probably want to take a few 'baby steps' before we launch into anything major... before we attempt to change any of the basic culture in your operation. Let's face it; you'll want me to better describe what it means to become more strategic, and what impact there may be on your business.

I've met with your entire staff, and placed some seeds of discontent – not with you or the Company, but with themselves. Let's let this dog hunt and see where it takes us. For the next monthly management meeting, throw them a bone – mention that you know that they've each met with me and you'd like some feedback, and see what happens.

The more interested and aggressive will bring some new ideas into the meeting. Some things that you've never seen before, and perhaps some changes that will be immediately useful. You OK with that?"

"Sounds like limited downside. I'll do it. The next meeting is a week from tomorrow. We'll start promptly at 8:30 AM."

January 4, 2014 - Specialist Attends 1st Staff Meeting

> *The right information is key
> *Listen to the organization

Don awakened at 5:00AM, about 30 minutes before the scheduled alarm, filled with anticipation as their first staff meeting of the new generation assembles today. He quickly dressed, rushed to the Sub-Zero refrigerator column, poured and drained a glass of fresh orange juice as he sprinted to the door. The gym, 15 minutes from the house, would be filled with hard-bodies this morning – gladiators readying for the lions of business.

His standard battery of medieval stretching, pulling and pulsing devices awaited his enthusiastic attack. Despite challenging these machines for years, he had never conquered or outlasted them within his routine. Today the nubile Jasmine, a 20-something co-ed, was startled by his enthusiasm, and surprisingly could not keep pace on the nearby machine.

"Wassup old guy? Taking some testosterone these days? Don, I've never seen you so hyped."

"Just a big day at the office, Jas. ... Not sure I've been this excited in a few years."

Don's 45-minute routine included about 30% more reps than usual. Throughout the exercise ritual, he thought about the notes jotted after his first meeting with Joseph. Perhaps this was a new beginning. After a quick shower, he ordered a triple-threat fruit smoothie at the concession. The intense flavor of the combination of fresh fruit - blueberries, strawberries, bananas, kiwi - peach yogurt and orange juice were invigorating and the perfect way to cap the exercise routine.

At the office, as a sign of the changed focus, Don had a tray of mixed bagels and a selection of herbal lite-cream-cheeses centered on the conference table. A stainless steel carafe of Barista Prima Italian Roast – yes, double caffeine for all – awaited the *game show contestants*. Who would have the right answers today? Who would have the right questions today?

Joseph arrived and immediately noticed Don's healthy glow. "Ready to launch, Don?"

"The countdown has begun."

Surprisingly, the entire staff arrived by 8:20. Each projected a different energy than the traditional bored ambivalence. Allison was on time? Don wanted to compliment her, but merely nodded acknowledgement and smiled briefly.

Don opened the meeting, inviting all to enjoy the healthy alternative to gooey, calorie burdened donuts, and stated, "You've all had a chance to meet with Joseph, and he mentioned that he's pushed your buttons. So let's get on with this."

Cynthia opened a manila file filled with stapled packets of information – numbers, color charts, and bullet points at the bottom of each page... clearly not the usual financial summary.

"Folks, as you know, I met with Joseph several weeks ago, and after the meeting, some soul searching and discussion with some area CFO's, I decided that I wasn't happy with the data that I discuss each month. It's just historical data – numbers to the nearest penny - that really doesn't help us understand the business and our decision-making. I'll ask for your patience with today's discussion. This is new for me, and of course new for you. No one has seen this information before, so there will be questions that need answers. I'm not trying to blind-side anyone, but want to get some feedback from each of you... does this kind of information really help, or is it a waste of my time. Overall, it takes about a half-day to put this together, but once we set up the models, the information will roll up in about 2 hours. If you like it, say so… if you don't, say so. If you need other information, ask for it. I may be able to get it for you. Let's roll."

Cynthia distributed the packets, and projected the first full-color slide using the LCD projector.

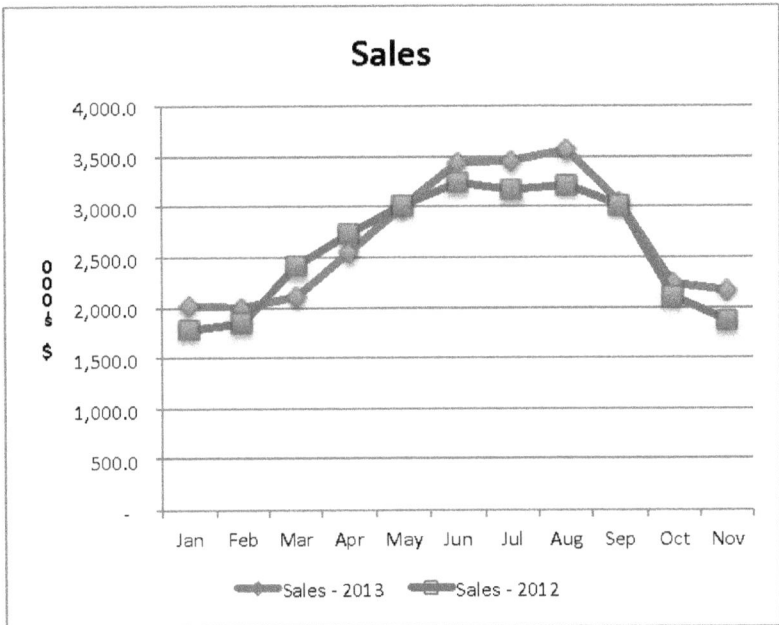

"We've all seen the financials to the nearest penny. Accurate, for sure, but after talking with Joseph, I decided to look at things a bit differently. When I looked at the monthly numbers, you can't help notice the bigger seasonal pattern in 2013… and I honestly couldn't tell you why it happened."

Stephen tapped his pen on the conference table and chuckled, "You honestly don't remember the hoops we jumped through to get Johnson Health Clinic to use our device? C'mon Cynthia – take some Alzheimer's meds and get with it." The entire team laughed – especially Cynthia – since she was the savior of the deal. How can you forget that you postponed 2 days of your vacation to work through contract terms to get this account?

Gross Margin %

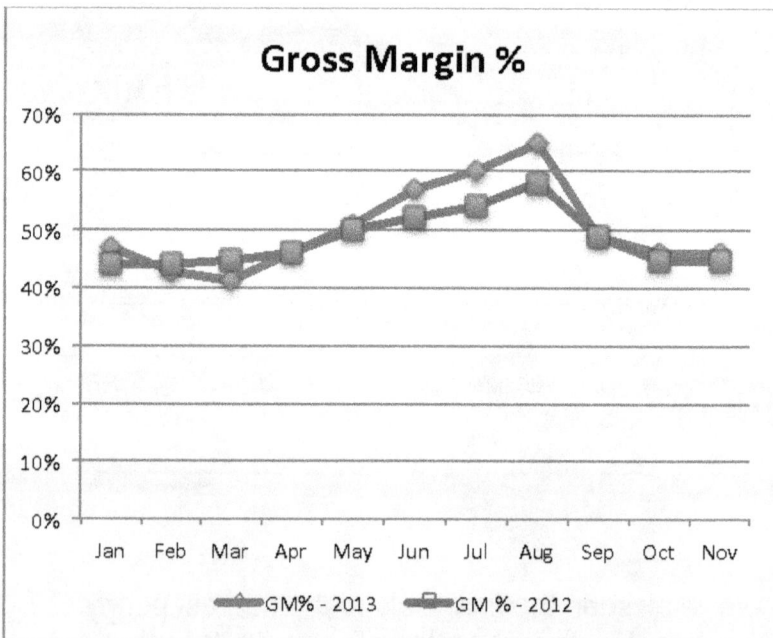

Cynthia continued, "And here is the gross margin percent graph. I'm embarrassed again. Increasing margins from 50%+- to mid 60's is huge. If we could ever figure out how to make that happen year-round, we'd have to buy a corporate jet to manage the earnings down!"

As part of the margin explanation, JB immediately discussed overhead absorption and the seasonal impact on earnings. Stephen also shared that the Johnson account had favorable margins – if we met the delivery commitments.

Joseph, no longer just an observer, posed the question, "So how do we smooth the seasonal pattern? Seems like the absorption thing would provide year 'round benefit. And what if we just drew a Gross Margin line at 57% across the entire year and said, 'What will it take to get us here?' That would add a million bucks to profit. Talk to me JB."

JB's brief manufacturing discussion included 75% unintelligible analysis for most of the execs, but Cynthia started writing notes on the white board that folks understood.

Don noticed that the team was also scribbling notes on the pages. He leaned into the presentation as if watching Picasso creating an original masterpiece. Initially the team was apprehensive with the new information, but since it wasn't merely a page full of numbers, the display captured their interest. They seemed more engaged and less defensive than usual.

Cynthia's packet included graphs of SG&A spending, Days Sales Outstanding, Inventory Turns, and Cash Flow. Gaining confidence with each chart, she boldly challenged the team: "What happened?" and "How do we make this better?"

After 30 minutes, Cynthia gratefully surrendered the floor with a smiling close, "Thanks team. I guess that this kind of information may be useful for us to manage better. Look, we all know I have limited information, but these graphs present ready information. What else do you think would be useful? I may be able to get the info. Hey, bagels for everyone!" Cynthia was positively bubbly.

Stephen and JB tossed a *knuckleball* to the team and changed their presentation order. Stephen opened his manila file and, just as with Cynthia, had a few pages printed for distribution. He slid the thumb-drive across the table and asked if Cynthia could load the "Cust" file PDF.

Don gazed at Joseph as if to say, "What the heck?" Joseph shrugged, knowing that Stephen was about to take us on a journey.

"Soooo, as we all know, Joseph was sent around to make us all feel bad about how we run the business, and it worked. I decided to do some digging with the info that we have available. Nothing too serious, but I took the Y-T-D customer sales file for 2012 and 2013, and did a high-low sort. Now JB tells me that's a Pareto analysis. I always thought that a Pareto was an Italian sports car, but that's a sales guy talking.

The reason for high-low? I just wanted to check out some of the major customers – I used the top 10 - to see what's happening. Check this out.

000's $	2013			2012		
	Amt	% Tot Cust	Cum	Amt	% Tot Cust	Cum
Boston Children's	2,878	10%	10%	2,767	10%	10%
Atlanta Children's	2,677	9%	19%	1,798	6%	16%
Seattle Pro Sports	2,675	9%	28%	2,122	7%	24%
Cincinnati Sports Meds	2,187	7%	35%	1,656	6%	29%
Charlotte Sports Medicine	2,017	7%	42%	1,985	7%	36%
Chicago Memorial	1,454	5%	47%	1,208	4%	41%
Stratford Hospital Service	1,212	4%	51%	988	3%	44%
Johnson Clinics	855	3%	54%	687	2%	47%
Charleston Spine Clinic	577	2%	56%	945	3%	50%
SanDiego Ortho	-	0%	56%	588	2%	52%
Subtotal	16,532	56%		14,744	52%	
All Other	13,012	44%	100%	13,663	48%	100%
Total Sales	29,544	100%		28,407	100%	

"Our Top-10 customers account for more than half of our business. We had some big winners, and a few losers. What do you see?"

Allison's eyes widened as she studied the chart. "Anyone notice that the largest sales increase was in a children's hospital, and it's the only *children's* on the page? What's going on Stephen?"

Margaret chimed, "Boston, Seattle, Cincinnati and Chicago all have both professional baseball and football teams. People are all wannabe jocks?"

Don's eyes narrowed, his forefinger tapping his cheek while biting his lower lip asked, "What the heck in San Diego and Charleston? I didn't realize they were in the tank?"

"All good questions team. I'm ashamed of myself for not focusing on these broad trends and questions much earlier. I've conditioned myself to say 'No information available' and I've become far too complacent just looking at the totals. Totals are up so life's good. Not! The shading – greens and blues are good, reds are bad.

Allison, I don't have a clue why Atlanta children's is up. I can't even explain why a children's hospital is one of the top 2 accounts. You're the med-brains in this team. Can you call some of the doc's at Atlanta children's and help me understand what's going on?

And Margaret, great catch. For sure they are all professional sports cities, and I'm going to check out what's happening to the populations in these burgs. Another thing that bothers me is that there are other dual sports cities not on the list – think NYC. I can't believe we didn't see this before, but – well, sales are up. No excuse, Don. It's just a bullshit statement that I'm ashamed of.

The San Diego drop isn't as bad as it looks. Stratford bought San Diego Ortho late last year, so they really didn't get a full year of the Ortho deal.

Don, unfortunately I don't have a clue about Charleston. I owe you an answer.

Can I share something else with you folks?

While we don't have all the information that we need to run the business, there are many points of information available – it isn't pretty to get it, but it's in the system. Given these revelations, I'm going to do some data mining to discover more pearls of wisdom. While I don't think we can afford a full time analyst, I'm calling the local university to see if I can get an Excel Stud to do some grinding for me. Shouldn't be cost prohibitive, and considering what I've just discovered, it's a no-brainer."

Stephen's confession and mea culpa were accepted, since the entire team was in a similar state. They recognized their complacency, built on the precarious fact that total sales were up.

Stephen discussed several other revelations, and decided that his self-immolation was complete. Self-consciously he focused on the tray of bagels, avoiding others' eye contact, selected a cinnamon raisin, and smeared a healthy layer of cheese and chive across the split bagel.

Don plucked a whole grain bagel off the tray and pinched a chunk of bagel. Before a nibble, he invited JB to discuss his manufacturing operation.

JB was slouched in his captain's chair munching a bagel, arms resting comfortably on the dark wooden surface, his large belly exaggerated by his posture. Slowly he rearranged his frame forward so that his forearms rested on the conference table.

"We are doing just great, Don. Manufacturing operations are humming along, and customer satisfaction continues in the low-to-mid 90's. I know that you like comfortable safety stock levels, and we are there.

No major issues with the vendors… we cleared up the mess with the China vendors, and have increased the on-hand stock just in case they give us trouble again.

Overall manufacturing variances are within reasonable levels, and the shop guys are doing a great job.

Not much else to discuss … and to keep the overall meeting on schedule, that's all I've got this month. Next."

Joseph warned Don that JB might provide a positive report that didn't include much specific information or accountability. He mentioned several areas that Don may want to probe to highlight that a new culture is born in Jackson Manufacturing.

Don thanked JB and followed with additional comments. "Thanks JB. Very brief update indeed. Hey, I was strolling around the plant last week and spotted a few things that – well can we get some additional information"

JB was about to chomp into a fresh bagel, stopped, mouth agape at Don's question. His eyes widened, and his expression changed quickly from self-satisfied to perplexed. He placed the bagel on the tray, and, while thinking of a response, selected a napkin to wipe the imaginary crumbs from his chin.

As if a theater actor playing Macbeth, he smiled broadly and very confidently responded, "Anything you need, Don."

Don recalled the briefing provided by Joseph, and began the discussion with a few brief questions in rapid fire.

"JB, I noticed that some of the line associates weren't wearing the required safety glasses in some high risk areas. And also, in the buffing cell, it seemed that many of the parts stored in the bins must have originated in the Cromagnon era with that layer of dust. Are those parts still usable?"

JB's eyes darted around the room checking the expression on the other team member's faces – each somewhat startled by the direct questions. He clutched the wooden arms of his chair and nervously slid forward in two jerking motions, nesting his large paunch against the table.

"Great questions, Don. The safety glasses – well, we both know that the technicians cannot maintain the tolerances required with those inexpensive safety glasses in place. We can't afford the scrap that results from sloppy work, so we just wink at the regulations and move forward.

And as far as those parts in bins." He laughed nervously and began fidgeting with his pen and scratching haphazardly on the legal pad. "Well sure those parts are usable. It's our conservatism and concern for stock outs that requires that cushion. You know your dictate – never run out of stock."

"JB if you had a choice of better glasses or an OSHA fine and lawsuit from an accident, do you think that OSHA penalties would cost more than better safety glasses?

"No contest, Don – new safety glasses." JB, visibly upset and embarrassed, took the smeared bagel and plopped it on his plate, rattling the plastic against the table. Grabbing the plastic knife with his sausage like fingers, he slashed the bagel into quarters, selected a chunk, and devoured it like a hungry animal.

"I have a few other questions – we can take care of those offline. Margaret, anything significant to report?"

"All's quiet, Don."

"OK folks, thanks for your input. You've all had a chance to meet with Joseph, and I think he's put a burr under your saddle. I'll ask Joseph to leave the room - take a break. Grab a coffee, Joseph, now we're going to talk about you a bit. Feedback from both sides is the way I like to go."

Joseph thanked all present for their input, rolled his chair away from the table, and quietly left the conference room. "I'll follow-up with you later Don."

The room was silent – people nervously doodling on scratchpads, repeatedly clicking roller-balls, smearing herbal cheese mindlessly in swirling designs on the split bagels. The team felt somewhat uneasy at the meeting format changes.

Don's broad grin put them at ease.

"Folks, that was a great meeting. Cynthia – how the heck did you come up with that information? Better yet, what can we do with the info to make this place run better?

Stephen - feel good about identifying those key customers and sales trends. Sure we might have discovered those things earlier, but today is a new game. Let me know what you find out.

JB – I can't explain it – I know my mantra has been lots of inventory is good and you've followed the guidelines. But when I saw that layer of dust – well I have to question my own policy. I still don't have a clue what's best or how to get there – and I need your help.

The past few weeks have been an exploration for me – stale old dog who's been running this Company for more than 30 years. Many of you folks have been right there with me throughout the good times and disasters.

I've had a few martinis with Joseph, and am not sure what to make of him. I do know that this team is important to me. What do you think of Joseph? His experience? His approach to a business? Talk to me folks."

Margaret was silently rehearsing the words to the Beatle's song "A Hard Day's Night" until she heard, "Talk to me folks."

Uncharacteristically, she immediately shared her thoughts.

"Don, Joseph has been around the block. During the discussion, he asked some very tough questions. Some – maybe off base – but others? Well, maybe I should have known answers. It seems that he's a big-business guy... I questioned, 'how will that help us?' I still don't know. But he did get me thinking about some – let's say – higher-level HR issues.

He was professional … his questions were more about the future than where we are today. We just haven't asked ourselves those questions before, and I'm not sure if that's good or bad."

Don responded, "Better or best, Margaret."

A red-faced JB, hands wrapped in a tight fist and extended onto the table, glared at Don, and cut off more discussion with Margaret. "Don you put me on the spot today, and I didn't like it. I've been managing this plant for what - maybe 8-10 years - and you've never challenged my capabilities before. Is that something Joseph put you up to?"

JB's harsh response and curt question had the impact of a Molotov cocktail in a crowd of teenagers. He fumbled in his pocket, grabbed a Joya de Nicaragua and bit the end off as if ready to light up.

"Settle down JB. Yes, I'm changing things a bit, but I'm not sure how, when or what will change. You folks probably haven't noticed that I'm not 25 years old anymore. Well, I don't know what that means, but for sure, it is tough for me to think about running this business 20 years from now."

"You going to sell-out?" Allison chirped.

"Here's everything I know. I don't plan to sell the Company, but we all know I haven't found the Fountain of Youth. We – and that includes the entire

110

management team – and I have done a good job during
the past decades. Well, if I'm not a puppy anymore, and
a successful business must look out beyond the next
payroll, we have to think differently. And quite honestly,
I don't know what I don't know. … Been within the four
walls for the past 30+ years.

I started talking with Joseph several weeks ago, and
asked him to spend some time with each of you.

Now, I want to hear what you think of Joseph. … The
good and the bad. Make it sharp and to the point."

Cynthia was twirling several strands of her ponytail, and
unemotionally offered, "I agree with Margaret that he
asked some tough questions. I didn't know the answers
and yes, I was embarrassed. We talked about the
systems, and information. Not a wish list of things that
we couldn't get if we put in SAP/ERP, but things that
may be readily available. While he's a Fortune 500
exec, he seems very practical, and able to dial down
expectations and adapt big business stuff to our size
Company. Should we hire him? … Guess I'd like to
know what the goals of engagement would be."

Using a pure clinical approach, Allison mentally churned
through a series of alternate hypotheses of what could
be done if Joseph worked with them. "He is unbiased,
asks open ended questions and allows *us* to finish
sentences and thoughts. He seems to have a process
that allows us to answer our own questions. From my
view, he figuratively cracked me on the side of the head

and said, 'If you're R&D, what have you developed lately?' Well, we've developed nothing new … and then we started to pick apart why not. Did it hurt to talk about my lousy performance in R&D? Sure it did! But did it help me understand my complacency? Sure it did. Don – JB – Stephen, I've got some ideas about some new product direction… when can we get together?"

Cynthia merely held up the new analysis and said, "More to come… not sure what or when, but Joseph pressed some buttons that got me thinking."

"OK – thanks for the balanced input. JB – get rid of that cigar… don't stink up this room.

We are a team and I want us to explore *good-better-best* together. I'm not sure what that means, but I think that after only a few hours with Joseph, we know that we can improve.

I'd like to ask Joseph for a plan about how to help us improve. Once I get the plan, we'll talk about the approach together so that the team can make a good decision. I wouldn't be here without your support, and I guess at this stage of my career, I'd like you to help me out. Thoughts?"

Sequentially, they agreed that it would be worthwhile to get a plan from Joseph.

"As Don got up to leave, he turned and said, "Thanks for your support folks."

After Don's departure, the team nervously looked around the room as if scanning for someone with a pistol, and nearly simultaneously started speaking. The momentary cacophony quickly muted to a single question, "What just happened?"

Stephen reasoned that Don was acknowledging that life is finite, and he had never considered, "What's next after the business?"

Margaret quietly paced gazing at the gently waving row of cattails along the watershed near the facility. As a flock of mallards landed in a flurry of flapping wings and thrashing water she quietly speculated that Don had just graduated from middle-aged entrepreneur to a full-fledged baby-boomer who recognizes his limitations. "I don't expect that he's going to go off the ledge and sell the place, but he seems to be taking a thoughtful approach to a challenge that he's never experienced before. I honestly think his timing may be right – well ahead of a critical event driving any decisions."

Cynthia added, "He's been good to us for many years. Let's assume he'll continue to be considerate of the team – and guard his future as well. The value of this business is tomorrow – future profits and cash flow. To think the Company has value without a well-managed operation going forward is quite naïve."

She immediately felt selfish – self-conscious of her remarks as if her future – all their futures – were most important in this discussion. She had momentarily abandoned the Company priorities and was ashamed. "What I meant to say…" and her voice trailed off to a whisper. The ducks were now roaming on the glassy surface creating silent v-wakes marking their progress.

JB, without any shame, stated, "Well, I don't like the change."

Stephen gestured palms-down in a motion to settle the emotion, "Look, we really don't have any downside to give Joseph some space. He hasn't done anything that threatens any of us. He's experienced and seems to have a solid analytical approach to this quandary of entrepreneur *graduation*. My suggestion – let's get with the program and support Don. It's his Company and each of us has a vested interest in the Company's continuing success. Let's hear the plan, and remember, Don asked us what we thought. He didn't just dictate the program."

All nodded in agreement, although JB was obviously displeased as he shredded a bagel into crumbly shards on the plastic tray.

January 5, 2014 - Specialist Feedback to CEO

> *Prep for sale timeline
> *Prioritize major issues

Don rearranged his office before Joseph arrived. Two easels with thick pads of self-sticking sheets stood at attention on the window side of the office. The easel's narrow metal tray was lined with multi-colored marking pens. The conference table, arranged as if it were a Staples marketing display, included two yellow legal pads positioned square with the captains chairs, an array of Sharpie's, a rainbow of various sized sticky-notes, a fresh carafe of dark rich coffee, and a half-dozen Dasani's.

The scrubbed clean office white-board awaited a torrent of notes from a spirited discussion about *tomorrows*.

Joseph was pleased as he entered this thoughtfully prepared arena.

Don welcomed Joseph with a warm handshake and hand on the shoulder as if they'd known each other since childhood. Don resolved to share his deepest concerns about the future as if Joseph were his Father Confessor. "So how would you like to proceed, Joseph?"

"Is that the dark roast coffee? If so, let's pour some energy to kick this off."

Don eagerly unscrewed the carafe and poured two generous cups of steaming dark refreshment.

"Don, this is a big step for you. My guess is that you've never done anything like this before. I think today, we just want to explore an approach to the future... maybe identify some key activities, some timelines, and resources required. You ok with that as today's goals?"

Don inhaled deeply, nodded, and said, "You're driving, Joseph. Let's get on with this."

For the next four hours, they talked about business outcomes. The brainstorming process ranged from an eruption of concepts to quiet conversations with sharpies hustling across a page. Three constant themes dominated the discussion:
  1. Current performance
  2. Future profitability

3. Transition

Current performance was a gnarly discussion with
challenges focused on accountability, market awareness
including competitors and competitive products, and
predictability. Occasionally Don was defensive and
upset with the direct questions that Joseph posed. As
emotions erupted Joseph defused the passion by
diverting to a neutral topic – vacation travel,
grandchildren, quiet Blue Ridge sunsets. His masterful
facilitation chaperoned Don through a three-dimensional
maze of speculation, fact, and personal sensitivities. To
be effective, Joseph mined 37 years of history, while
refreshing memories ranging from euphoria to despair,
from inspiration to melancholy. This collage of
experience was the foundation for moving forward to
tomorrow's alternatives. The historical good days were
proud moments radiant in the detail of accomplishment.
Bad day's memories were indistinct – dulled by time –
mere placeholders in the archives.

Throughout the discussion Joseph scratched multi-
colored notes across the flip charts – reds indicating
risks, and blues and greens opportunities. Filled pages
were sequentially numbered and pasted to any vacant
wall space around the office – and a few sheets covered
the office windows. Multi-colored, numbered *post-it*
action items were pasted near major section headings.
From afar, this rainbow mosaic of words, shapes and
colors may be viewed as the haphazard scribbling of a
three-year old, but to Don this represented a revelation
of thought for *tomorrows*.

Don held up his hand as if stopping traffic. "Let me just think about all these charts for a moment, Joseph." He scanned the first few flip-chart pages, stood and repositioned several of the post-its on the charts – not to change the sequence or flow, but more to personally touch the concepts… a tangible action to confirm their validity. His unblinking eyes never strayed from the notes while his hand unconsciously touched his temple. How can it be this simple? Know where you are - know where you are going and know resources required. Estimate time to complete. This isn't a business case. This is a flight plan into instrument conditions where there are some unknowns. The planning process itself minimizes flight risk, the periodic reporting confirms the current status and allows the pilot to adjust activity so that the plane safely reaches the destination. And Don would never fly without an IFR flight plan.

Joseph unscrewed and sipped a Dasani while Don was absorbing the concepts. As Don approached the charts and adjusted several of the colored stickers, Joseph knew these embryonic concepts were flowering into Don's future vision of what could be.

It was clear that Don's historical zeal for the Company had waned over the decades, and he was neither driven by growth, nor attuned to the marketplace and competition. By the end of the session, Don understood that Jackson Manufacturing was a solid Company with eroding market presence… perhaps with a limited future. And *future* was critical for Don – selling the

Company or not. Monetizing the Company's future was Don's retirement.

Planning and accountability were essential to his future, but historically he opposed such administrative time-wasters as not entrepreneurial... not profit oriented.

Reporting – other than cash balance in the bank – were part of the 'accountants full employment act' and designed to obfuscate results. In the past, if he wanted to discover performance, he just asked the right person.

His entrepreneurial DNA needed immediate gene therapy, and Joseph was the expert to help him identify and implement change.

Using his iPhone, Joseph took pictures of all the charts and emailed them to Don. He also sequentially peeled the flip-chart pages from the wall, stacked and carefully rolled them to ensure that the post-its stayed properly positioned.

1/09/14

Keys to
Valuation

1. Future Cash Flow

  1.1 Base

  1.2 Growth Engines

    1.2.1 Inside ——→ Licensing

    1.2.2 Outside ——→ Acquisition

    JV

Hockey sticks

Line of business reporting: Sales/ Margins   Trends!!

R&D

RISK

+

++

+++

Revenue sources; product aging

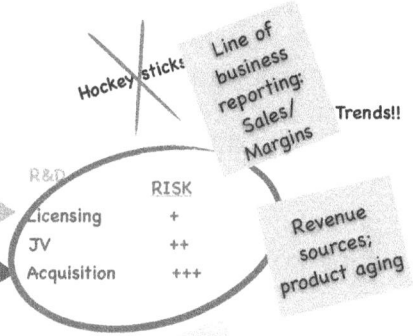

2. Credibility ✓

  2.1 Historical performance

  2.2 People

  2.3 Process

  2.4 Plant/ assets

  2.5 Product

  2.6 Market

Spending analysis ~2/3 year history

* Planning effectiveness
* Reporting
* Business dashboard
* Trending
* Analysis

The master document was straightforward, with about 10 primary points, structured to highlight importance, and a few post-its.

"This was quite a session today, Don. I'm blown-away by how much we have accomplished, and at your willingness to take the punches that I've thrown. Today was quite outstanding. What would you like to do next?"

"…Gotta tell ya, I have a completely different appreciation of how to run a business. I'll call it a theoretical knowledge at this point because I understand the concepts, but I don't know how to make it happen. By comparison to this management process, I've been a blunt instrument … a 19th century management artifact that in spite of myself has done – well, I'll say ok – but really maybe not.

Two questions – how do we get the team to understand these concepts, and how do we get the Company to run using this process?"

"Let's understand that this is not an easy process to implement, Don. We'll have to change personal habits – habits that are thoroughly ingrained. Habits are tough to change.

We have to introduce new concepts and we have to train the executives what to do and how to do it, all the while satisfying customers and beating the competition.

When we start down the path to progress, there will be failures. We will make mistakes, and they will cost you money. When we identify a failure, we have to celebrate the discovery and immediately correct the problem. Emotions will be high as some of the execs will immediately grasp and implement the required changes, while others may be slower to learn – or perhaps intentionally drag their feet – not to intentionally sabotage the project, but to reinforce their sincere belief that we are moving in the wrong direction. At that point, you have decisions to make.

The process takes time... to be effective, you may be in execution mode for 1-2 years. During that time, you will likely be improving your market value and marketability every quarter. But it takes work, and the journey takes tenacity... dedication to the process despite short-term setbacks.

So for example, when JB starts to sift through those overflowing bins of dusty materials, you will likely have write-offs. Not because you just created bad product, but because your process *recognizes* the bad product immediately. You may also have to invest in new equipment... maybe hire outsiders to help you implement process improvements ... maybe train your employees."

"So let me see if I understand this. Quite often a business selling price is a multiple of earnings, and you want me to take an earnings hit as I change my processes? Sounds to me like my valuation will be going down and it will cost me twice – once because earnings are down and once because my business will be less desirable."

"Correct if you only present GAAP earnings, but when we prepare financials, we will present earnings to reflect ongoing operations, then the incremental investments made to improve the business. So for example, if you clean up the manufacturing processes to minimize scrap and actively manage the manufacturing process to prove that the process is under control, we can identify one-time write-offs as such and adjust earnings. Of course, in the negotiation process the other side can always argue for the reduced earnings to be used as the base price, but if you have accurate and timely reporting demonstrating performance, you have a strong negotiating position. Remember, we are selling future earnings, not historical performance. And future earnings are estimates supported by credibility.

And, by the way, if you choose not to sell the business, what's wrong with long range improved profitability?"

"Joseph, you make it sound so simple."

"It's pretty straightforward, but remember, culture change is not without pain. I've seen the best people – the 'A' players - embrace the changes that we're discussing because it allows them to boast about their performance. Those 'B' and 'C' employees often don't want the changes, because their poor performance is front and center... cannot be hidden any longer.

...Just human nature..."

123

"So what do you suggest, Joseph?"

"Review the notes from today, Don. Think about the journey, and some of the pitfalls we've discussed. It will be a lot of work, but I think that you'll see in the long run, it is the only way to protect your future... your tomorrow's.

When we do it right, your executives will grow in their careers, and your employees will grow in personal value, and very likely increase their earnings when performance based systems are in place.

Let's get together in a couple of days and talk through your thoughts. If you're in agreement, we can then take the staff through our notes and see if we can gain consensus."

The next meeting was set for Wednesday at 9:00 AM.

January 22, 2014 - Specialist to CEO & CFO: Next Steps Reporting

> ✳Improve reporting
> ✳Business dashboard
> ✳Key performance metrics
> ✳Planning

Don welcomed Joseph. "Well, Joseph, the last few hours that we spent discussing how to better manage a company were extremely valuable. From 30,000 feet, I can appreciate that it is a fairly simple process – something that I never paid attention to before. And your cautionary statements about points of failure and high emotions were, let's say, balanced. This isn't Alice in Wonderland where everything will go smoothly, but I see how the business would be more saleable and perhaps at a higher value when we can demonstrate that we can not only promise, but also deliver better results.

125

How would you like to proceed?"

Joseph opened a file and tabled the broad guideline they developed last time so that both could observe.

"Let's explore what I'll call Stage 1:
- Improved reporting
- Internal Analysis
- Key Metrics
- Planning

While we'd like to have perfect information, my guess is that your system can't provide *perfect* information. In step 1, I review reporting available today – whether it be daily, weekly or monthly – and then look at your planning."

Don leaned back in the chair, and with a broad grin said, " And what will you do after the first 15 minutes? I honestly think that you've seen everything we've got. Daily reporting? Weekly reporting? You're kidding, right?"

"OK – then it seems that we may have some opportunity to crank things up a bit. Improved reporting is a way for you to push responsibility down through the organization, and hold people accountable. If we do it right, there should be minimal effort to gain exceptional results.

I'd like to spend a few more hours with your execs – perhaps 1-2 hours with each – and basically identify what they believe to be the most important metrics to measure their performance. ... How they know whether they are doing well or poorly.

If these folks are good, they've already identified the items and have an informal mechanism in place. We'll elevate the metric to a more formal process. The first step will be to establish available reporting immediately – that means within 1-2 weeks. I'm not sure if it will include daily, weekly or just monthly, but let's define my deliverable as improved reporting within 10 business days from now, while consuming only 2+- hours of your execs time. Deal?"

"Deal!"

Don thought, 'Interesting how Joseph is unafraid to define deliverables right up front, without really knowing much about the Company – doesn't have a clue about our systems. Gutsy move... really no downside for me except for a few bucks.'

"Don, can you drop an email to the folks letting them know that I will be meeting with them?"

Don's email introduced Joseph as a consultant who would help the Company focus on cash flow and profit improvement, and strategic issues. Meetings would generally be one-on-one and require no more than 2 hours. The email implored all, "…be candid…Joseph has access to any Company information."

The next day, Joseph met with Cynthia. She brought the same reporting and planning files as the first meeting, but the files were not stacked as a barrier to discussion, but rather presented so that both could review the information during the discussion. Her easy manner displayed a comfort with the process, and encouraged a collaborative effort. As she opened one of the files, she asked, "How shall we proceed?"

"Before we start pawing through the pages, Cynthia, tell me how you know the business is doing well or poorly?"

"The key for me is cash flow – cash balance and revolver, receipts and disbursements. I download a daily cash report from the bank that includes all the details. If it's close to my plan, life is good. If it's off by much, I have the accountant check it out.

I also get a daily sales number, and a listing of any significant credit adjustments. I have a target daily sales number – modified a bit by seasonality – and I don't expect any major credit adjustments."

Joseph nodded agreement, selected a marker and started drawing on the white board, while encouraging Cynthia to continue.

Metrics	Daily	Weekly	Monthly
– Manufacturing			
–PPV		✓	
–OT Spend		✓	
–W/O variance		✓	
–Orders	✓		
–Backlog	✓		
–Headcount			✓
–DSO			✓
–Inventory Turns			✓

"We don't get much daily info from manufacturing, but we do have some decent information on a monthly basis. So, for example, JB always checks out the Purchase Price Variance – mainly because of the raw material price volatility. He is also a real bird-dog on other variances such as overhead spending, labor utilization and oh-my-god, you can't believe how he tracks overtime spending."

"So on those spending variances, are they managed only monthly, or are there postings to the ledger every day?"

"For sure there are daily entries as each work order is closed."

"So does that mean you could provide – let's call it a weekly report on key variances?"

While Cynthia nodded agreement, she anxiously watched Joseph's scrawling across the white board. As the graphics took shape, she leaned into the chair with eyes wide and a discreet smile. Joseph took raw numbers and gave them life. Data that was easily available transformed into easily interpreted information.

"Cynthia, this is a rough sketch of how you might want to present information. And I really don't know what makes the most sense, but you're in the business. Think through what is easily available and how the team may be able to use the information. Maybe you'll want to use some real numbers and review the information with the other execs. Once you find the right set of information, why not pass it by Don to see what he thinks?"

Daily Sales Report

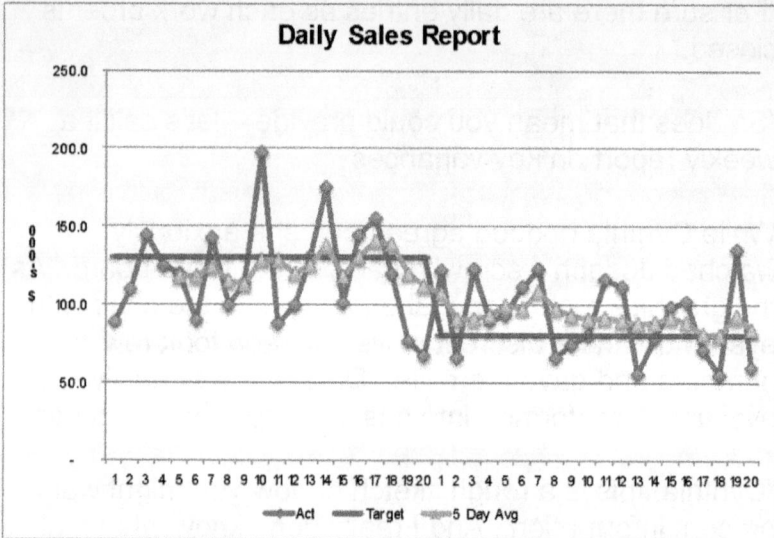

"I scratched several lines on the chart and show two months of activity. When something unusual happens – example of $200,000 of sales on the 10th day – add a note to the chart. Real information that management can act – or react to. Thoughts?"

Cynthia jumped to her feet, grabbed a green marker and quickly added several lines to the chart. Her attitude was energized as she quickly brainstormed a dozen categories – from sales of kits, to a listing of variances, to credit memos issued.

Metrics	Daily	Weekly	Monthly
- Kit Sales	✔	✔	✔
- Knuckle Sales	✔	✔	✔
- Margins	✔	✔	✔
Manufacturing			
- PPV		✔	
-OT Spending		✔	
- W/O variance		✔	
Orders	✔		
Backlog	✔		
Headcount			✔
DSO			✔
Inventory Turns			✔

"Now when you create these reports, be careful not to build an administrative monster. You'll want to limit information to what is important to the team. And you'll also want to limit the reporting to what can easily be obtained. I know that you have some systems limitations."

"Got it!"

Joseph was pleased with Cynthia's grasp of the concepts. Her initial selection of metrics and timing looked reasonable, but information availability would be one of the keys to selection. Cynthia would also have to discuss the selected metrics with the execs, who may object to some of the information. Reporting forces accountability.

As a final step, Joseph discussed information flow and how reports should reflect level of responsibility – more detailed for supervisors and managers – summary information for upper levels of management. He shared a planning template slide that described the concept.

ABC Company, LLC

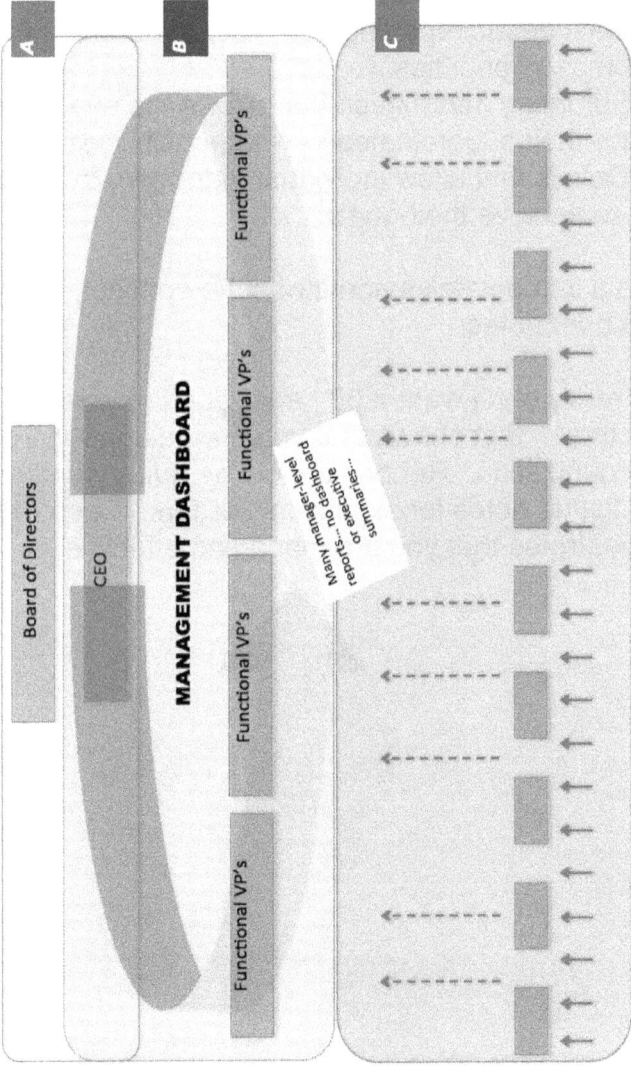

A

Board of Directors

B

Functional VP's | Functional VP's | CEO | Functional VP's | Functional VP's

MANAGEMENT DASHBOARD

Many manager-level reports-- no dashboard or executive summaries...

C

A = Least detail, reporting summary information focused on Company priorities.
B = Summary information that allows the executive to monitor their subordinates key responsibilities.
C = Details that allow individual managers to act and react to achieve their goals.

Cynthia immediately understood the concept, and wrote some brief notes.

"You really don't want a 50 page report to go to 'Directors' – that shows that you are delegating work up the organization. Reports should be quickly understood and include notes for significant matters. Crisp reporting demonstrates that you are managing effectively."

January 20, 2014 - Specialist to VP Sales: Next Steps

> *Sales Strategy
> *Customer/channel classification & priorities
> *Pipeline management
> *Resource allocation

Stephen's office lair screamed of sales and marketing. Shelves showcased performance awards, memorial photos of Stephen arm-in-arm with beautiful models at trade-shows, or perched on Hawaiian cliffs – Calloway drivers extended as if posing for a statue – with professional golfers such as Bubba Watson. Office décor was bright and cheery – a positive feng shui throughout.

The neatly organized desk and credenza were laid out to provide creative space. A quiver of multi-colored sharpies and a pad of graph paper signaled an innovative executive who was unafraid of thinking outside the lines.

The white board was barren except for 3 lines – "J&J– New Jersey; Stryker – Ohio; DePuy – Minn".

"Morning Stephen. Is this a good time?"   Joseph always jealously guarded the executive's time. He wanted to ensure that when they met, there were no other priorities diluting their concentrated discussions.

"You bet – c'mon in." Stephen guided Joseph to the round conference table – empty except for the tray with several bottles of Dasani.

The script was typical – "…tell me how you run your business…"

Stephen's description of his management process was carefully scripted as if he were on a sales call. He described each individual in the sales force, their strengths and weaknesses, and how he developed their regional sales targets using the Company goal as a guide. He explained that if the Company goal was to increase sales by 5%, each region's goal was set at 7% over prior year to create somewhat of a contingency – a cushion to cover a region's shortfall.

Joseph introduced the concept of sales pipeline, and managing the customer portfolio using the A-B-C method, concentrating on existing and potential customers. They also shared thoughts about customer turnover, and various techniques to maintain customer awareness.

Defining A-B-C actual and potential customers allowed Stephen to focus the Company's limited resources on the greatest potential sales areas. Simple Pareto analysis ranked existing customers from high to low annual sales, based on historical annual volume, and required sales executives to estimate potential sales volume. In the initial analysis, the ranking of A-B-C was intuitive rather than scientifically based. During the discussion, Stephen agreed that an individual customer with historical/potential sales volume of $500,000 or more would be classified as an "A" customer. Annual sales volume of less than $25,000 would be considered a "C" customer, and all others would be classified as "B" level. The same sales range would be used for potential customers.

"Stephen, let's be clear, there is nothing magic about $500k or $25k. They're somewhat arbitrary to help you focus your limited resources.

Classifying customers by annual sales volume allowed the Company to prioritize sales and marketing efforts based on likely profitability. Stephen agreed that this type of detailed customer analysis could be completed in a few hours, as long as precision was not required.

Once the initial segmentation was defined, Joseph posed the question, "So now that you have a listing of targets, how do you define sales goals – and let's not forget about allocating sales/marketing resources to the lofty goals established."

Since Stephen was the Sales and Marketing VP, all promotional efforts were his responsibility. Once again, his spending resources were allocated by Cynthia and Don – frequently the prior year plus a percent – usually less than 5%. His planning process was straightforward. Each expense category - such as Compensation, Advertising, Internet, Trade Shows, and T&E - increased by the target percent.

Joseph challenged Stephen, "How the hell are you going to significantly increase sales with a 5% increase of resources?"

"Hey, don't lean on me, Joseph. That's not the question that I am paid to answer. My challenge is – for example – get a 5% increase in sales with a 5% increase in spending. Don has never asked for more, nor allowed more spending. Don't bust my chops, eh!"

"OK, let's change the question, Stephen. If Don were to say, 'I want a 15% increase in sales' what would you do?"

Stephen was speechless. In a decade, he had never dealt with such a challenge. He was upset with this ridiculous speculation and summarized, "Bullshit! Won't happen, so why waste our time?" The only sound for the next few minutes was Stephen's nervous clicking of his fountain pen cap.

"Hey Stephen, you've blocked out 2 hours. Let's play this out and see where it goes."

Joseph sketched a matrix on the board that had column headings of A-B-C and rows describing various spending categories such as compensation, advertising, trade shows, T&E, collateral material etc. He asked Stephen for round numbers of spending by category, careful not to get too mired in minutia.

"What's a sales rep cost?"

"I've got a half-dozen reps that have different levels of experience. ...Far too difficult to categorize cost. Heck, a newbie has a base of $35,000 plus commission, while my best guy has a base of $60,000. You just can't have a single number for the reps."

"So is there a target total compensation for a rep – all in, including commission? And T&E and fringe?"

"Never looked at it that way. I guess that we expect a rookie to get about $25,000 of commission if they do a decent job. Some may get a lot more."

"What if we just say a rep costs $100,000 annually, including fringe, travel, base and commission. How far off could we be for back-of-the envelope planning?"

"That's not a stupid number. Should be ok for back-of-the envelope."

Joseph guided the discussion to round-number analysis covering the expense categories, achieving his goal of a macro analysis. Jackson used direct selling as nearly the exclusive mode to promote the knuckles.

"Stephen, how have you used the Internet, and trade shows to promote the product and increase sales. The reach and teaching capability of these promotional modes could help increase product awareness – maybe increase overall sales."

"You just don't get it, Joseph. We are a simple, mom and pop organization built on 20th century technology. There has never been a need to expand sales – or even introduce new products – since Don is doing just fine. He makes a good buck, pays his bills, and meets payroll – without fail. Stop pressing my buttons for alternatives."

Occasionally, he challenged Stephen with a 'what if' question, and pressed for answers until Stephen was agitated. "What if you had an extra half-million to spend on sales & marketing? What would you spend it on, and how much extra sales could you get?"

Jackson Manufacturing hardly touched the International markets with more than 6 billion people, and while Stephen clearly understood the market potential, he had no International experience.

Stephen gradually lost his defensive posture, and seemed to enjoy the pure speculation. It didn't cost anything to scratch alternatives on the white-board, and some of the ideas were brilliant – and never before considered. They also identified some incredibly stupid concepts, but it didn't cost anything except a few minutes of already allocated time.

In a flurry of activity, they wrote, erased and modified entries repeatedly, listing spending estimates and action programs across the A-B-C *current* and *potential* columns.

Brainstorming… what a concept.

After several hours of discussion and white-board penmanship, Stephen enthusiastically saw ways to improve his management process.

Once they explored the A-B-C customer categories, Joseph concentrated on the trade channels, such as distributors, Joint Ventures, manufacturers representatives. Stephen was thoroughly familiar with the attributes of the trade channels. As they conjured alternatives to direct sales, Joseph puzzled over why many of these lower cost, minimal risk alternatives were not used. The consistent response was, "No money for development."

Once the broad spending allocation matrices were reviewed, Joseph focused on customer pipeline, closing cycle and success ratios. Stephen was familiar with the processes, but only applied the principles informally. He saw little benefit in documenting and formally managing such a process.

Although these were not final analyses, Joseph snapped photos of the white board and sent a copy to Stephen.

| | Customer Classifications | | | | | |
| | A | | B | | C | |
	Actual	Potential	Actual	Potential	Actual	Potential
Direct Resources						
Direct Sales						
Distributor						
Catalog						
Website						
Other						
Indirect Resources						
T&E						
Trade Associations						
Public Relations						
Government PAC						

Trade Classification (US &/or International)					
Direct		Distributor		Wholesale	
Actual	Potential	Actual	Potential	Actual	Potential

Direct Resources
Direct Sales
Distributor
Catalog
Website
Other

Indirect Resources
T&E
Trade Associations
Public Relations
Government PAC

"OK Stephen, let's discuss customer pipeline. What is your normal closing cycle – for example, from first point of contact to closing? And also, what is your success ratio?"

"We don't use such a regimented process, Joseph. Our process is informal, and it has been for years. Thus far, it works. Not sure why I would change anything."

"I understand your concerns about too much administrative BS. It's not so much the perfect model, but thinking through the marketplace and current and potential customers might be helpful as you allocate limited resources." Joseph scratched out a quick sales funnel, with 5 sections, on the whiteboard. "I'm going to

be arbitrary when I create some of these sections, but I
want to explore how it may be helpful for you. If it isn't
helpful, no worries." His diagram included a section for
"A" Potential, and "B" potential customers, which were
assumed to have different sales cycles. He also
identified different success ratios for "A" and "B"
customers, explaining that "A" potential's may be more
difficult to close.

At the base of the diagram, he listed some activities to
be completed during each phase of the sales pipeline
process, again, identifying different activities for "A" and
"B" customers.

One feature that would be consistent throughout the
pipeline process is something called "Internet Search".
"This thing called 'Internet Search' can be used for your
existing customers and for potential customers. Set up
a Google search for Company names, and anything that
pops up in the web – basically anything printed in a
newspaper or other public media – will be referenced for
you. This gives you the chance to drop a known exec or
sales contact a brief note of – perhaps congratulations -
upon signing a new contract… hiring a new exec …
expanding offices etc. It may be a great reason to keep
in touch with the exec.

Look, the pipeline process and overall allocation of
resources may not change how you run the business,
but personally I'd rather play on a whiteboard to see if
something makes sense, rather than spend real money
trying something before I simulate the process.

145

These two analytical methods can give you the ability to manage the sales process more effectively. You can ask each of your reps for a listing of all "A" potential customers within their region, and ask for them to manage the pipeline process on at least 5 "A" potentials each quarter."

Joseph left the whiteboard and walked to the desk for a Dasani. "Interested?" as he raised a bottle. As Stephen nodded, Joseph lofted a bottle across the desk to a catch worthy of a tight end near the goal line.

"Once you've sketched out the process and probabilities, you just have to manage the pipeline to get the desired results. So let's say you need an additional million dollars of sales, you define an "A" potential account as one with $500,000 annual volume, and your process proves out a 5% success rate, you need to identify and call on 40 potential "A" accounts (40 accounts @ $500,000 annual volume with a 5% success rate…voila… $1 million of annual sales.

Now we both know it doesn't work exactly like that, but when you think through the process, I think that you'll see how it will make your job easier."

This was an ideal time to let these concepts sink in. Stephen sipped the water, while unconsciously toying with the bottle label.

"Look we're not going to be able to sketch out an entire pipeline process today. I only ask that you consider this kind of analytical process to see if it will work for you."

"... Sounds simple enough, but where do I get the ratios?"

"If you don't have success ratios defined, use your gut ... intuition... to begin the process. All the ratios and processes should be continually updated to reflect reality, but don't' wait for perfection to get started."

Sales Pipeline Management

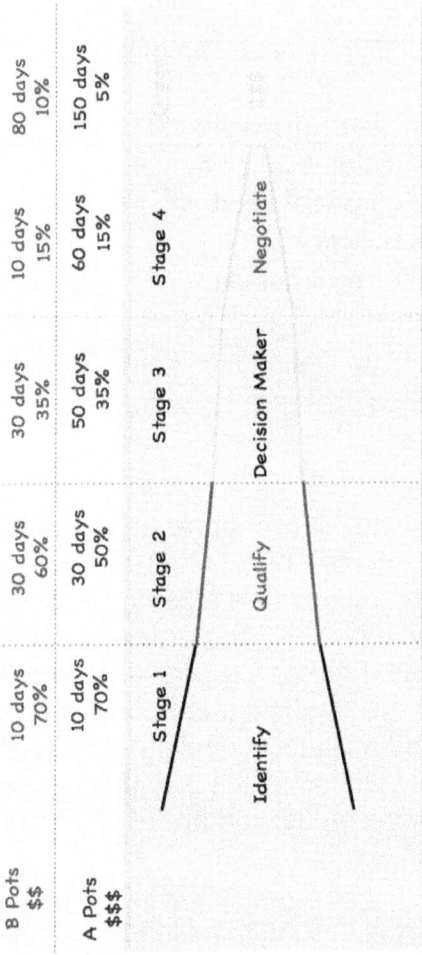

	Stage 1	Stage 2	Stage 3	Stage 4	
B Pots $$	10 days 70%	30 days 60%	30 days 35%	10 days 15%	80 days 10%
A Pots $$$	10 days 70%	30 days 50%	50 days 35%	60 days 15%	150 days 5%

Stage 1	**Stage 2**	**Stage 3**	**Stage 4**
Identify	Qualify	Decision Maker	Negotiate

Internet Search

B Pots $$
- Initial contact – Director +
- Office visit
- Follow-up mailing
- Phone contact

- Lunch
- Meet engineers
- Follow-up mailing

- Lunch – +Officer
- Meet engineers
- Follow-up mailing

- Lunch – +Officer
- Reference clients
- Proposal

A Pots $$$
- Initial contact – Director ++
- Office visit
- Follow-up mailing
- Phone contact

- Lunch – Director ++
- Meet engineers
- Follow-up mailing

- Lunch – +Officer
- Meet engineers
- Follow-up mailing

January 22, 2014 – Specialist to VP R&D: Next Steps

> *R&D pipeline management
> *Prioritization based on market & financial returns
> *ID development, manufacturing & launch requirements

The 8:30 appointment with Allison, at her office, would give Joseph the chance to see her on home turf. Her office was an interesting mix of mad scientist and well organized professional. Her neat and orderly desk contrasted markedly with her conference table, stacked with scientific journals, bio-medical text books, a 9"x12" artist's sketch book, and a Black Moleskine Folio with the black ribbon marker placed about one-third through the volume, and a 1" wide red ribbon about half through the folio.

Several landscape photos of a lush, rolling landscape, and several more personalized pictures of hikers stacked high with over-stuffed backpacks and broad smiles.

Allison's smile and warm handshake welcomed Joseph into her office. As she guided Joseph to the conference table, she retrieved the three placemats that she outlined several weeks before. "I've thought a lot about our last discussion and decided that I should be more aggressive, until Don says '… back off…'

Let's take a look at the last summary.

Description		US	China	Other
			(Millions $$)	
Youth	✓			
Male	✓		75	50
Female	✓	20	45	150
Women	✓	50	25	50
Men	✓	30	80	80
Obese	✓	75		

		Materials			Production Method		Circuitry	
	Pure	60/40	40/60	80/20	Machined	Cast	Selenium	NanoTech
Titanium		Potential Breakthrough		90%				90%
Tantalum	50%							

"We have the opportunity to help patients live better, more enjoyable lives. Our products can extend meaningful hobbies and open new lifestyles to so many people.

If we engineer things better, we can also improve profitability for Don. He hasn't challenged us on any of these fronts. You did, and initially, I was not happy. But after I thought about your challenge, I decided, why not.

After looking at some of our brainstorming on these exceptionally well-designed place mats." Her broad smile beamed her playfulness in this brainstorming mode. "I've concentrated on several areas for development. Obesity is the root of killing more Americans than almost any other controllable disease. The disease's progression is almost self-fulfilling, since once obese, the joints and skeletal structure wears down more quickly, and individuals exercise less, leading to more obesity. We need to concentrate on more structurally sound fittings, with more durable alloys."

"It sounds like you've done some serious thinking about this. But let's back up a bit. You've got a lot of stuff in this office. What do you do with all this information?"

She took him on a virtual tour of the office, including some proud discussion about her hiking adventure on the Camino de Santiago. The desk photos were Spanish landscapes, and pictures of several new acquaintances she met on the trek. Her enthusiastic discussion of the Camino adventure described a most creative time of her life. Twenty-five days of hiking across a foreign land - alone and without reservations - stripped her mind of cobwebs and clutter. While she attributed no revelations to the trek, she was reinvigorated upon her return.

As she described the conference table landscape, she identified the stacks of journals – some with the plastic wrap in tact, while others were obviously well used with page corners turned, yellow stickies referencing important sections. The diverse library included biomedical journals, as well as cabinet-making and engineering metallurgy periodicals. The blend of sciences portrayed a creative, solutions-oriented mind not constrained by traditional thinking.

Joseph asked to explore the sketchbook and the folio to help understand why she used so many notebooks. The artist's sketchbook was pure brainstorming and included many pages with asterisks - one, two or three in the top right corner to indicate importance - and a number of pages with heavy dark diagonal lines from corner to corner. Such "x'ed" pages were of no value – after initial review, a pure waste of time. Allison knew that brainstorming results ranged from garbage to absolute brilliance, and used her own unique method to label appropriately.

As Joseph scanned the "***" pages, he noticed that many seemed to be a close fit to potential product line expansion at Jackson. Some of those pages also identified competitive products that might be an ideal product line extension for the Jackson line.

"Tell me more about "***" pages, Allison."

"Absolutely lovely ideas – but beyond the scope of anything Don wants to do. But as I read the journals and just dream about 'what could be', many of these seem so right – a perfect fit for who we are. We're not a conglomerate - we're a simple mom & pop shop that makes a few bucks by serving patient needs. Sure, I'd like to make some of these things happen, but with a 3-5% spending increase, where are we going with these dreams?" As she spoke, her enthusiasm waned and her attitude dissolved to a wistful gaze."

"Have you asked Don about any of these 'triple-dip' ideas?"

"No – just never seemed like he would be interested."

"Well, let's spend a few minutes and just talk. First of all, where do you encounter these ideas? For example, do half of the ideas originate with a journal review? And once you identify an idea, how do you vet the concept to give it substance?

Joseph posed numerous questions to understand her creative methods, and as he suspected, she had a routine that frequently developed potential products and improved production methods.

"And tell me about the Folio. Looks a bit neater and better organized than the artists sketch pad."

The black Moleskine had the attached black ribbon, and also a bright red ribbon – something that could be used to wrap a ponytail in blustery conditions. "And the ribbons, Allison?"

"You are a curious soul, Joseph. The first section of the folio represents materials, the second section represents new designs, and the third section – yes, highlighted with the red ribbon – are the approved products that others make, that I'd like to get in our product line."

As she flipped through the sections, the notes in this book were noticeably neater and better organized than the rough sketches and notes in the sketchbook. Each section seemed to follow an individual template of information. The first section included a brief description of the concept – whether an exotic metal, or new product – and how it might improve the Company's performance. The next section seemed to highlight sales volumes over a 3-5 year period. Surprisingly, these values were listed in millions of dollars. The third section highlighted development costs, including likely capital spending and research costs.

She explained that she had little knowledge of sales and marketing costs, and – at best – guestimates for manufacturing costs. Her numbers were scientific in their basis – best available information – but not substantiated by any extensive research with other executive staff members.

"So Allison, if you could pick three projects to investigate from this entire folio, which ones would they be?"

When she selected the projects, Joseph challenged her selection criteria to determine the extent of her knowledge and confidence level to bring the products to market successfully. Allison understood the metallurgy and design technology, was familiar with market characteristics and manufacturing challenges. She lacked familiarity with pricing, product launch programs and costs.

"You've got some great structure in how you consider developments. Have you ever considered sharing the ideas with others on the staff?"

"I did several years ago, but then we all concluded, 'Why Bother? No development money."

"I like the clarity of thought when you focus on new product development. You've identified many of the criteria to make a successful investment decision. Can we play with the concepts on the white board?"

Allison reached into the office refrigerator, selected two Dasani's and shared one with Joseph, who after an hour of discussion could use a break.

She was intrigued with Joseph's manner and approach to development. At each stage, he repeated the question, "Have you talked to Don?" Interesting approach… was he trying to make her uneasy, or encourage her to challenge Don?

Joseph selected three dry-erase markers – black, red, and green, and started to write on the whiteboard. "Joseph, if you write on the board, we won't be able to transcribe the info easily – I use the board frequently for concept development and erase anything on it."

"No worries, Allison – I'll take a picture and send you a copy – if we create anything of interest."

Allison chuckled at his modesty – of course we'll document the ideas developed, otherwise why bother with the whiteboard. Joseph has certainly done this before.

Joseph talked while he was writing, encouraging Allison's input about the concepts. Words and concepts flew to the board – some remained while others instantly disappeared.

At the conclusion of the hour, Joseph's drafting could have been the basis of a new product development thesis.

Project Description:			
	2 years historical	**3-5 years future**	**Terminal Value**
Cash Flows - outbound			
Capital			
Expenses			
Development			
Launch			
Maintenance			
Cash Flows - inbound			
Revenues			
Earnings			

Development Timeline

Market Potential
US
International

Competitive discussion

Launch & marketing discussion

Allison was surprised at the thoroughness of the analysis... from project description to development costs, capital and manpower required, to estimated P&L for the next few years.

Joseph emphasized that precision was not critical, but sufficient information to make a good decision was essential. As an example, he mentioned that in the concept development stage, it was pointless to estimate profitability over a 5-year period to anything closer than plus-or-minus $100,000. If a project made sense at the development stage, more precision would be required, but he mentioned that since probably 75% of the projects could be eliminated in a first pass evaluation, considerable time would be saved just by 'chunking it out' to the nearest $100,000.

Yes, she thought, an expeditious way to plan.

Overall, Allison was an impressive executive who conquered her frustration with the Company's lack of imagination by personal research and hobbies that challenged her both physically and mentally. Her trek to Spain for the solo 500-mile stroll cleared many cobwebs.

"Say, that is an interesting charm, Allison, what does it represent," referring to the gold charm on her necklace.

"Greek symbol for 'Pi'. It is an *irrational* number – something that in decimal form goes on forever, and never repeats itself. To me it represents a quest for knowledge that never ends. An enigma. The concept fascinates me."

January 25, 2014 - Specialist to VP Human Resources

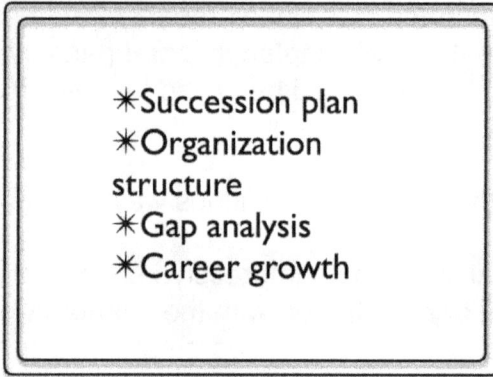

＊Succession plan
＊Organization structure
＊Gap analysis
＊Career growth

Joseph read the email he received from Margaret, the Human Resources executive. "Would be good to meet with you next, if you can adjust your schedule. MC"

Joseph was intrigued that she took the initiative to adjust the schedule, and of course accommodated her request. They met for lunch at the local J. Alexander's, since the restaurant had large tables, a quiet atmosphere and discreet areas for confidential discussions.

Margaret met him at the reception area and the attractive young hostess with a genuine smile guided them to a quiet section of the restaurant.
January chills forced both to bundle… Joseph in a traditional Burberry Trench Coat topped with a Harris

Tweed cap, and Margaret in a burgundy, double
breasted lambskin coat accented with burgundy
shearling gloves and a Gucci silk scarf. As coats and
accessories were stacked in the booth, they both were
pleased with the restaurant selection.

"Good afternoon, my name is Mickey." The trim auburn-
haired waitress garbed in black, no doubt a local college
student, explained the lunch specials in such careful
detail that she could have been a writer for Conde Nast.
When questioned about the standard fare, she
passionately described the delicate wine sauces, the
light crispness of the fish and chips, and the bold flavor
of the black bean veggie burger. Margaret's eyes
widened and, somewhat embarrassed, admitted to
dieting after the holiday festivities.

After a few minutes discussing the cold January
weather, they scanned the menu for the best selection.

Mickey returned with two iced teas and quickly jotted
their order, confirming their selection with a chef's
eloquent description. "…The Caesar salad with herbal
crostini, seared fresh, wild caught Alaskan salmon, and
a cup of portabella mushroom soup made with a dash of
sherry, topped with a dollop of sour cream…"

"… And for you, sir, the seared Ahi Tuna, field greens
with a wasabi and cilantro vinaigrette. Would you like
some fresh bread, or perhaps the herbal crostini to
accompany?"

Margaret seemed more confident today, one hand resting comfortably on the heavy dark oak table, the other swirling the lemon droplets into the tea with a straw. Looking up from the mini-whirlpools in the tea, she said, "Glad that you were able to meet with me, Joseph.

I've been interested in your approach with our team for the past few weeks, and wanted to give you some feedback. As you might imagine, as the HR representative, folks often consider me their father confessor or rabbi. Whatever they tell me stays with me. That said, I've got an obligation to the Company and to Don, who has taken good care of all of us.

So far, you've talked with Cynthia, Allison, and Stephen. Each of them mentioned that you seem to know your business, and that you like to challenge them... push them beyond their traditional borders, and sometimes figuratively 'stick your finger in their eye...'

Sounds like you may be creating some energy in this business. And Don has been getting some positive feedback from each of them – some of the feedback has been unsettling... forcing him to rethink some of the strategies.

I wanted to catch you before you met with JB. He's a tough guy who has been working in factories for decades ... has a Mechanical Engineering degree from Purdue, but, well, we all know that he's gotten a bit stale – I guess like the rest of us, but he's more of an independent and immovable monolith – perhaps the only one in the business who really knows the manufacturing, except Don.

He's also heard about your approach from the rest of the folks, and is building an arsenal of information to keep you in your place, and out of his space.

Personally, I am very happy that you've been poking at this carcass of a business that we all love, but know something needs to change. We've all had these discussions before, but life's so good here, we've never known what to change, and didn't want to disrupt our happy little lives, in our warm and fuzzy environment."

"So Margaret, it's interesting that you've bared your soul to me. Do the others know how you were going to share this information with me?"

"It's my style – do whatever I can behind the scenes to help make this Company more successful."

"Great – and thanks for the heads-up with JB. Well, tell me about yourself and how you run the Human Resources function."

The steaming cup of mushroom soup arrived exactly as described – a lightly seasoned dollop of sour cream floating, centered in the cup.
"Mickey, that soup looks so good, may I have a cup as well? Margaret, please enjoy."

As lunch progressed, Margaret confessed that her role was primarily one of compliance with Federal, State and Local personnel regulations, processing payrolls and commissions, and monitoring performance review processes. She mused that since personnel costs totaled more than 60% of non-materials cost, she should be doing more, but was unsure what should be done.

"The business – and the associates – are in the *today* frame of mind. We are all doing well, since Don is so generous, and the whole team seems to have settled into an ozone layer that doesn't demand much. … Comfortable like a well-worn set of shearling slippers. As I talk to folks, there is some kind of undercurrent that I can't quite identify – not a negative or detrimental tone like sabotage – but an uneasy feeling… some kind of unrest.

We've noticed that several of the younger engineers have left in the past year, and haven't gotten clear insight into their reasons for departure during the exit interviews."

"So, let's say you are in charge of all the people in the Company. What do you think should be done Margaret?"

By this time, Mickey showcased a tray of desserts suitable for Henry VIII. Shamefully, Joseph and Margaret, unable to resist, selected the day's special – a silky smooth cheesecake with velvet graham cracker crust topped with plump cherries drizzled with a cognac reduction.

Margaret agreed that espresso would be an ideal complement. "And Mickey, can you bring some paper and pen... not a small pad, but something that we can create with..."

"We really don't have a *tomorrow* vision... a guide that tells us where we are going and in broad terms how to get there. As a result, we live day-to-day – which isn't bad but it's a bit unsettling."

"So what do you want to do about it? What if you were in charge?"

"It seems that somehow we need to describe where we are going and how we are going to get there."

"Here's some paper. Let's sketch out the things that you think are important."

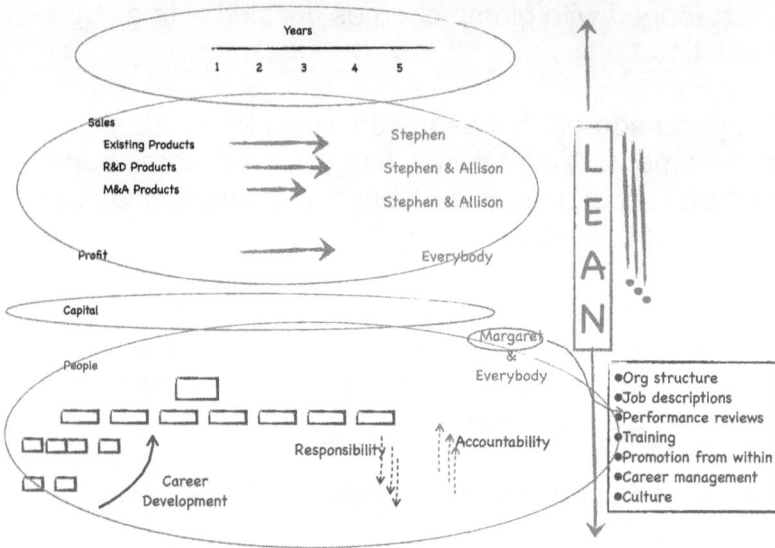

During the next hour Margaret and Joseph sketched out concepts that Margaret thought were important to the Company – things that she considered *tomorrow*. After some debate, they resolved that *tomorrow* wasn't a month or a year, but many years, because to really have an effect, programs took 2+- years to implement.

They focused on three areas that Margaret, surprisingly, defined as critical – Profit & Loss, Capital Spending, and People. Rather than just explore concepts, Joseph insisted that Margaret put names next to each major category. Initially, she was opposed to assigning names, since this was Don's Company, not hers. Joseph explained the concept of team, and unless everyone had a common understanding of Company goals – including Don – it would be impossible for the team to effectively deliver the goals.

She identified the product offering gap, and with some coaxing, expanded the sales needs to include new products developed through R&D, and those that must come from outside. Yes, Stephen and Allison must be responsible since they *own* those functions.

As Joseph explored the Profit concept, it was clear that if everyone weren't committed to Company goals, profit goals would not be achieved. And if goals were not properly communicated with measurable checkpoints, the team could not work together effectively.

Margaret was very comfortable discussing organization and personal development. Despite her limited education, her passion for strategic human resources issues was evident. She was reluctant to fully participate in earlier discussions about P&L, Capital, and new products, but her enthusiasm for HR positively bubbled.

She gave Joseph a thorough lesson in Human Resource process, and focused on keys to effective HR management. Organization structure was a cornerstone of success, especially when staffed with the right people. Once the structure and people were in place, personal goals must be coordinated so that the Company objectives would be met - easily done through proper job descriptions and effective performance reviews. Reviews must be done on time, and be thorough and honest so that the employees can personally contribute to the Company success, and develop their real world value. She insisted that employees needed career development so they received more than a paycheck.

She also scratched out an over-riding program that covered all functions – "LEAN." While she was not expert at the process, she had trained enough to understand that the process makes a Company more effective by doing the right thing, in the right way, every time. This would also eliminate waste throughout the Company – making the Company a better place to work.

It was clear to Joseph that Margaret thoroughly understood the Human Resources responsibility, but had never practiced the techniques to improve Company performance. When questioned why, Margaret replied, "We don't have the money to invest, no one has asked for her advice, and change was frowned upon. Other than that, we'd make some changes."

Exhausted, she leaned back, breathed a deep sigh, and folded her hands as if to say, "Lesson complete."

Joseph pressed, "And now what?"

"I think that's why you're here, Joseph. You've gotten input from almost everyone. Maybe some good ideas… maybe not. You've got this hodgepodge of concepts, observations, knowledge and known gaps. I'm thinking that you'll assemble this mosaic into a picture that we can all appreciate and understand… and begin to improve. So you tell me what's next."

"Each of you has been very cooperative and shared your ideas with me. You folks all have a keen understanding of what must be done, but we need an organized approach to make the team function as one. It's up to me to convince Don that change is necessary.

Hey, Margaret, this has been a fabulous lunch – sorry we killed so much of your afternoon."

January 29, 2014 - Specialist to VP
Manufacturing: Next steps

```
✳Lean manufacturing
✳Key metrics
✳Waste & rework
```

Three inches of fresh powder draped tree limbs creating frosted skeletons throughout the city. City metro buses chewed the fluffy powder into lumps of brown sugar tracing routes along city streets. Traffic, slowed to a crawl, delayed Joseph's arrival to meet with JB.

Today, Joseph abandoned traditional professional attire and dressed in Khaki whipcord pants, Gore-Tex backpacking boots, down vest with a Gore-Tex ski jacket. He was determined not to be cold, and decided that ruining his shoes just wasn't worth the effect to be gained. He also thought dressing down for the rough and tumble JB was a worthwhile gesture.

When he arrived in JB's office, JB recognized his advantage and sarcastically said, "Glad you could make it, Joseph. I've got so much to do; I decided to arrive early to get some other things done. No worries that you're 30 minutes late."

… Insert knife between the third and fourth rib, twist slightly to shred the costal cartilage and inflict severe pain while keeping the experimental animal alive… advantage, JB.

Joseph offered, "Sorry JB, there is no excuse for me to be late. I apologize for messing up your day."

JB's lighted Nicaraguan wafted smoke from the glowing tip recently cleared of a long nub of ash. He resembled a steam engine with 3 quick puffs on the cigar, and then, after a long draw, exhaled as if to fumigate Joseph of dreaded insects.

Fortunately, Margaret's tip, and Joseph's intuition prepared him for such an intellectual assault. … Battle lines drawn.

Joseph decided to reset the battle lines, and focus on facts to realign the meeting dynamics. "JB, can we spend our time today discussing your operations – let's get to specifics if you don't mind?"

"I like the way you think, Joseph. Direct … to the point … no bullshit. You ever work in manufacturing? You seem to have that results orientation of a manufacturing jock."

"Yes, I've spent some time in operations… gives me a bit of background – enough to be dangerous –when I'm talking with experts like you. Do you have any financials or charts that can help me understand how you mange this operation. I can tell you, Don likes the results that you've delivered over the past few years."

Without any hesitation, JB fired a question. "Is Don going to sell the place?"

"Let's say that Don has recognized his vulnerabilities… knows that he's not going to live forever, and wants to understand strategic options. Hey, several weeks ago we toured the facility… thanks for the tour. Today, I'd like to understand how you manage the operations. What kind of data do you look at to understand that your process is under control?"

"I don't clutter my mind with too much information, Joseph. I'm sort of a traditional manufacturing VP who knows the process, knows the people, and manage from the top down. Sure I get weekly spending reports, and the month end financials come out after 3 weeks – not much value in them at that time. I rely on walking the floor to manage. The floor managers keep me up to date on what's happening. I try to keep the main product cost at about $435.00, and everything's ok with the world. Check this out – 6 month's of data – all keyed to $435.00/unit."

171

	Jan	Feb	Mar	Apr	May	Jun
2011						
Units Produced	3,233	3,121	2,984	2,656	3,012	3,333
Direct Labor	498	445	435	487	401	511
Direct Material	566	546	576	576	563	498
O/H Spending	344	354	346	431	365	354
Scrap	11	14	54	32	22	32
Cost/Unit	435.51	430.95	454.76	562.50	441.24	408.94
2012						
Units Produced	2,998	3,012	2,888	2,945	2,601	3,798
Direct Labor	498	422	411	343	522	511
Direct Material	477	487	490	655	687	497
O/H Spending	344	401	356	387	377	387
Scrap	11	12	14	21	21	11
Cost/Unit	439.96	434.93	435.25	470.29	609.77	367.30
2013						
Units Produced	3,233	3,121	3,012	2,800	3,224	3,123
Direct Labor	512	498	477	412	518	489
Direct Material	455	481	399	409	576	497
O/H Spending	398	422	378	404	405	409
Scrap	11	14	23	63	11	19
Cost/Unit	422.21	448.89	416.33	437.50	464.95	446.69
Scrap						
Dept 100	0	0	2	1	0	0
Dept 200	1	1	1	2	0	0
Dept 300	5	3	4	3	8	14
Dept 400	5	10	16	57	3	5
	11	14	23	63	11	19
	5	10	16	57	3	5

"That is one serious spreadsheet. Sometimes the numbers jump around a bit. What happens then?"

"I check out the reasons, fix the problem and get on with it. Don knows I'm on top of things."

"Last week Don asked about the dusty parts. Any thoughts?"

"He sniped at me a bit... I was ...well, I was angry about that question ... he should have asked me before the meeting so that I could find out the answer.

I had one of the engineering folks check out a few of those bins. We had some bad parts in them, but they told me that was an exception... not typical."

"And so what are next steps?"

"Well, we'll write off that scrap, and yes, I'm going to have all the bins reviewed to find out if there are any more problems. And yes, I was surprised about the scrap. The guys usually write-off scrap immediately when they spot it."

JB does not review departmental reporting, and although he grudgingly complies with Cynthia's accounting requirements, always considered the detail accounting requirements to be a waste of time. He concentrates on Material Cost and Price Variance, Direct Labor, and Overtime Spending. As long as his average cost is about $435.00, he considers his job well done.

"JB, would you mind if I asked Cynthia for some departmental information for the past few years? We won't bother any of your department managers."

"Have at it Joseph."

After another 30 minutes of JB blowing smoke rings, tipping ash into the crusted ashtray, and sipping a Diet Dr. Pepper, Joseph closed the meeting.

The brief meeting with JB progressed exactly as expected. JB's bastion would not be breached. He believed his operation was performing at an acceptable level, and no outsider could dictate otherwise.

During the next few days, Joseph asked Cynthia for some manufacturing departmental information – previously unused data stored in the ERP system for nearly a decade. It seems that JB was not entirely truthful about what he has available for his management.

February 2, 2014 - Specialist to CEO: Formulate a Plan

```
*Reporting
*Metrics
*Organization assessment
*Delegation of responsibilities
*Strategic plan
```

"Don, thanks for meeting with me. I just wanted to give you an update, and thought the club might be the best venue. I'd like to brainstorm about your business."

"Shall we have the Irish coffee's to launch this?" Not waiting for an answer, Don waved at Sandy.
"Interesting outfit today, Sandy. I'm not sure what to make of 'Punxsutawney Phil' shirts."

"Groundhog Day, and we thought after this miserable winter, it was worthwhile to stir things up a bit. Do you like the outfit?"

175

"Definitely stirring things up – will this day repeat itself-repeat itself – repeat itself – over and over again?" A pause for laughter, and none surfaced. Don self-consciously ordered. "Joseph, shall we have the Irish coffee?" A nod and the order was placed.

Joseph decided that it was the perfect time for candid discussion of his findings. "OK, Don, I've touched the next level of detail with your team, and just want to talk about your expectations. We can improve your current operations, improve earnings and cash flow, and reduce capital requirements. We're talking about a culture change, and you experienced the first sensitivities at the last management meeting when you cornered JB.

When the culture change is fully implemented, you may find different team members, because some of the team will not – or will be reluctant – to change. You select the team members that remain, depending on how committed you are to culture change. I can describe the impact if the team is not working together and the potential costs to you.

If we change the culture to more of a performance orientation with accountabilities and delegation of responsibility, you may find the business more enjoyable, and you may have more spare time for hobbies and time with the family. Again, you get to make those choices.

If we do this right, the value of your Company will increase, and the marketability will improve significantly if you decide to sell the Company. Basically, the only downside may be some fractured relationships with the current management team, and those decisions are purely yours. I can guide you through the entire process, if you like.

Guidance? Heck, I can develop a plan to improve Company performance as quickly as possible, so that we can get immediate buy-in by the execs. Measurable improvements are great validation of success.

You and I can modify the plan to meet your needs, and then we begin execution."

Sandy, catlike silence in her crepe sole shoes, excused herself and stretched to serve the Irish coffee.

"I know that you gentleman have a sweet-tooth, so I scooped a few oatmeal cookies from Chef John, who encouraged me not to charge for them. …Hope you like oatmeal."

The Irish coffee, buried under a tall swirl of fresh whipped cream dusted with a whisper of cinnamon, smelled of Irish whiskey and robust roast coffee. The flared glass double walled mug showcased the layers that begged to be mixed.

Don skimmed the swirled whipped cream to smooth the mound to a simple cone and enjoyed the concentrated cinnamon flavoring. Once the cone reached symmetry, he mixed the layers that quickly moved from a barber pole design to a solid mocha color.

"Develop a plan and let's see where it takes us. Any initial thoughts?"

The conversation, interrupted only by sipping the Irish and munching the cookies, ambled for more than an hour.

As is customary, Joseph sketched out the rough plan on a placemat.

	Quarters					
	1	2	3	4	5	6
Improved reporting	✔			✔		
Establishing performance metrics	✔					
Organizational assessment		✔		✔		
Delegation of responsibility		✔		✔		
Strategic Plan	✔				✔	

Joseph summarized the conversation. "We'll want to improve reporting as quickly as possible. Your business, like virtually all middle-market companies, measures accounting *stuff*, and doesn't measure activities that will help you manage better. We won't be adding dozens of pages, but rather summarize specific information that the execs can manage with. If we do it right, *you* will also have better information to manage with. Once the – I'll call it master report – is identified, we can concentrate on key performance metrics. The team develops reports - not me - because I don't really know what is most important in your business.

Metrics and reports will lead to the strategic plan, which at first will be somewhat rough... new process to the team... and require you and the executives to look outside the four walls. We'll look at competitive conditions, competitors, and the macro environment."

Joseph paused to measure Don's reaction. Since there was no adverse reaction, he continued. "Throughout the process, we'll gain a better understanding of the organization's needs and capabilities. Here's where you get to make some choices that will affect the future of the Company. We may find resource gaps that can be filled with training, or perhaps can't be filled by the existing team. You get to make decisions once again.

Reporting, key metrics, organization and strategy are not static items, since the competitive world is continuously changing. If we are smart, we'll adjust to important market changes.

Don, this will be challenging, and if we do it right, should not be too stressful and will improve Company performance. The key is that you are in charge throughout the process – you make the decisions about where we go, and how fast we get there.

This is your Company... your process... and your future."

"So Joseph, how many of these culture changes have you done before?"

"Quite a few here in the US, Europe, and Latin America."

"And your success ratio?"

"This may sound stupid, but every one of them met the owner's desires, because this is their process. I facilitate their decision making, and they take the process wherever they want.

I can say that in every case, the management of the Company improved, but perhaps not to its potential. The owner's decision."

"What is an example?"

"In some cases, family harmony is far more important than profitability. In some Companies, unqualified family members held key positions that the owner was unwilling to change."

Don winced, shifted uncomfortably in his seat and while taking a deep breath mumbled Robert, Chip and Janelle.

"Don, you get to guide this Company through a process that will reliably demonstrate future profitability. That credibility will come from planning, executing the plan, and by holding people accountable to meaningful metrics, well beyond profitability compared to the prior year. While it may initially appear to be more work, you'll find that managed delegation of authority and responsibility will reduce your personal workload, while giving you more control.

Over the next year-or-so, you'll see increased earnings and previously unforeseen opportunities captured by your team. When your business operations can be reliably planned, you will have a more marketable operation, if you choose to sell the Company.

There will be some early wins, but the process of culture change requires time and consistent follow-up to ensure it is sustainable. Once processes are fully implemented and the team is focused on the right objectives, you'll discover how much opportunity there is in this field.

Oh, and one other thing. When we begin the process, reported earnings may suffer initially. Not only from incremental investments in business improvements, but because past errors surface. Remember those bins of WIP in the factory? Well, I doubt all of that is good product. We'll see. JB is looking at the product to determine its best disposition.

Any questions?"

"Let's get on with this and see where it takes us."

February 4, 2014 - Specialist to CFO: Improved Reporting

```
*Management information
*Key metrics
*Timely/accurate/
consistent
```

"Cynthia, it was good to get your invitation to meet today. What's up?"

"Hey Joseph, thanks for adjusting your schedule." Her discomfort and nervousness were obvious, but Joseph always allowed executives to find their own way to share a concern. "I'm a bit embarrassed about this. For years, I've considered it my job to make sure that Don gets what he asks for. Well..." She shifted in her seat as if seated on nettles. "Well, I haven't been doing my job. After our last discussion I did some soul searching and then started to think about the CFO's responsibilities. My job isn't to just give the boss what he asks for. Don depends on me as the finance professional to give him what he asks for, sure, but also to give him what he needs to run the business. I'm the finance pro, and that's my job." As she talked the pace and intensity of her words increased. "So I'm not too impressed with myself," she concluded.

"OK. It's good to do some self-reflection, Cynthia. So now you're not happy with your performance. What's next?"

"It's time for performance, and I'm searching for some guidance. I've had the chance to dredge some information from the ledgers, assemble some draft statements, but before I go out on a limb with new *stuff* and look stupid, wanted to pass things by you – sensibility check. Do you mind? I haven't reviewed any of this information with the rest of the staff... wanted to be sure it makes sense."

With that, she flipped through several pages of information mined from the system. The well-thought pages had notes describing her objectives and each saved space for input from the responsible executive. This exceptional insight into the business was superb. As Joseph beamed while scanning the pages, he raised his eyes, looked over his glasses and said, "Magnificent! Outstanding insight into the business." Cynthia took a deep breath and sighed agreeably.

They carefully reviewed each page, challenging each other about content and presentation. Joseph was deeply satisfied with her depth of understanding and ability to present Company information in a clear, concise manner.

Don jotted notes on some of the pages.

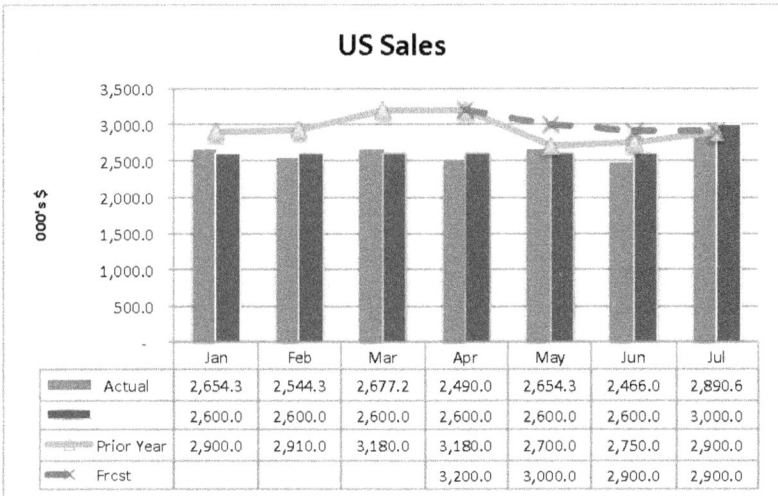

US Sales

	Jan	Feb	Mar	Apr	May	Jun	Jul
Actual	2,654.3	2,544.3	2,677.2	2,490.0	2,654.3	2,466.0	2,890.6
	2,600.0	2,600.0	2,600.0	2,600.0	2,600.0	2,600.0	3,000.0
Prior Year	2,900.0	2,910.0	3,180.0	3,180.0	2,700.0	2,750.0	2,900.0
Frcst				3,200.0	3,000.0	2,900.0	2,900.0

I like the comparative to Budget, Prior Year & Forecast.

Might consider adding a 3-month moving average…

maybe even a gross profit line.

Consolidated
Month:

Kryzinski	Current Month			Year To Date				
(000's US $)		Favorable (Unfavorable)			Favorable (Unfavorable)			
	Amt	Forecast	Prior Year	Amt	Forecast		Prior Year	
		Amt	Amt		Amt	%	Amt	%
US Sales								
Units to Customers								
Avg Selling Price/1000								
Avg Cost/1000								
Metals Purchases								
Sales								
US								
Export								
By-products								
Total Sales								
Gross Profit- (Standard)								
US								
Export								
By-products								
Total G.P.								
Variance From Standard								
Total Gross Profit								
GP %						n/a		n/a
SG&A								
SG&A % Sales						n/a		n/a
Interest								
Pretax Profit								
Profit After Tax								
Cash Flow								
Headcount								
Capital Spending								
Inventory Turns								
DSO								

Notes:

Example Co - Consolidated
Month:

Kryzinski

	Current Month				Quarter to Date				Year To Date			
			Favorable (Unfavorable)				Favorable (Unfavorable)				Favorable (Unfavorable)	
			Forecast	Prior Year			Forecast	Prior Year			Forecast	Prior Year
	Amt	% Sls	Amt %	Amt %	Amt	% Sls	Amt %	Amt %	Amt	% Sls	Amt %	Amt %
US Sales												
Units to Customers												
Avg Selling Price/1000												
Avg Cost/1000												
Metals Purchases												
Sales												
US												
Export												
By-Products												
Total Sales												
Gross Profit- (Standard)												
US												
Export												
By-products												
Total G.P.												
Variance From Standard												
Mexico City												
Rochester												
Purchase Variances												
Total Variance												
Total Gross Profit												
GP %			n/a	n/a			n/a	n/a			n/a	n/a
SG&A												
SG&A % Sales			n/a	n/a			n/a	n/a			n/a	n/a
Interest												
Pretax Profit												
Profit After Tax												
Cash Flow												
Headcount												
Capital Spending												
Inventory Turns												
DSO												

Notes:

186

Should we graph Average cost per unit and unit throughput? How can we use this information to forecast better? Need to explain Volume and Rate Variance calculation... what is basis?

Hours Worked

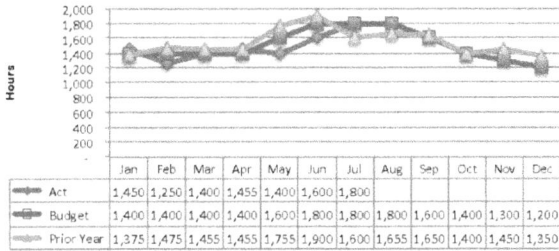

	Jan	Feb	Mar	Apr	May	Jun	Jul	Aug	Sep	Oct	Nov	Dec
Act	1,450	1,250	1,400	1,455	1,400	1,600	1,800					
Budget	1,400	1,400	1,400	1,400	1,600	1,800	1,800	1,800	1,600	1,400	1,300	1,200
Prior Year	1,375	1,475	1,455	1,455	1,755	1,900	1,600	1,655	1,650	1,400	1,450	1,350

Down Time

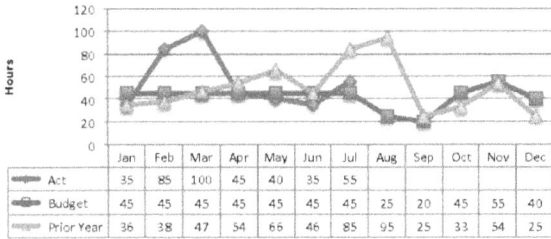

	Jan	Feb	Mar	Apr	May	Jun	Jul	Aug	Sep	Oct	Nov	Dec
Act	35	85	100	45	40	35	55					
Budget	45	45	45	45	45	45	45	25	20	45	55	40
Prior Year	36	38	47	54	66	46	85	95	25	33	54	25

Production Variances

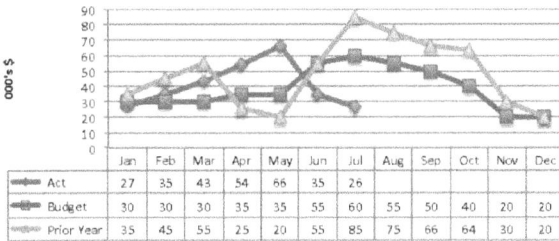

	Jan	Feb	Mar	Apr	May	Jun	Jul	Aug	Sep	Oct	Nov	Dec
Act	27	35	43	54	66	35	26					
Budget	30	30	30	35	35	55	60	55	50	40	20	20
Prior Year	35	45	55	25	20	55	85	75	66	64	30	20

Notes:

Where do we get "Plan" information? Where do we get forecast information?

Maxwell

Metals Purchases

Legend: Steel, Aluminum, Other, Consumption

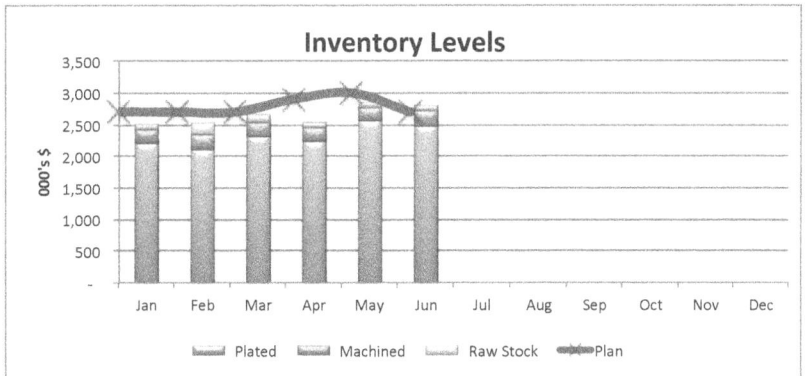

Inventory Levels

Y-axis: 000's $

Legend: Plated, Machined, Raw Stock, Plan

Notes:

Interesting blend of information on these pages. I wonder why they have not included Titanium as one of the key metals purchased?

Johnston

Accounts Receivable Aging

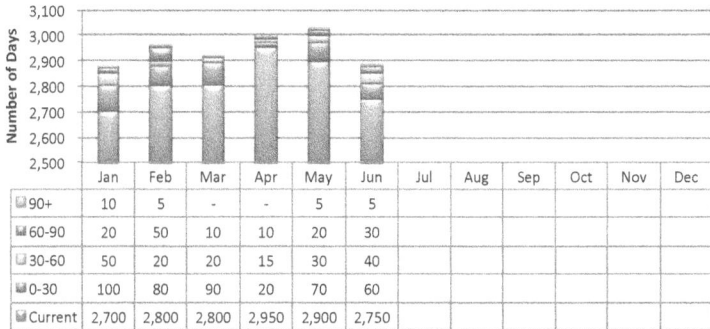

	Jan	Feb	Mar	Apr	May	Jun	Jul	Aug	Sep	Oct	Nov	Dec
90+	10	5	-	-	5	5						
60-90	20	50	10	10	20	30						
30-60	50	20	20	15	30	40						
0-30	100	80	90	20	70	60						
Current	2,700	2,800	2,800	2,950	2,900	2,750						

Days Sales Outstanding

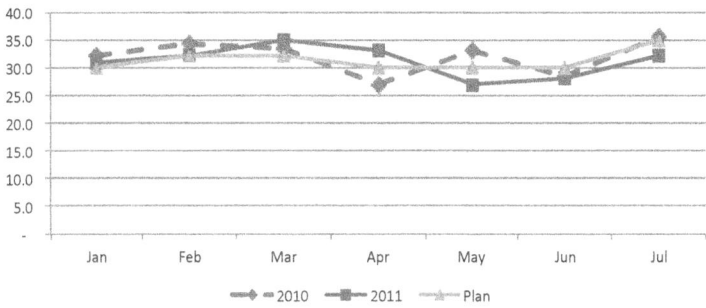

Legend: 2010, 2011, Plan

Notes:

Excellent – some exposure for a key element of cash flow!

Example - Consolidated
Month:

(000's US $)

	Amt	Inrease (Decrease)				
		Budget			Prior Year	
		Amt	%		Amt	%
Current Assets						
Cash	(113.2)					
Cert of Deposit						
Accounts Receivable	2,890.3					
Inventory	10,396.8					
Prepaid Expenses	40.3					
Total Current Assets	13,214.2					
Fixed roperty Plant & Equipment						
Total Fixed Assets	27,399.8					
Total Accumulated Depreciation	(19,753.4)					
Net Fixed Assets	7,646.4					
Other Assets	143.4					
Total Assets	21,004.0					
Current Liabilities						
Line of Credit-short-term	4,337.0					
Accounts Payable	746.3					
Accrued Expenses & Withholdings	1,175.4					
Currnet portion of LT Debt	525.2					
Total Current Liabilities	6,783.9					
Long term liabilities						
Term Loan	4,264.6					
Grant						
Other Long Term Debt						
Current Portion of Long Term Debt	(525.2)					
Total Long Term Debt	3,739.4					
Subordinated Debt	823.4					
Total Liabilities	11,346.7					
Equity						
Common Stock	350.0					
Retained Earnings	9,307.2					
Total Stockholder Equity	9,657.2					
Total Liabilities and Equity	21,003.9					

Notes:

Excellent – detailed cash flow information! Especially good that they compare to budget.

Example Co - Consolidated Cash Flow
Month:

(000's US $)

	Amt	Increase (Decrease)				
		Budget			Prior Year	
		Amt	%		Amt	%
Operating Activities						
Net Income						
Adjustments to Reconcile Net Income						
Depreciation						
Gain/Loss on Sale of Fixed Assets						
LIFO Reserve						
Changes in Operating Assets						
Dec (Inc) Accounts Receivable						
Dec (Inc) Inventory						
Dec (Inc) Prepaids/Other Assets						
Inc (Dec) Accounts Pay						
Inc (Dec) Accruals						
Net Cash from Operaating Activities						
Investing Activities						
Purchase of Property & Equip						
Proceeds from Sale of Asset						
Net Cash Used by Investing Activities						
Financing Activities						
Line of Credit-Short-term						
Industrial Revenue Bonds						
Grant						
Term Loan						
Undisbursed Proceeds from Bond Issue						
Other Long Term Debt						
Notes Payable Shareholders						
Accounts Payable - Shareholders						
Dividends						
Sale (Redemption of Stock)						
Net Cash From Financing Activities						
Net Change in Cash						

Notes:

Cynthia explained that the information was easily available through the system, and once people agreed on the items to be reported, these statements required less than a day to prepare.

She insisted that the closing cycle must be reduced to report within 10 days. Reporting beyond 10 days seemed like a wasted effort, since the team can't change tactics with data more than a month old.

Joseph was extremely pleased with Cynthia's self-assessment and proactive response to poor performance.

"What would you like to do next, Cynthia?"

"Review the information with the team to be sure that no one is blindsided in front of the boss. Hey, Joseph, without their buy-in this is going nowhere."

"And if someone says they don't want the accountability in detailed statements?

"It's my job to provide information that will help them manage their business segment. Some of the particular items in these reports can be adjusted, but I've got to give them and Don the tools to manage."

During the next 5 days, Cynthia reviewed the information with each executive. All were pleased to receive information, and created a short-list of additional requirements. JB surprised Cynthia – he liked the information that would show performance.

She scheduled a review meeting with Don to get his input.

Joseph was pleased as the team matured.

February 12, 2014 - Specialist Attends 2nd Staff Meeting

```
*Positive reinforcement
*Don't shoot the messenger
```

Don and Joseph met briefly before the staff meeting to establish expectations. Each staff member would explain their respective reporting, and perhaps outline next steps to complete and additional information required. Joseph explained that Cynthia was the driver for reporting improvement, and she was personally very dissatisfied with her previous lax performance. "Don, she has taken charge and done an exceptional job identifying Company needs and reviewing report improvements with the rest of the staff. It would be good to acknowledge her efforts."

The meeting, scheduled to start at 8:30, was in full attendance by 8:20. The cast was somehow different, but Don couldn't yet identify the reason.

Don launched the meeting 5 minutes early with the offer of refreshments, now limited to a selection of Greek yogurt, a blushing fresh fruit tray with plump strawberries, grapes and chunks of freshly cut pineapple, honeydew and cantaloupe, dark steaming coffee and a selection of teas.

Each executive, allotted 30 minutes to discuss their function, used the LCD projector to explain their reporting goals and the shortcomings of information. Cynthia provided an introduction to the improved reporting, admonishing her previous performance. Don quickly interjected, "No need to beat yourself up. We're all in this together, Cynthia."

"Don, we've been developing some new reporting during the past few weeks and wanted to do a process check with you to be sure that we are on the right track. We'll review the schedules with you, knowing that all the information is not available today – but we'll tell you when we expect to get there.

This is somewhat new territory for us, so we will make some mistakes, and ask for your patience during this process. You OK with that?"

Don nodded and gestured to continue.

As the team noshed on the healthy snacks, Cynthia orchestrated the performance as she shuffled the wireless mouse and laser pointer among the staff.

In his best presentation voice, Stephen eloquently launched the process with darting laser dots, several slides and a discussion about how they need to think differently about the business. Reporting should be expanded to include Export since the opportunity was significant and without separate reports, the Company wouldn't give Export the proper attention. Stephen also wanted to manage pricing, and supplemental product sales more aggressively. This required better planning and some additional administrative process within his sales force, but considering the growth potential, it was essential. Although the draft reports compared results against the prior three months averages, future reports would compare to an updated forecast. Once the Company had a six-month trend of metrics, Stephen would develop forecasts to measure performance.

"In addition to these reporting changes, we're reviewing current and potential customers, classifying them into meaningful buckets, and developing some metrics to help us manage better. We'll be defining a closing cycle and more aggressively managing the process – if you're on board with the concept.

This is a completely new process, and we're going to make mistakes. I'll ask for your patience as we stumble through the development. As we dig deeper into the process, we may need some investment dollars to continue. I've been researching CRM systems – they don't come cheap, but I think they may be justified. What are your thoughts, Don?"

"Wow! The way that you've explained the new approach is a revolution of change. Radical – and I can guess that you are right about mistakes. But as long as we carefully consider the outcome before we make major investments, I'm ok with it."

"And by the way, I may need several additional sales reps in the future."

Don smiled as the rules of engagement were being developed. "Right on – as long as they're justified. I would have been disappointed if you didn't ask for more reps, considering how we're rethinking the business."

JB took charge next. Don puzzled over what was different about JB at this meeting. At first, he thought JB would be grumbling about the lack of doughnuts – not so. Then it struck Don that JB wore a starched button-down shirt, with pressed pants – not a polo shirt and sweater with chinos. Interesting. Posture perfect, JB discussed key reporting elements, highlighting areas Don had never before considered.

In two pages, JB explored the financial highlights of the manufacturing operation. Manufacturing, no longer limited to a single cost of sales number, included variances to 'standard' spending and purchase price variances. JB sheepishly admitted that the Company, due to its smaller size, never developed standards, but rather worked using averages. As long as the average total cost made sense, all was ok. Since the Company achieved a 'critical mass' he thought that we needed

more sophistication. Don took particular interest in the
graphs of hours worked, Downtime, and Variances from
average, and asked if such information was available by
week – or perhaps by department. "I'll check on that
Don," JB replied, now concerned that he had opened
Pandora's box.

"Inventory levels… do we really have $2.5 million of
inventory out there in the factory?"

"Yes Don – we've been heavily stocked to avoid any
service delays. We're going to check into that a bit
more to see what we can do."

JB's revolutionary change startled Joseph, and Don was
speechless at the *born-again* JB. Cynthia guided the
remaining financial discussion for another 15 minutes
encouraging the executive team to share potential
improvements.

It seemed that the reporting discussion was complete,
since they reviewed the P&L, receivables and inventory.
Cynthia noticed that Don was preparing to leave and
said, "Not so fast, boss. We'd like to talk about new
product development. Allison, you're on the hot-seat."

Don resettled into his seat, puzzled by Cynthia's
directive.

"Don, I'd like to talk with you about new product
development. You know, we haven't spent much effort
to introduce new products during the past – what can it

be – 5 years? Well, I'd like to propose a change to that. I've got some ideas, and Stephen has some great insight into new products that we can produce in our shop. He has access to the customers, and he's a good listener. He has a list of product improvements and enhancements.

I've got connections with other companies' R&D folks, and to nearby universities developing new products. We'd like to share a development process with you and get some feedback."

Jackson Manufacturing Inc.
New Product Development Checklist

1. Product Description

2. Market Conditions

	Market Share (By Year)		
	1	**2**	**3**

Key Competitors (List)

3. Product Development *(Description of Process)*

4. Investment Required

		YEAR	
	1	**2**	**3**

Capital
  R&D
  Sales & Marketing
  Manufacturing

5. People

6. Expense
  R&D
  Marketing
  Sales Training
  Advertising
  Manufacturing

7. Approvals

Marketing	_____	R&D	_____
Finance	_____	CEO	_____

"Let's spend a few minutes discussing each section. "

Although allotted only 30 minutes, Allison guided a thorough discussion of development concepts that reflected the insight of all the critical execs. The framework included market size and growth, sales considerations, competitive analysis, and manufacturability. Timelines would include the names of those executives responsible to perform each task, dates, and estimated costs – whether expense or capital. Each member of the team would be responsible to approve the proposal, giving Don confirmation that they believe they can deliver on time and within budget.

"Don, this is a change in how we do business, but we'd like to give it a try. The Company won't have to spend anything on any project, until you approve the concept. We think that this will help the Company prosper – and it might be a helluva lot of fun."

Don could hardly contain his exuberance. Emotionally he felt like he just completed a double black at Vail – a super thrill to hear the engagement and new ideas.

"Folks, I can only say, 'I'm impressed.' During the past few years, I think I've become too complacent. You've stepped up the game, and, while there'll be no spending carte blanche, I think that if you put the effort into proposals and more aggressive management, I have to do the same. Let's rock!"

And with that, Don rolled his chair back, stood and momentarily stretched his legs and arched his back to chase the stiffness away. He walked around the table and shook each executive's hand and said a simple, "Thank you," and left the room.

Team members scanned the room for mutual assurances that they had just launched a major improvement for the Company. Joseph quietly nodded his head, confirming their wonderful progress. "Well done folks. You folks are impressive in your zealous approach to improvement. You all did a great job this morning – and I didn't hear one complaint about the lack of those corpulent, calorie laden, gooey chocolate covered grease missiles we call donuts. Could this be a new generation of leaders we have assembled? Congrats to all – now to execute."

Joseph mimicked Don's departure with a congratulatory handshake to each, and quietly left the room.

Self-satisfied, each team member relaxed, smiled and understood that they now had to deliver... but they hadn't had this much fun in years. They were energized.

April 4, 2014 - CEO Grasps Strategic Planning

*Strategy = Team effort
*CEO to define broad goals
*Concise planning timetable

After a month, Joseph had another private meeting with Don to check on progress. Don enjoyed breakfast meetings, especially when scheduled at the North Branch Diner, an art-deco remnant from the 40's. This casual eatery served the best breakfast platters, served on beige heavy-duty wide-rimmed commercial china – the kind that bounces on tile floors and never chips. Coffee mugs, with handles thick as a patron's thumb, always steamed with fresh hot coffee from first serving to the relentless automatic refills.

Janey, the owner, spotted Don and Joseph slip into the vinyl covered booth, grabbed two mugs of coffee and a pair of menus. "Coffee guys?" as the filled cups settled on the table without spilling a drop. In a single motion, the menus were opened, and slipped effortlessly in front of her guests. ""A heart-stopper, Don? ... And what would you like sir?"

Joseph quickly scanned the menu and read the 'heart-stopper' description. "Three eggs as you like them, atop a mound of fresh, home-made prime-rib hash spiked with a dash of jalapeño peppers and scallions, with toast or English muffin."

Both nodded agreeably, Don ordering over-easy, while Joseph requested poached.

After they compared notes about the recent Polar Vortex that paralyzed the region, Joseph questioned, "How's business, Don?"

"It is an interesting time. Everyone really got cranked up a month ago, and they have been working their tails off – seems like nights and weekends – to meet their commitments. They're like Seal-team 6 on a mission – maybe to prove something to themselves – that they've still got it – or maybe to prove something to me.

Whatever the reason, things are happening. It's as if we've drained the swamp, and just as you said, some ugly things are surfacing. Just last week, JB 'fessed up to nearly $125,000 of WIP problems. Some of those products in bins on the floor had some hidden flaws - bad product that we paid the crew to produce.

And the team has started talking about investments in data systems – from CRM to ERP – alphabet soup that could cost me a half-million to get up and running. Let me tell you, those numbers were heart stoppers, just like Janey's hash."

"And how have you handled these revelations?"

"… Can't really complain about it, since we wound them up and cut them loose, but it's tough to be positive with the kind of money they're talking about."

The banter continued to wander aimlessly - more of a penitent speaking with a father confessor than Don seeking advice or approval.

"We've made a lot of progress, and Cynthia has assembled new report templates so that we have historical data to support metrics. Using the metrics as a base, we've been able to forecast with a reasonable comfort level. By reviewing historical trends, seasonal patterns etc. we've got a solid foundation for what we've described as the base business, and focus most of our attention on changes that we can make to build the business.

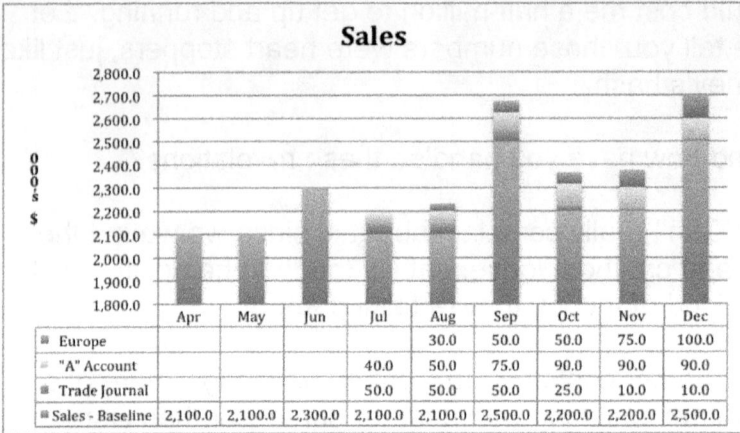

Sales

	Apr	May	Jun	Jul	Aug	Sep	Oct	Nov	Dec
Europe					30.0	50.0	50.0	75.0	100.0
"A" Account				40.0	50.0	75.0	90.0	90.0	90.0
Trade Journal				50.0	50.0	50.0	25.0	10.0	10.0
Sales - Baseline	2,100.0	2,100.0	2,300.0	2,100.0	2,100.0	2,500.0	2,200.0	2,200.0	2,500.0

Don wrapped both hands around the heavy mug as much to warm his hands as drink the coffee. After a few noisy sips, continued, "Using the historical charts, we've identified a business baseline that, without any major management intervention, we can routinely achieve. Once we identified the baseline, we let the managers and directors manage the business – with some guidelines, of course." He smiled modestly. We now try to spend our time making a difference... a real executive role. Sounds pretty simple, but we need to document some procedures so that the VP's don't get buried in day-to-day stuff."

"And do you have those procedure requirements on anyone's schedule? Prioritized? Timelines?"

"Not yet, Joseph. ... Open item."

Steaming mounded platters of food arrived just before they focused on the spending charts. The food was plated to look like a cartoon character – eggs staring back as eyes with a button nose on a mélange of hash, with toast points as eyebrows. … A clever presentation with a devilishly light scent of toasted bread.

A splash of Tabasco… Don gripped the knife and fork and slashed the golden yolk, Don said, "This looks superb, Janey."

Carefully marrying the whites and yolks with clumps of hash, Joseph heartily agreed and joked, "… heart stopper for sure!"

"Check out the "A" account impact, Joseph. Stephen has analyzed actual and potential customers as you suggested, and made 'A' accounts a priority. We checked out the potential A's, evaluated our resources, and will really beat up on a few. We've estimated a 90-day closing cycle, and have forecasted a new account will begin in July. Look at that impact! Do you have any idea what that will do to our earnings?" His enthusiasm was only overshadowed by the destruction of his 'heart stopper' display.

Spending

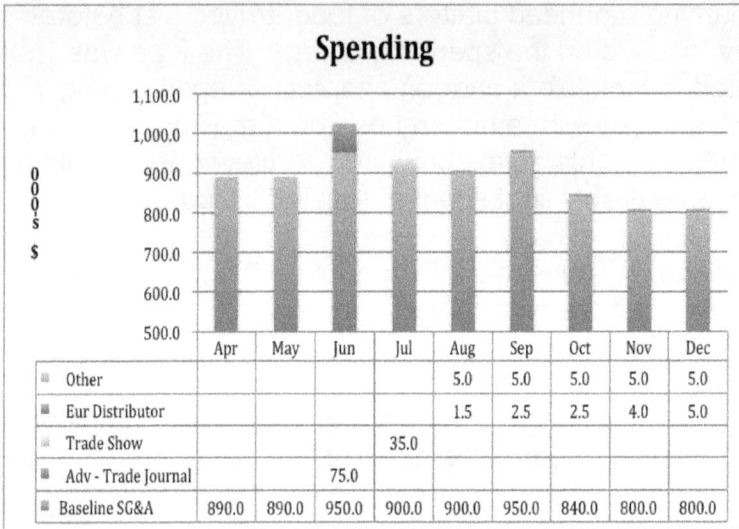

	Apr	May	Jun	Jul	Aug	Sep	Oct	Nov	Dec
Other					5.0	5.0	5.0	5.0	5.0
Eur Distributor					1.5	2.5	2.5	4.0	5.0
Trade Show				35.0					
Adv - Trade Journal			75.0						
Baseline SG&A	890.0	890.0	950.0	900.0	900.0	950.0	840.0	800.0	800.0

Don continued, "We've used the same approach with spending. Cynthia calls this baseline forecasting. Here's the deal. If we don't make any decisions, a relatively fixed level of spending just happens every month. A key variable is the number of weeks in a month, but otherwise, we don't arbitrarily hire and fire people… the monthly rent is the same, utilities don't vary much etc. As executives we need to identify things that make a difference. Look at the Trade Journal Advertising sales. The journal hits in June, and we expect a bump in sales starting in July. Now, it really isn't that precise, but we've checked history enough to know that there will be a bump. So far, without actual results, this is somewhat speculative, but it's better to sketch this out on paper, since it doesn't cost anything to plan, and we select the best alternative, with a backup plan of course."

"Backup plan?"

"You know that I'm somewhat conservative, and Cynthia gets a gold medal for moderation. We've put these basic programs in place, but we also have some backup switches to pull to get sales or reduce expenses to meet our profit goals. For example, we have only one 'A' planned, but we really have three potentials in the pipeline. Out of the three, we expect to get a run-rate of about $90,000/month. Cynthia's spending also has a fudge-factor – a contingency built in that we can use in a pinch.

Joseph, do you have any idea how predictable this becomes with this kind of planning? One other thing - if we pull this off, these few programs will increase earnings by about $200,000 annually. Well, if I was to decide to sell the Company, and we used a multiple of 6X, that would mean selling the Company for an extra $1.2 million? This is somewhat incredible – if we pull this off."

"So do you want to sell the Company?"

"I don't need to make that decision now, but if I do, the earnings will be there."

Don was thrilled with the Company's progress. "What do you suggest for next steps, Joseph?"

Janey cleared the table poured some fresh java.
"Janey, some paper and a pencil please." She offered
some pages from her order pad, but Joseph asked for
some large sheets. Extra placemats and a sharpie
arrived in minutes.

"I think that now that you have some better reporting, it
is a good time to start strategic planning."

Joseph explained an approach to strategic planning that
was straightforward. He scratched notes across a
selection of place mats, each sequentially numbered in
the top right corner.

Joseph's broad confident strokes with the sharpie
confirmed that he had done this kind of analysis before.
His list was straightforward, logical and seemed to be
complete.

I.   Vision/mission

II. Company Background
  a. Who & what we are
  b. Industry
  c. Products
  d. Structure

III. Competitive analysis
  a. Macro environment
  b. Company strengths & weaknesses
  c. Competitive assessment

IV. Financials
  a. Company P&L's
  b. Product line P&L's
  c. Regional P&L's
  d. Balance sheets
  e. Capital spending
  f.   Cash flows

V.   Action plans
  a. What to do
  b. Who will do
  c. When will it be done
  d. Benefits of execution

1

Joseph discussed each element of the strategic plan so that Don understood the depth of analysis and discussion expected. "Don, there is no such thing as a perfect strategic plan. There are many alternative strategic planning processes, but this simplified approach works well in middle-market companies. Extensive outside research is not essential, but if there are gaps in the required information when the plan is done, research assignments are defined as deliverables for the executives. The facilitator will steer the executive team through the process. An effective planning process should span no more than 3-4 weeks, and require no more than 3+- days of any individual executive's effort."

At one point, Don pushed back saying, "Some other companies that I know have spent months working on strategic plans, and in the end, didn't have much other than a wordy, blue sky document that didn't deliver anything. Others spent a few days in a resort strategizing – nice time for the execs with a little golf and great food... nice warm and fuzzy ideas on some flip charts, but no action. Why would this be any different?"

"Accountability and linkage to financial statements... P&L's, Balance Sheets, Capital Spending, and Cash Flows. Timelines with names and dates. Let me continue, and I'll show you the difference."

Over the next hour, Joseph explained the outline.

"The vision and mission are directional statements designed to guide the Company's energy...they are not dogmatic statements but rather a description of what the Company wants to be, who are our customers and what markets we serve... a timeless and long lasting guide. Strategic plans include Company background as a frame of reference – where they've been and how they got there. The background can be somewhat inspirational. Don, you started in your garage 25+ years ago, and now you've got a $30 million Company that sells product around the world. Gives me goose bumps just to say it."

Joseph continued, "Once those first two steps are complete, the team will analyze the business conditions – macro analysis - what's the US and global economic reality – recession, slow growth? What countries may be opportunities and what is required to compete in them?"

Don raised his index finger, "What if we don't want to expand internationally?"

"Then you make the decision not to. It's your Company, Don, and that's the purpose of the strategic plan. Let's say you put some pressure on Stephen to increase sales, and he decides that export sales to South Africa would give him the sales growth he needs to meet your expectations. If you don't have written guidance – for example, the strategic plan saying 'no' to international expansion – Stephen might expand to include distributor sales in South Africa. And let me tell you, distributor sales in South Africa may not be a good idea, given the liability risks you assume as a US Company.

Or perhaps you, the Company owner, decides that you want to expand to South Africa, and you explore the opportunity in the strategic planning process. You may discover that it requires a major long-term commitment, and a contract with a distributor is onerous, but you still want to proceed. You've discovered the issues, made a conscious decision to proceed, and you haven't spent a dime on the project while thinking it through – minimal risk to scratch out the issues before you blast onward."

Don replied thoughtfully, "Sort of a simulation on the whiteboard – low risk. And if we don't know some of the critical elements required to make a product decision, Stephen gets a task to research the issue before we make any commitments." He mused, nodding his head and quietly deliberating, "Expansion with controlled risk...I like it."

While attempting to remove the empty plates noiselessly, a blob of blackberry jelly dropped on the diagram. Apologetic, Janey wiped – no smeared – the stain across the competitive analysis.

"Competitive analysis reflects the team's market knowledge - specific competitors, competitive conditions and macro analysis about where the market is going. Here's a question for you Don. Who are your top 5 competitors, and why are they good? And when you answer the question, how do we compare to these competitors on each of the items you identify."

"C'mon Joseph, we know our markets very well. I've been in the business for more than 25 years and we've been successful. That gets into far too much detail."

"OK, then let me suggest that you have several very large competitors including Stryker, Johnson & Johnson, and DePuy. From a resource point, they can easily swallow you – basically put you out of business if they choose. They have incredibly trained sales executives, extensive regulatory compliance functions, and are well connected to all the major hospitals and clinics. They are global in reach, and have exceptional medical research staffs. How do you beat them?"

Mounting a counterchallenge, Don quickly responded, "Well, we don't go head-to-head with them. We have historically concentrated on the Talus and Navicular, and we concentrate our marketing efforts on the smaller regional hospitals. Think Wal-Mart – they became the largest global retailer by concentrating on the small burgs that Sears and K-Mart ignored. We have built relationships with the MD's that perform the surgeries, and have close affiliations with smaller, less prestigious research universities, rather than our employing large staffs of MD's in research."

"And what other *replacement bones* fit your niche? Will you only do foot bones, or are there replacement bones that the J&J's won't spend time developing?"

Joseph was intentionally accelerating the tempo to stir emotion.

"Sure there are – we just haven't identified them yet."

"And when will you do so?"

Don's fists tightened, and the vein in his temple began to pulse. He lashed out, "When the timing is right, Joseph. You know, I don't need to answer your questions."

"And if you launched another *bone* within your defined niche, would sales and earnings increase. And if sales and earnings increased, would your Company be worth more? Perhaps even get Jackson Manufacturing above the radar so that J&J would like to acquire the Company? Perhaps even get a bidding war between J&J and DePuy?"

"Yeah, yeah, yeah – I get it. Back off…"

"I've been pressing your buttons today, Don. Let's understand, this is your Company, and you can do whatever you like with it. My role, if we continue, is to help you identify options – branches in a decision tree that you get to manage. If you want to grow the Company, we can identify ways to do that… if you want to sell the Company, we can help think through the options and processes that you might want to do. You're always in control."

221

"So tell me about the financials in this strategic plan."

"Good question. Let me ask you, how do you feel about the financials that Cynthia has delivered in the last month?"

"It is surprising how much information we have in our systems. I always considered Cynthia's job to be *keep the financial controls* so that we don't get stupid… *satisfy the bank*, and *manage the extra cash* that we've generated.   And whatever you do, Cynthia, don't get in the way of those that operate the business. During the past few months, she's actually identified trends and opportunities that we've never seen before. Using that information, we also have a better view of where we may be able to go. When I saw the potential impact of the new "A" account, I was shocked."

"Exactly. You're benefiting from more effective financial management. We use the same concepts in strategic planning. That is, identify risks and opportunities, identify a sponsor – someone who is responsible to perform tasks – and hook some numbers to the tasks. The numbers are capital, working capital, expenses, sales and profitability. The beauty of the process is that the team sees how the various tasks inter-relate, and can accomplish your vision. They do that on a whiteboard, with active participation by the entire team, and you haven't spent a dime thinking through growth opportunities. Can you think of a better way to get the team engaged?"

"Theoretically, sounds good, Joseph, but think about our team. Many different personalities. Some shy folks. What if they don't engage?"

"That's my job, Don. I don't allow shy participants. Have you noticed how you've gone from casual conversation to – well, you got a bit angry, didn't you?"

"I'd like to look at an actual example plan – generic of course. Can you do that?"

As Janey freshened the coffee, Joseph eased the iPad from his portfolio, tapped the touch screen, and served the information to Don. "I've got a generic example to share with you, Don. There are really only six example pages."

"Check out the broad language – not fluff, but directional. ...Metal fabrication, engineering and product design. So what will this Company do when an opportunity in injection molding pops up?"

"Based on this vision, pass the opportunity."

"Exactly! The Vision doesn't have to be pages long – just enough to frame where the Company will go. The next slide is one way to display strengths and weaknesses. How do I know these?

Example Company Vision

Example Company will be recognized as a leader in the metal fabrication, engineering and product design industry. We will be a company that you can depend upon 100% of the time. As a team we will be effective, efficient and credible. Our employees will continue to upgrade and expand their technical knowledge to deliver a higher value-added product to our customers. Our customers will trust that when they are in need of service, Example Company will provide them with the technical and product assistance immediately. When customers call they will receive the correct answer from a qualified source, immediately. Example Company will build relationships with our customers through proactive communication. We will be seen as a business partner, who delivers results, not excuses.

Description	Strength	Weakness	Opportunity	Threat
General				
Training				
Management Training			○	
Technical Training - Design Software		○		
Technical Training - Factory Automation		○		
Cross Training				
Standardized Procedures		○		
Product Development				
Personnel	○			
Technology/IT Platform	○			
Lean Design Practices	○			
Facilities			○	
Culture	○			
Website				
User Friendliness			○	
Custom Order Capability				○
Sales Management		○		
Professionalism versus competition				
Sense of Organization	○			
Systems				○
Internet Competitors				○

Don took the bait. "Is that my cue to say you're not smart enough to know those in every business?"

"Exactly! I don't know the strengths and weaknesses but you and the executives do. My role is to coax the information from the execs. Sometimes I'll get them angry – you've seen that – sometimes I flatter them –

but when I'm done, people are satisfied that the major strengths and weaknesses are on the table."

Competitive Mapping

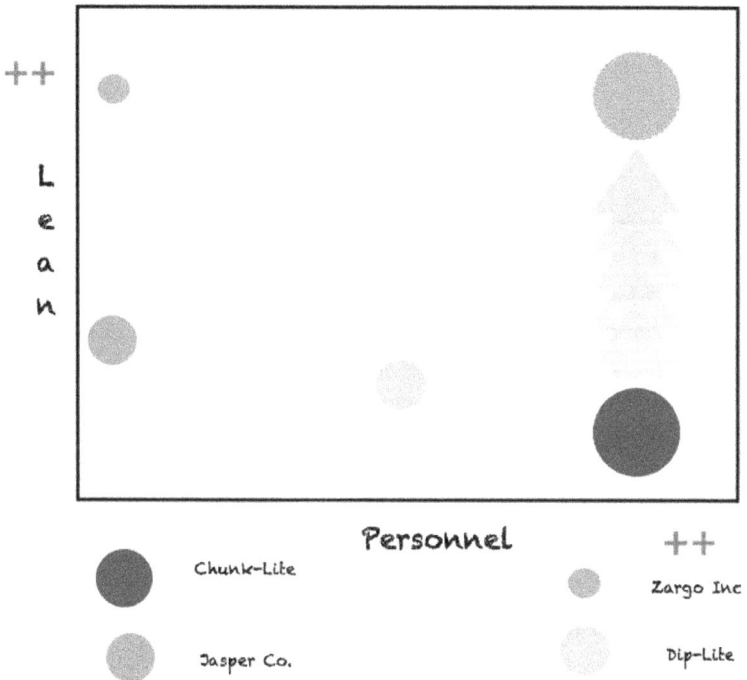

"This is another example of how to graphically compare a company to competitors. The area of the circle reflects relative size, and the strength or weakness is identified on the axis. So in this case, Chunk-Lite is 2-3 times the size of their key competitors, and they have a very strong organization – Chunk Lite's circle is at the far right on the Personnel axis. Chunk Lite is very weak in Lean Business Practice, and one of their strategic goals is to improve "Lean Business Practices"."

"I get it. The arrows indicate their growth goal. So, in this situation what if they wanted to buy Zargo?"

"Why would they do that?"

"Zargo is smaller and has exceptional Lean Business Practices with weak 'Personnel'. Might be cheaper for them to buy the competitor, absorb or learn their Lean expertise, grow the Company with the sales acquired, and migrate the Lean expertise to Chunk Lite."

"Exactly. You've got it, Don. And notice how quickly you could draw the conclusion from the imagery presented."

"The next two pages go together."

Description Johnson Total Company	2009 (Act)	2010 (Act)	Plan						2012	2013
			2011				Tot Year			
			1st	2nd	3rd	4th				
Number of Units Sold	12,050	15,900	8,550	10,200	10,200	12,450	20,340		24,800	30,100
Number of Direct Headcount	7	8	8	-	9	9	7		8	8
Number of Kiosks	-	-	-	8	4	7	7		8	11
Custom Designs	-	-	-	-	-	50	50		80	100
Revenue/Job	2,159.3	1,915.5	907.0	968.6	1,051.0	900.7	1,939.0		1,943.3	1,878.2
Gross Profit/Job	736.7	624.5	287.4	294.4	322.1	282.9	603.1		554.8	488.9
(000's US $)										
Revenue	26,020.0	30,456.0	7,755.0	9,880.0	10,720.0	11,214.0	39,439.0		48,193.0	56,534.0
Gross Profit	8,877.00	9,930.0	2,457.0	3,003.0	3,285.0	3,522.0	12,267.0		13,758.0	14,716.0
GP%	34.1%	32.6%	31.7%	30.4%	30.6%	31.4%	31.1%		28.5%	26.0%
Selling General & Admin	7,008.0	6,731.0	1,573.0	1,744.0	1,952.0	1,918.0	7,185.0		7,522.0	7,854.0
Profit Before Tax	1,869.0	3,199.0	884.0	1,259.0	1,333.0	1,604.0	5,082.0		6,236.0	6,862.0
Profit After Tax	281.0	974.0	151.0	292.0	425.0	347.0	1,216.0		1,523.0	1,856.0
DSO	55	53	55	55	52	51	52		50	48
Inventory Months on Hand	4.0	3.0	3.0	3.0	2.5	2.3	2.5		2.5	2.3

Key Programs

Growth

Market Share

Ref	Description	Due Date	Responsible	Spending	
				Capital	Expense
1	Assess organization clerical staffing needs	Q4 2011	Anderson		
2	Develop & implement improved cost accounting for custom design shop	Q4 2011	Delvechio	50	15
3	Develop a comprehensive marketing plan to sell custom designed products	Q4 2011	Johnson		
4	Develop a Website for the Custom Design business	Q1 2012	Dilson	35	
5	Develop key metrics to effectively monitor the Custom Design Business	Q4 2012	Anderson		

Ref	Description	Due Date	Responsible	Spending	
1	Assess organization clerical staffing needs	Q4 2011	Anderson		
5	Develop key metrics to effectively monitor the Custom Design Business	Q4 2012	Anderson		
2	Develop & implement improved cost accounting for custom design shop	Q4 2011	Delvechio	50	15
3	Develop a comprehensive marketing plan to sell custom designed products	Q4 2011	Johnson		
4	Develop a Website for the Custom Design business	Q1 2012	Dilson	35	

"We talked about hooking financials to programs, since without accountability, you really don't have an incentive or a process to measure achievement. The Business Segment financial summary includes P&L and other metrics that can be controlled by the program sponsor – in this case, look at the top left corner – Johnson. He owns this "Total Company" program, including deliverables that he can manage such as Inventory Turns and DSO. His policies and execution will allow him to reach these goals. In this presentation, we set financial goals such as Gross Profit, number of units sold, average price, as well as headcount. Mr. Johnson asks for specific resources, and promises specific returns to the stockholders.

We also highlight – directionally – market share goals, and specific actions such as to launch and grow a new Product Line ZZ. One compact summary page for 'Johnson' that leaves little to the imagination about his commitments.

The next page - do you remember how I said names and dates – includes specific deliverables by individual and date to be completed.

These are just examples of what can be. The strategic plan can take many shapes, but this seems to work well in the middle market, and for a company of your size the plan might be 10-15 pages deep."

Don leaned forward and expanded several of the pages by pinching the iPad screen. He puzzled over how a business could be summarized in such a simple presentation... accountabilities defined... names, dates.

"Fascinating. And how long does one of these plans take?"

"This would be a few hours of discussion with each executive, and perhaps a 2-day meeting offsite to shake out the details."

"So, let me see if I understand this. We get the team together to talk about the Vision, financial goals, competition, strengths and weaknesses. After a few days of effort, I get one of these plans, that tells me the expected financial results in 3 years, and includes specific deliverables of how I will get there. And if I want to be a $35 million annual revenue Company, and we can figure out how to get there, it might happen?"

"If the plans are reasonable, with appropriate contingencies, and folks are accountable and actually execute, that's right."

"And if they don't execute?"

"You won't make it, but that again is your decision. If they don't execute reasonable plans, then you haven't held them accountable."

"Does this really work?"

"Yes and no. The point of failure in strategic planning is the lack of disciplined execution. If you don't enforce the accountability, it will fail. Of course with the

232

financials, you will understand how much failure costs you."

"In the case of a sale, it could be a multiple of 5-7 times earnings, right?"

"Exactly."

"And if I don't want to sell?"

"Your strategy reflects that."

"Send me a copy of these pages and I'll get back to you early next week." He scanned the restaurant for Janey, waved at her to get the check.

April 21, 2014 - Specialist & CEO to Planning the Offsite

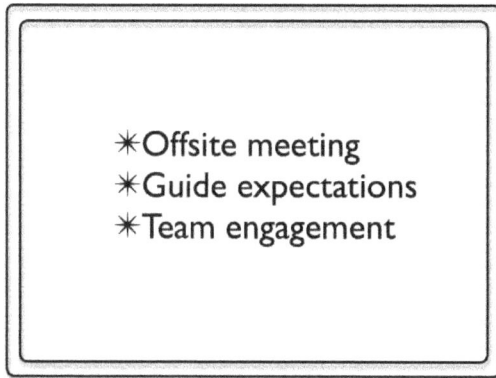

*Offsite meeting
*Guide expectations
*Team engagement

Joseph has been extremely busy during the past 3 weeks. Thus far, Don has officially launched the strategic planning process, and Joseph has completed initial and follow-up meetings with each of the executives.

At Joseph's first meeting with Don they identified business intentions including Company strategic goals, market presence, financial goals, and the possibility that Don would sell the Company within the next 3 years. This first iteration was merely to shape out the future, knowing that based on the team's input, all intentions could be modified.

000's $	2012	2013	2014	2015	2016	2017
Sales						
Baseline	19,566	19,233	18,788	18,500	20,000	21,000
Billings/Peterson					500	1,000
Knuckles	10,041	10,779	12,226	14,455	15,055	16,476
International				500	750	750
New Product				–	250	500
Total Sales	29,607	30,012	31,014	33,455	36,555	39,726
Gross Profit	15,692	15,306	15,119	17,505	20,405	20,241
Total GM %	53%	51%	49%	52%	56%	51%
Baseline %	47%	43%	42%	45%	46%	47%
Billings/Peterson %					55%	51%
Knuckles %	66%	65%	59%	60%	64%	54%
International				60%	67%	68%
New Product					60%	60%
SG&A						
Sales	6,997	7,122	7,255	7,500	7,800	8,300
R&D	750	785	815	1,555	1,950	2,150
Admin	3,162	3,213	3,200	3,759	3,065	3,350
Other	1,912	2,015	2,212	2,465	2,676	3,014
Total	12,821	13,135	13,482	15,279	15,491	16,814
Pretax Profit	2,871	2,171	1,637	2,226	4,914	3,427
% of Sales	10%	7%	5%	7%	13%	9%
After Tax Profit	1,436	1,086	819	1,113	2,457	1,714

Cash	2012	2013	2014	2015	2016	2017
Capital Spending	560	750	1,500	1,500	1,500	2,000

	2012	2013	2014	2015	2016	2017
Accounts Receivable	8,522	12,122	10,989	9,895	8,778	8,500
Accounts Payable						
Inventory Balance	–	–	–	–	–	3
DSO	96	135	119	99	80	72
Invnetory Turns	2.5	2.7	3.5	4	4.5	4.5

A draft P&L and major cash flow items demonstrated
significant potential growth that initially looked

impossible. Individual assumptions to reach those goals seemed reasonable, but when summarized, Company results were startling.

Key assumptions and notes included:

- New product introductions would increase sales by $2.5 million and would focus on niche bone replacements in wrist, hips and elbows. Expect development through existing University research and acquisition of orphan products from fringe companies.
- $.5 million data system investment needed to grow... 2014/2015.
- New programmable machining centers required in factory to reduce cycle time... $1.0 million investment in 2015/2016
- Lean manufacturing initiative required in manufacturing to reach inventory turn goals and improved margins... increased admin cost of $.5 million in 2015
- Expect $.5 million inventory write-off due to lean thinking in 2014
- Improved sales process, expanded sales force increase sales by $2.5 million
- Expand export sales/globalization to increase sales by $2.5 million
- Price increase in 2015 due to service & delivery improvements...$1.0 million
- All programs prioritized and will be implemented incrementally as profits improve

- Improvements in data systems, and billing/accounts receivable processing to reduce DSO
- Write-off of bad inventory and lean manufacturing to improve inventory turns

"Don, the draft P&L is startling, but when you look at the assumptions, they're not stupid – especially when you consider the amount of contingency we have baked in. On the one side, I'm nervous, but since programs will be rolled out based on what we can afford, I think we have the process under control."

"Joseph, I can tell you that I've never looked at the business like this before. I've been focused on monthly profitability and cash flow. When you pulled me back from the details, and forced me to look at the big picture, I can only say, 'holy crap' - this is achievable." His eyes flashed with excitement as he considered the big items that he never would have identified without the intervention. Joseph warned him that once they thought strategically, he would see the business through a different lens.

Before the off-site meeting, Joseph and Don scripted how the meetings would proceed.

"Don, you'll set the stage by discussing the basic elements of the planning process, including the vision/mission, a bit of history – successes and failures – and then how we will talk about the competitors, strengths and weaknesses. I've already sensitized the team to those challenges. I've also challenged them to think about how we can grow by 25-30% in the next three years. They were each initially surprised when I coughed up that number, but after a few questions about competitors, new products, price increases and process improvements, they decided the challenge wasn't completely stupid."

"Got it. I'm also going to share my concerns about my continued ownership – this boomer's getting old. I don't want the elephant in the room to be ignored, and I want them to know how important they are to the future of the Company. And of course, that part of the strategic plan is to understand how we can make them an integral part of the future success – through stock options or grants, bonus programs etc. We don't have the answers yet, but that will be my responsibility, working with Margaret, outside experts and the rest of the team to be sure that we do the right thing."

The meeting was scheduled to begin at the University Club, 8:30, starting with a continental breakfast of fruit, yogurt, and a selection of muffins and bagels. Surprisingly, all arrived by 8:10, and were ready to proceed at 8:30.

Don welcomed all to the first strategic planning session for Jackson Machinery Inc. As he scanned the participants, he noticed some changes.

JB was no longer slouched in the chair, with his rotund belly snuggled against the table's edge, but rather he sat nearly erect in his chair. He also did not smell of cigar smoke, looked a few pounds lighter, and wore a starched shirt with neatly pressed pants. A flesh-toned adhesive patch was affixed to his left forearm. Could that be a nicotine patch? His weekly reports were frightening at first, as he highlighted the thousands of dollars of obsolete or unacceptable parts previously stored in dust-covered bins scattered around the factory. Fortunately, Joseph prepared Don for the upcoming write-offs as a normal condition of improvement. JB was now more proactive on the floor, attempting to make things better, while still managing largely using his old paradigm. What's next for JB?

Cynthia was smiling and positively bubbly in a private conversation with Allison. Cynthia's self-confidence ratcheted to peak levels as if an all-star athlete competing on an Olympic speed skating oval. As always, neatly coiffed and conservatively dressed, she seemed more at ease with the business than at any time in the past 8 years, despite her increased financial management responsibility – a responsibility she personally developed and confirmed with Don.

No shortage of self-confidence, Allison's traditional tardy performance and distracted scientist look morphed into a focused scientific development executive who was on a mission. She adopted the posture of 'push Don until he says no'. Her collection of new product concepts was so extensive that during the past few weeks, she provided a steady stream of new product development ideas concentrating on existing and potential markets, using new materials and designs. All were identified through her relationships with local universities. Don asked her to work with Stephen to get better consumer insight to avoid squandering limited resources. Don puzzled over Allison's dramatic change as if going from a caterpillar to butterfly. Where has this dynamo been hiding for so many years?

Stephen, the ultimate professional, continues to expand sales, but at a pace we've never experienced before. At our weekly meetings, he now highlights the customer pipeline – never discussed before - and trade channels that we are mining. He now seemed to be working more closely with Allison in the product development mode. Surprisingly he included her on some sales calls with the major second-tier hospitals and surgery centers. This had never happened before.

Margaret has recently become more active in business discussions demonstrating a more proactive role in the Company. Several times, as she pressed for more involvement in establishing performance goals and linkage with rewards, she referenced local companies that had successfully changed their reward systems. Normally she avoided business discussions, apparently preferring to concentrate exclusively on tactical matters such as payroll, health care benefits and pay structures. In recent one-to-one meetings, she has pressed for a comprehensive executive compensation plan that considers longer-term incentives for key executives, and succession planning. Don wondered, 'Where does she come up with that stuff?'

Could all this progress be the result of Joseph's prodding and service enrichment process?

"Good morning folks. Today is the first day of our strategic planning session. During the past few weeks, you've each spent time with Joseph, who has apparently been very successful in stirring things up. Well, today and tomorrow, we're going to mix the pot once again. We're going to start with something that I personally found incomprehensible even two weeks ago. But with Joseph's guidance – and should I say prodding…" Don chuckled, gazed at Joseph, and nodded an acknowledgement almost imperceptibly. "… We have been thinking like a different Company. It seemed a shame to let all this creativity meander throughout the Company without lending a bit of focus to the process. Hence, the strategy session begins.

Joseph will facilitate the process, and he has assured me that there are no topics off the table. Occasionally, you'll see me squirming in my seat when he gets into delicate tissue, and I hope he'll be gentle with all of us… especially me.

I can tell you that during discussions with Joseph, he's made me darned angry… very nervous… very concerned. But every time, he seems to read my emotions, knows where the hard edge lies, and talks me off the cliff. Our job is to push *him* to his limits – as he said – no topics off the table. So let's have at it!"

Don gestured to Joseph that it was now his meeting, while Don moved to the refreshments, peeled the cover from a Greek Yogurt and scooped some fresh strawberries and blueberries into the plastic cup. Paired with a cup of steaming coffee, he slipped comfortably into a seat at the far end of the conference table.

Joseph had the PowerPoint's preloaded for an immediate and effective start. After challenging each of them to be open-minded, and be prepared for some challenging discussion, he launched the P&L. The team examined the projected P&L, mouths agape and stunned speechless. Joseph's questions, delicate as a fully charged cattle prod, were designed for discomfort.

"So Stephen, what do you think?"

As the slide launched, Stephen leaned forward, elbows on the table and hands folded almost as if in prayer. His eyes darted across the years, and his head almost imperceptibly bobbed – perhaps not in agreement, but in amazement. "His only comment, "…interesting…" After a moment's pause, he looked at Cynthia and said, "Quintuple profits in the next 3 years?" and left the question hanging in the air.

Cynthia spotted the Gross Margin increase from 47% to nearly 60%, looked at JB and said, "Do you buy this margin increase?"

Don shifted nervously and played with a strawberry, continuously coating the berry in the yogurt, as there appeared to be rebellion. Stephen observed, "…but we get a 30% increase in selling expense. I like that, Don."

While trying to avoid being negative, JB, without a hint of body language, said, "We can't cut costs that much."

Allison offered a slight solution, "…new products… new alloys … new markets?"

On cue, Joseph interrupted, "OK, we've captured your interest. Now our challenge is to make something happen. Of course, we could just as easily increase sales to $50 million, don't you think?"

With that figure, people almost disengaged completely from the conversation – Cynthia sipping a coffee, while JB carefully picked the raisins from a bagel. Allison started to flip through the presentation booklet.

"Ah-ah, Allison, no reading ahead. Let's play this out folks. What if I gave each one of you an after-tax check for $1 million if we could reach $50 million of sales in three years, would you give up?"

Shy Margaret, spoon in hand, raised her hand from the table as if to wave to a professor, and said, "Let's buy a company!"

"Perfect!" Joseph complimented her on the completely outlandish idea that solved the problem. "Why not?"

"Because we haven't done so in the past," Cynthia said without looking up.

"So what... nothing off the table," Joseph responded.

Don, with a concerned look, challenged Joseph, "I appreciate your creativity, Joseph, but we can't afford to buy a company."

"Why not? Just because you don't have the money in the bank?"

Steely eyed, Cynthia replied, "Yes."

"And does that mean we can't partner with investors who like our business potential, like the results that we have? Do we need to own the whole thing, or can we borrow the money, Cynthia."

"I suppose there are alternatives."

"Folks, we can't get through this process suffering with outdated paradigms. Now, that doesn't mean we have unlimited funds, but it does require us to think differently. We don't want to stretch to $50 million of annual sales, but we do think that we can reach $39.5 million. Reasonably. During the next two days, we will explore who are our competitors, strengths and weaknesses of both, and macro factors like the economy, export markets, pricing strategies etc.

Now, in fact, when we've completed the thorough analysis, we may discover that the $39.5 million is unachievable, but it will only be after we've examined all the major Company factors. We may discover that our vision and mission will take us to markets never before considered. We may discover major advantages – like our flexibility and responsiveness - to be key strengths, linkages with university researchers to be vital competitive advantage.

Let's approach this meeting as one without any barriers. It's my job to keep the process on track. For the next two days, this is our schedule," as he projected the slide on the screen."

Today

8:30 – 9:00	Introduction
9:00 – 10:30	Vision/Mission
10:30 – 10:45	*Break*
10:45 –	Functional discussion – Organization, people, processes; strengths & weaknesses
10:45 - 11:15	- Finance & IT
11:15 – 12:00	- Manufacturing/Ops/Logistics
12:00 – 1:00	*Lunch*
1:00 – 1:30	- Legal
1:30 – 2:00	- Human Resources
2:00 - 2:30	- Sales
2:30 – 3:15	- R&D; New Product Development
3:15 - 3:30	*Break*
3:30 – 5:00	Strengths & weaknesses: prioritized

245

Tomorrow

8:00 – 9:00	Discussion – macro environment; economy; globalization
9:00 – 11:00	Discussion – Competitors; mapping
11:00 – 11:15	*Break*
11:15 – 12:30	Products; substitutes; etc.
12:30 – 1:30	*Lunch*
1:30 – 3:00	Key initiatives

He continued, "Throughout these two days, it's my job to keep us on track. And believe me, I'm not foolish enough to think that we can accomplish 100% of everything required in two days, but we'll get through enough where the shape of things to come will be evident.

As we explore the future, we're going to identify things that must be done. Some within the bounds of reality – others that may not fit the available resources. But we won't let that stop us… that is exactly what the 'parking lot' – those flip charts along the wall – are for.

Nothing is off limits. We won't be critical of another's comments or suggestions, since we are problem solving.

One last thing. No one caught the expected changes in DSO or Inventory Turns. Those two simple metrics will generate millions of dollars of free cash flow… money that, if Don chooses, can be reinvested in the business... or used to purchase another business." Cynthia, with furrowed brow and a deep scowl, scratched a note on her pad.

"If we do our job right, during the next few days, we will open vistas never before seen, and in a positive team environment, discover a business that we never knew existed before. Questions?"

"I see legal up on the screen. Who's doing that?"

"We've called it an Administrative function, and assigned that to Cynthia. In this analysis, every function has a home... good Segway, Allison. You'll see in the next slide that we've parsed the Company into a series of cells. Each of you owns a group of cells. Anything that goes on in those cells is yours... people, processes, plant & assets, product, and market. I've set up the matrix knowing that everything must have an owner, but some of the cells are N/A – not applicable. Great question, Allison."

The colorful matrix jumped on the screen for the team's examination. "When you check out the matrix, you'll see separate lines for Finance and for Legal. If you're all in agreement, I'd like to assign names to each line. So, for example, Cynthia you have the Legal, IT and the Finance lines. Comfortable?"

She nodded agreement. Joseph continued to assign names to every line.

"Now let's spend a minute to look at the columns. Any thoughts on 'People – Inside/Outside?'"

Margaret fired the answer as if she were participating in the Final Jeopardy question. "Employees and Contractors."

"Great start. Anyone else included?" After a protracted silence, Joseph offered, "I'll suggest that anyone – person or organization – that the function has contact with is included. So, for example, if Cynthia interacts with the Internal Revenue Service, they are included as part of her responsibility."

Joseph continued, "Any thoughts on Process – Content/Application?"

"This is a pure guess, but would that mean a process that is well-developed and documented, and also used and monitored?"

"Excellent Allison. Anyone want to take Plant?"

"I'm guessing that location means any location, and maintained in an appropriate or usable way." Joseph responded, "JB, I knew that I could count on you to fill in the gaps. Yes, and Plant also includes any assets. So it means that we have the right plant/facilities and assets – including intellectual property, Allison – and the quality fits the need. … Properly maintained. So let's make up an example. If Allison is preparing a file for a patent application, her responsibility is to prepare proper documentation to effectively obtain the patent, and proper processes to maintain the patent.

Any thoughts why Cynthia's *law* line would extend across to Plant?"

Cynthia's head bobbed as she quietly concluded, "It's because I've got to be sure that all legal matters are proper – law is my responsibility."

Stephen mildly objected, "Wait a minute. It seems that we have double coverage and potential conflict when we have two execs responsible."

"That might be one conclusion," Joseph responded, "…or I might say redundancy, and a certain element of two execs cooperating to make sure that nothing falls through the cracks."

As JB munched a granola bar, eyes never wavering from the slide, he said as if talking to himself, "So that means that the Service line is mine… and I'm responsible for Inside/Outside People that would include vendors and customers…my processes related to those contacts should be at the right level … I'm to ensure that the facilities meet requirements…" and his voice trailed off to a whisper.

Know Your Potential Buyer ... ID keys to Value ... Critical Self-Assessment ... Focused Improvements

	B	I	N	G	O

1 Year - Great ...Implement Substantive Change   6 Month's - Caution ... Prioritize Changes   3 Month's - too late

1 Year	6 Month's	3 Month's

Define Buyer:
- Financial?
- Strategic?
- Unsure?

	People	Process	Plant	Product	Market
	Inside / Outside	Content / Application	Location / Quality	Current / Pipeline	Share / Growth
Company					
Logistics					
Operations					
Sales					
Marketing					
Service					
HR					
Technology/IT					
Finance					
Legal					
Other					

Rank top 5 strengths, based on potential buyer: 1 is best

With that, Joseph launched the Vision/Mission segment. Surprisingly, everyone thought the Vision was to be a *knuckles* company, recognized as a leader in the US.

Guided by Joseph, the team explored Company capabilities, executive team goals and Don's personal desires. After nearly an hour of animated discussion that ranged from the clearly unachievable *save humanity* to a far more practical, yet equally unachievable, "… provide any required artificial bones to baby boomers…" the team settled on some key words. The process itself included Allison pacing the floor in a frenzy of brainstorming concepts, to Joseph's marker slashing words – some with circles in red… arrows connecting concepts - across numerous flip chart pages. Joseph's frenetic pace and enthusiasm engaged all execs in a flurry of ideas that would condense like water droplets on a chilled glass of lemonade, to a single concentrated idea.

Once concepts were prioritized, Joseph applauded their unbridled efforts and congratulated each of them on the team's accomplishments. "I'll take these priorities and craft some words that try to capture these ideas into a single paragraph that describes our vision and mission. Let's have a coffee – hey, we're right on schedule. Bravo."

The team huddled in amazement at what they had accomplished in an hour. Five different functions, each with their own priorities, agreed on the critical elements of the Company vision and mission that would guide the

future of the Company. Margaret had one simple
question. "What just happened? Better yet, how did it
happen?"

JB was extremely pleased as he motioned to all to join
him in a healthy snack. Stephen motioned to JB's
forearm. "Hey JB, what's that patch on your arm?"

"Nicotine patch. ... Giving up the Nicaraguans. Decided
that I wasn't as healthy as I wanted to be. Changed my
diet as well... lost 7 pounds in the last month."

"Next thing you know, we'll be chasing you around the
gym, trying to keep up with you. Yogurt anyone?"

Coffee cups filled, individuals unsheathed their
smartphones and responded to voicemails and emails in
the few remaining break minutes. All seemed pleased
with the meeting's initial progress.

April 26, 2014 – HR: Offsite Functional Discussion

＊Organization structure
＊Personnel assessment
＊Gap analysis
＊Career growth

After a brief discussion with Don, Joseph marched purposefully to the front of the room, clicking the agenda to the screen.

"OK, let's get rolling. We've got a great start, but still have two days remaining. A bit of a schedule change. I've asked Margaret to start the session with the Human Resources discussion. Since Margaret is the first, let's be kind to her – with a wink and toss of the remote, Joseph relinquished control of the meeting.

"Good morning. Wow – what a great start," her voice quivering with nervousness. "I'm new to presentations and I don't have a lot of beautiful slides. I just want to share some information about the organization."

With that, she queued the first slide with the Organization Chart.

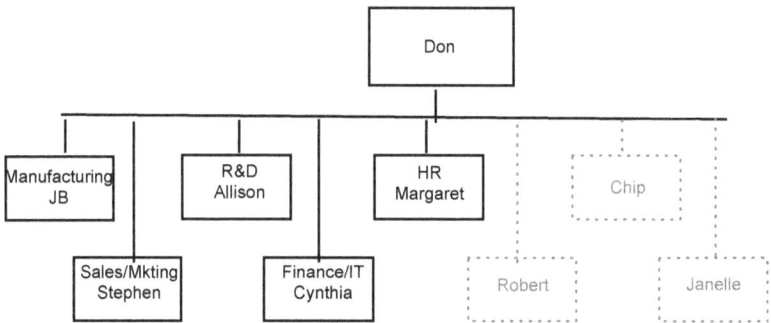

Following the guidelines, her 30-minute session covered People (including organization structure), Process, Plant, and Market- no impact on Product. Don immediately focused on the blue boxes and asked, "Why are those in Blue, Margaret?" Margaret stammered, her voice almost a whisper. "I'm not sure what they do, Don, but we know they report to you."

JB and Stephen exchanged nervous glances, raised eyebrows and discretely smiled. Margaret raised an issue that they were all concerned about, since Robert and Chip occasionally disrupted the business flow, referencing their heritage and place on the organization chart.

"Folks, they're family and they report to me for one reason. They're good people, and help me with research. Their role is not to interfere in the basic Company operations."

JB leaned forward, elbows on the table. "Don, sometimes Robert and Chip get on a personal mission. How do you expect us to handle their interventions? It's not the kind of thing we want to bother you with."

Joseph knew that delicate tissue was exposed. During the next 10 minutes he carefully guided the team discussion to ensure that Don understood the magnitude of the issue. Don was surprised at the examples. Joseph peeled a flip chart page, writing a heading in all capitals, "PARKING LOT" and listed "Robert, Chip, Janelle". "OK – we have some concrete examples. Don and I will follow-up on this later. Margaret, let's move on."

Relieved to move on, she quickly changed slides to a stark, black & white slide with a half-dozen line items. Although she and Joseph discussed these items extensively before the meeting, she was concerned about the team's possible reaction to the topics. As the slide appeared, she nervously peeked at Joseph, who nodded, and shaped the words, 'you're doing fine.'

Human Resources

Description	Rating	Discussion
Job Descriptions:	Needs work	•Standard template - developed •Not updated & current •New positions not documented
Performance Reviews	Needs work	•Standard formats developed - need improvement •Timely compliance - limited • Quality - limited
Employee Bonus Plans:	None	•Considered important - not competitive
Executive Compensation:	Needs Work	•Generally subjective •Stretch goals not incented •Linkage to Company goals limited
Succession Plan:	None	•Succession gaps exist

Throughout her discussion, Joseph encouraged the team to probe Margaret's topics and challenge themselves about the relevance and importance of each of the items.

The team enthusiastically debated the nuisance value and bureaucracy of Job Descriptions and Performance Reviews. JB, the most vocal, simply considered Job Descriptions and Performance reviews to be redundant, non-value added activities that slowed him down.

"JB, I understand how you might feel that way, since you measure each individual's performance based on quality output. But think of Job Descriptions as a way of planning how you allocate work among your subordinates. When you review all the activities that your function performs – from manufacturing to logistics and customer service – good job descriptions allow you to delegate balanced workloads and help team members develop their careers.

And performance reviews? Well, they allow you to measure not only the production, but you can include areas of personal improvement in a performance review. For example, you might want to require your staff to achieve Green Belt status in a 6-sigma program. They achieve personal career growth, while you have improved skills at your disposal."

After a spirited discussion, JB decided that the tools would allow him to delegate more responsibility, since improved reporting would enforce accountability.

All were intrigued by Margaret's Bonus Plan discussion. She explained that regional companies of similar size each had Employee Bonus plans, and that to remain competitive, the Company should consider adding such a plan.

"Why would we pay a bonus to someone for doing their job?" was the common question.

Can it be that Margaret anticipated these questions? She fired back with a quick smile, "Well, if you only want them to do their basic job, then the paycheck is absolutely enough. But with an employee bonus program, we can have some stretch goals that will improve overall Company performance."

Don felt conspicuously targeted by the "Succession Plan" topic, and could sense his face reddening. Joseph spotted the angst immediately and interrupted Margaret before her first sentence, to defuse the situation.

"Now, team, succession planning is a tough one. Let's think about each of the functional areas. So JB, let's say you win a $25 million lottery. What's the first call you make from Jamaica?" The entire team laughed and started to chide JB. "Gonna leave us just like that, eh JB? What about the $50 bucks you owe me?' joked Stephen.

"You folks get what I mean. Allison, if you decide on your next Spanish trip to use only a one-way ticket, what do we do? OK, Margaret, take it away."

"Thanks Joseph. You see what we mean when we say succession planning. It's not necessarily for your benefit – especially if you leave – but for the benefit of the Company. Do we all have successors in place?"

Uniformly the team responded, "no."

"So these are issues for us to resolve before we lose opportunity. Joseph suggested that I identify target dates for fixing these gaps, but when you look at the gaps, these are not my issues, but our issues. I think during the next few days, we should identify ways to fix these open items, and set up a timetable for each of us to adhere to.

Joseph, I think that's it."

Joseph immediately stood, and started applause, followed by the team applauding. The first review was complete, touching perhaps the most sensitive issues in the Company, without any major explosions. Joseph demonstrated his ability to manage extremely sensitive issues, focus on key items and get the team to accept ownership.

"Margaret, great job identifying the gaps in our Human Resources function. Did you folks notice that she didn't concentrate on minutia but rather on strategic items that

will help us achieve our Vision and Mission? Well done,
Margaret."

April 26, 2014 – Finance/IT: Offsite Functional Discussion

```
*Organization assessment
*Gap analysis
*Financial risk assessment
```

"Cynthia, Margaret is a tough act to follow, but we have confidence in your performance." Joseph slid the remote/laser combination across the dark wooden conference table.

Cynthia seemed to smile more now than at any time while at Jackson Machine – interesting. As usual, her bouncy ponytail bobbed as she took charge of the meeting. After inviting all to freshen their coffee, she flipped to her first slide.

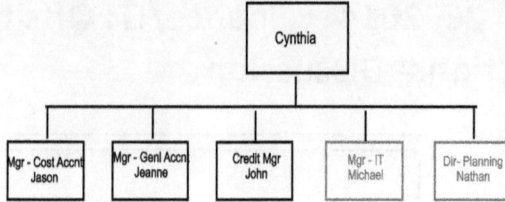

```
                                    ┌──────────┐
                                    │ Cynthia  │
                                    └────┬─────┘
        ┌──────────────┬────────────┬────┴─────────┬──────────────┐
┌───────────────┐┌──────────────┐┌──────────┐┌────────────┐┌─────────────┐
│Mgr - Cost Accnt││Mgr - Genl Accn││Credit Mgr││  Mgr - IT  ││Dir- Planning│
│     Jason      ││    Jeanne     ││   John   ││  Michael   ││   Nathan    │
└───────────────┘└──────────────┘└──────────┘└────────────┘└─────────────┘
```

Assessment
- Experience
- Performance
- Depth of Tech Knowledge
- Management skills

(B) (B) (A) (C) (C)

· ·

Potential

(A) (?) (A) (C) (C)

· ·

Promotion Timeline   12 Months   (?)   (?)

· ·

Process Assessment   (C)   (B)   (B+)   (D)   (D)

Open Items

★Succession Planning
★Upgrade IT Manager
★Upgrade Planning Director
★

★Improve external financial relationships
★Improve reporting
Implement Lean Business Concepts
Upgrade data systems

★Implement Lean Business Concepts
★Upgrade data systems

"Joseph and I have spent some time discussing the department, concentrating on People, Process, and Plant – really the assets that we use to help manage this Company. This was not fun or enjoyable for me. I've been responsible for the department for 3 years, and their performance is a reflection of my performance, and executive competence.

Well, after looking at this organization and our performance for the past few years, I was not happy. Not because the people haven't done as requested, but because I've not been as demanding as I should have been. Well, I've upgraded my performance – raised the bar of what I need to do and what the department needs to do."

Joseph was standing at the rear of the room, and raised a hand gesturing Cynthia to pause. "That's a great start Cynthia. For the future, we're only going to allow 1 minute and 11 seconds for self-flagellation." After a short burst of laughter, Joseph continued, "We're all entering a new phase of growth... raising the bar ... going to the next level... We all know the buzzwords used by so many talking heads on TV. It won't be easy, as Cynthia discovered, but as we can see from her smile, the satisfaction of challenging our status quo is immense.

From my viewpoint, don't beat yourself up too much when you go through this exercise, because if you are honest with yourself, you will discover many areas where you can improve. In fact, next year at this time,

you'll be able to say the same thing – we need to
change some things.

I've talked with Cynthia about her self-assessment, and
think that she's done a fine job. Onward, Cynthia."

Joseph was always careful to let the executives feel like
a winner whenever they had done a good job.

"OK, Joseph, now I'm embarrassed at your compliment.
Let's get on with this so I can stop blushing. I've looked
at People, Process, and Plant, and I've discovered
some gaps in need compared to existing resource."

For the next 45 minutes she shared her assessments.
Surprisingly she identified two of her direct reports that
have not - and likely could not - perform to the standard
required. In particular, she believed that the Information
Technology Director and the Planning Director would
not be capable of growing with the Company. These
conclusions surprised both JB and Margaret who voiced
their disagreement.

Margaret chirped, "I don't agree with your assessment of
both the IT and Planning Director. They have been very
helpful responding to my needs in Human Resources."
JB reinforced her opinion of those two. "Whenever I
need a special report from IT, Michael delivers. Not a
lot of fuss or complaining. And, while I don't spend a lot
of time with Nathan, he never misses a tick with me."

"I appreciate your viewpoint, Margaret and JB. But reacting to business questions is only one part of the new performance criteria that I've established. As Directors, I expect them to be more proactive… anticipate needs and establish performance standards so that urgent requests can be avoided. Lets take a recent example. JB, last week you asked for a report summarizing Knuckles work-orders closed during the past 10 days, right?"

Quite proudly, JB boasted, "Youbetcha… and Michael got the report to me within 24 hours. Quick turnaround, eh?"

"And have you ever asked for similar reports in the past?"

"Youbetcha … and received the report within 24 hours. This guy's good!"

"OK, JB. First, I'm glad that you are happy with the historical response times. In the *new deal*, we want to have the IT department meet with each of you and discover your information needs and not wait for the ad hoc requests that require us to drop everything to get you a special report.

After spending time with Joseph, I've recalibrated performance standards and redefined our role. Our role in finance and IT is as a Company resource. The finance and IT department don't work for me, *we* work for the Company. Our role is an internal service provider to serve the other functional areas' needs, as well as provide a financial management environment to protect the assets of the Company.

Proactive is a key word for us now. In the past, we could get away with a response to some questions by saying, '…not my job…' Well, that is no longer acceptable. We are part of a team that is competing in a very challenging global market. If we don't function as a key component of the Company team, then I – and we in the department – are not doing our job."

Allison offered, "Wow, did you ever drink the Kool-Aid! Settle down gal."

Joseph, leaning against the paneled wall near the flip chart in the back of the room, was pleased with the discourse. The team was challenging each other when discussing performance.

Joseph challenged the team, "Engagement – yes this is exactly what must be done to achieve peak performance. Anybody want to comment on the concept of 'internal service provider'? Anyone else have that role in the Company?"

Allison looked up from her doodled tinker-toy like chemical structure describing a fictional cure for cancer. "I've got a responsibility to the stockholders – that's you Don – to help develop a product pipeline that gives this Company some longevity… give this Company some legs. If we don't continuously introduce new products, the Company will become irrelevant... we'll go out of business."

JB was twirling his pen in small circles on the conference table surface. Without looking up, "And I guess it's my responsibility to produce first quality products to spec, at the least cost, so that we make a profit."

"OK folks, let's put some words on the Parking Lot." Joseph selected the red marker and in large bold capital letters, scribed SERVICE ORIENTATION. "Everybody ok with that note?"

After agreement, Joseph redirected the meeting to Cynthia. "Great stuff, Cynthia. Didn't mean to distract you from your presentation. Onward."

"And to close out the "C" evaluations, the Director of Planning needs to understand the business well enough to identify key metrics that will help us easily understand our performance. Once these measures are identified, we'll manage better – perhaps prepare a management dashboard for us all to use. Nathan does not seem to have the capability to do that kind of work. He's more of a spreadsheet jockey. A good technician, but I think we need more."

Margaret's furrowed brow and scowl tipped Cynthia. "Any questions, Margaret?"

"So does that mean you're going to fire them?"

"Not necessarily. Look, we're changing the specifications of the job. My approach is to define the new job requirements, provide training and let their performance define their future. My assessment of their capabilities may be wrong. We'll find out. The key to this approach is timing. If we were in the midst of a financial crisis, I'd have to move more quickly. I believe that we have 6-12 months to let this take a normal course of performance evaluation, since the critical need for the upgrade will be 12-18 months out, as we ramp up the business. Joseph and I looked at timelines, and capabilities, and I think that the department can perform effectively for the next few months without a turnover. If our performance suffers, we may make a change sooner."

"I think Alice is promotable from Credit Manager, but I'm not sure what to do with her. Joseph, can we put that on the Parking Lot so that I can keep moving?

When I looked at the *Plant* side of the business, I became very concerned about the IT environment. I think that we need new hardware and software. Our software has not kept current with the latest releases, which means we can't get the proper level of support if the system crashes. And the hardware is nearly 8 years old, and unable to accommodate many of the web features that may be useful to the Company. Don, this could be some heavy spending... perhaps hundreds-of-thousands of dollars."

Don was sitting quietly throughout the discussions. So far, he had 2 pages of yellow-pad notes… some with exclamation points… some circles… some things double underlined in red. When Cynthia mentioned the price of IT, the note jotted was in red, double-underlined, and circled with several exclamation points. Joseph noticed the highlighted notes. "Great observation, Cynthia. A system crash could be very expensive. I'm guessing that your recommended action is to have a qualified review of the IT environment and not just plow ahead with spending." Joseph wanted Don to understand that a thorough analysis would be completed before any proposal would be prepared.

"For sure, Joseph."

"Cynthia, can you talk a bit about "Lean Business Concepts? For some reason, I thought that Lean was a manufacturing process, and not for accountants and finance folks." Joseph knew how well the concept would apply to finance, but wanted Cynthia to explain how finance could benefit. If she could explain the concept to the team, she understood the process. She quickly sketched a process map, while discussing the elements.

Expense Reports

"I always considered the benefits of Lean Manufacturing to be exclusively manufacturing operations. Several weeks ago I met a Lean Business Consultant at a local Association for Corporate Growth meeting. This guy is fully dedicated to the Lean Business process. Over lunch, he scratched out a simple process map that described what he called an assembly process. In 15 minutes, he demonstrated how lean thinking could improve any process. Sure the guy was a bit of a zealot, but two days later, a complimentary copy of his book – I think it was called, "The Fearless Front Line" - showed up in my mailbox. Gofigure.

I read the book that weekend, and decided to check out the process mapping described. Stephen, remember a few weeks ago you mentioned that expense reimbursements took weeks? I decided to sketch out the T&E process as a pilot project. In about an hour this T&E mess was charted on a white board. I've 'x'ed out the processes that we combined to a single step, and overall, we've reduced turnaround time by up to 3 weeks." Cynthia proudly pointed to the sketch on the flipchart with so many red x's boasting of steps eliminated.

"Yes, we were embarrassed, but not so much that we didn't change the process. Stephen, how are the expense reimbursements looking these days?"

"Fast – like lightening compared to a month ago. So that was how you did it. Do you think it would apply to sales operations?"

"Everything we do is a process. I'm no expert, but it seems that lean thinking should work on any process. Give that guy Ray Attiyah a call- he'll take you to lunch to talk about the process. And since we accelerated the reimbursement process, we may be able to avoid cash advances. More to come on that.

So let me summarize – we have a lot to improve. I'm unhappy about the current state, but believe that we can significantly improve the financial management of the Company by focusing on priorities - specifically outlined on the slide.

"Thanks Cynthia. Excellent job overall. I particularly like how you approached the staffing questions. I noticed that you only evaluated your direct reports – I assume that you will tackle other layers in a complete organization review. You went a bit overtime, but the extra time was well worth the investment. That work you did on lean was superb. It doesn't sound like an overpowering, or time consuming challenge, and the benefits from that simple exercise are incredible. Any comments?"

JB leaned forward, faked his fist pounding on the table and boasted with a smile, "Hey, you're taking away my thunder!" The entire team burst into laughter.

Joseph strolled to the front of the conference room, noting that it was 11:45. "Hey folks, we've had a great morning session. We've covered a lot of material, and we're a bit behind schedule – but considering what we've covered, that's a good thing. Let's break for an early lunch – that will give you a chance to catch up with emails and phone calls. Back here ready to go at 1 – on the dot. JB will take us through manufacturing."

With that, the team scattered to rest rooms, and corners of the conference room to respond to phone messages, and read emails.

Don raised his coffee cup to the team in a congratulatory motion. "Great start – thank you for the efforts."

Don and Joseph huddled in the back of the conference room. "What's your initial reaction, Don?"

"Well, I've heard some things that I've never heard before. Lean Finance? What a concept. The part that surprises me is the easy implementation. I always viewed these buzzword programs of the month as just hocus-pocus. It seems that there may be more to it.

And the way folks have beat themselves up.   I'm surprised at the stark honesty of their – shall I call them shortcomings? These issues have been inside the Company for years, and no one ever mentioned them before. That bothers me."

"OK – let's look at that for a minute. Just in the past few weeks, we've asked the execs to look at the business from a completely different vantage point. We've pressed them to improve their areas… not just operate within a budget. Think about how the Company's been managed. Budgets set by you and Cynthia using massive spreadsheets, with a predetermined target that – might I say – was quite conservative to protect against the downside?

Now you've opened the question to, 'Help me manage better,' and you are asking them for creative problem solving, better ways to manage the business in their particular specialty. Said another way, 'Ms. Finance expert, what should you be doing differently to improve the business?' You should always get a different answer. That doesn't mean, however, that you must give them what they ask for. Your response will depend on your risk tolerance, available resources, and overall strategy. For example, if you plan to sell the Company to a strategic buyer, you may not want to invest a half-million dollars in a new data system, since the strategic will likely load your business onto their systems."

"Sure, I see how that might happen. But how do we know what we should do if I decide to sell?"

"Excellent question. We don't know, but will have to make educated guesses about the future. Each decision will be made with imperfect information – a calculated risk. Each decision is yours to make, and our role is to provide as much information as possible to provide a reasonable basis for the decision. Let's get some lunch."

April 26, 2014 – Manufacturing & Customer Operations

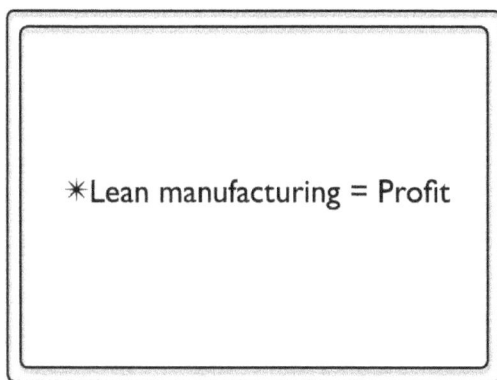

$*$Lean manufacturing = Profit

JB called the meeting to order with a simple, "Let's get going."

"We have a lot to cover, and I'll do my best to finish in 30 minutes. And before I start, let's all admit that I'm not good at presentations and being in front of a crowd."

Although not accustomed to leading meetings of his peers, he was not nervous, and his gruff personality took charge immediately. In some ways, he might be considered intimidating, but familiarity with his personality disarmed such bravado.

"We'll talk about Manufacturing, Operations, and
Logistics today. Since I have 3 areas, I'm not sure how I
ended up with only 30 minutes, but let's go. Just as
Margaret and Cynthia have covered People, Processes
and Plant, I'll do the same. Probably since Joseph
coached us to do so..." As those words lingered, JB
tossed a brief salute to Joseph.

"Up front, I'll tell you I don't have any fancy charts," as
he launched the first slide. "Just simple, straightforward
manufacturing information. Cynthia, you stole some of
my thunder. I wanted to be the first to talk about Lean
Manufacturing.

	JB			

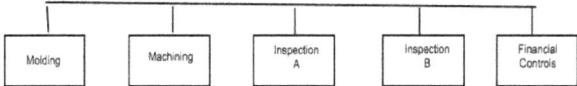

	Molding	Machining	Inspection A	Inspection B	Financial Controls
Headcount	47	84	7	7	3
Overtime	$345,042	$275,880	$57,780	$112,470	$35,564
Percent Spending	37%	47%	7%	6%	3%
Rework Spending	4% of COS	7% of COS			
Scrap Spending	4% of COS	7% of COS			
Materials Spending		$23,525,450			
Inventory		$8,525,450			

LEAN BUSINESS

"For the past few years, most people have talked about the Toyota Manufacturing Method. Well, Henry Ford invented the whole thing, and he wrote about it in a book called, 'Henry Ford: Today and Tomorrow'. He wrote the book in 1926, and I was surprised when I found it. I will tell you that the folks at Toyota perfected the process, and there are many consultants who preach the Toyota gospel.

I've just started reading about it, and I've met with some consultants just to acquaint myself with the ideas. Cynthia, that Ray Attiyah seems to be pretty good. What's your take? Yay or Nay?"

Cynthia gestured with a thumbs-up, confirming her positive impression of Ray and his book. JB stopped momentarily to quench his thirst, draining a small Dasani.

"I've started to look at what *could be* in our shop. For me to do a thorough job, I'll have to spend a lot more time on the methods, and maybe hire those consultants, if you agree Don. But for now, let's look at some highlights based on today's knowledge.

I won't read all the numbers to you, but we've spent more than $800,000 on overtime in the past year. Historically, my main concern has been to get the product out the door to the customers – at any cost. But when you read the books, a question about timing and product flow screams at you. Said another way, if our process is under control, we shouldn't need so much overtime. Why is that so important? Well, through November, we only earned a pretax of $2.5 million. Don, I'm not saying that I can save $800,000 of overtime, but if I could, that would increase profits by 30% - just looking at overtime.

And, I'm ashamed of myself, but until the past few weeks with Joseph's persistence, I was able to gather some scrap and rework numbers. I was shocked. All in, we have more than $2 million of scrap and rework being done."

By this time, Don was fiercely scratching notes on his yellow legal pad. Bright red circles around large block lettered notes – SAVINGS!!! After a moment, he pushed his chair from the table and purposefully walked to the refreshments, selected the largest chocolate chip cookie from the glass platter, took a small bite, and smiled. Thinking to himself, 'Joseph was right when he said that I should guard my emotions during these first meetings. I might be surprised – maybe even angry – but don't shoot the messengers.'

JB awaited an explosion after his disclosures – silence hung like a dense fog in the room. Allison cast a nervous glance toward Cynthia, raised eyebrows as if to say, 'Hang on!'

After consuming the chocolaty confection, Don said, "Great stuff, JB. What else have you got?"

Somewhat startled, JB continued. "And we spend about
$23 million for materials. We concentrate our purchases
with quite a few metals suppliers so that we don't have
supply exposures, and haven't put out a bid for quite a
while. We may have some upside with purchase price –
maybe through improved logistics.

We've kept a large supply of inventory on hand to avoid
stockouts. The Lean Business concept suggests that
we have too much on hand. If we believe in the system,
we may be able to move from 1.5 inventory turns per
year to as much as 3 turns a year."

Cynthia cleared her throat as if ready to speak, but
remained silent.

"Yes, Cynthia, that could be as much as an additional
few million dollars of cash flow each year. Guys, I'm not
promising these numbers, but want to let you know that
we are going to get into a project that helps us improve
the business. These areas seem ripe for the harvest.
The only open question is how much will we harvest.
After talking with a few folks, I am 100% convinced that
we can improve. …Just not sure how much."

Don was silent, but a small smile crept over his face.

"Now let's look at a few other areas. We have 17
people in inspection and financial controls. If you
believe the theory, we should be able to redeploy some
of that resource to direct production. We may have to
eliminate the headcount altogether. Don, I know how

reluctant you are to cut some of these dedicated people. These are your decisions. We'll get you the information that you need to evaluate the business."

Stephen was fascinated by the discussion, and the possibility that the manufacturing process might be streamlined to improve delivery cycle times. Joseph primed Stephen for this discussion with background information about improved cycle times, higher quality performance, fewer shipping errors, and perhaps improved product development cycle times.

"OK JB. You know if you create all this improvement, we may have more money available for R&D... maybe some new products will be released, and we might improve service levels – not that they are bad now – but improved order cycle times might make us more competitive. Heck, with new products – maybe some that can be easily launched in International markets – we just may need more manufacturing people – not fewer. I have to tell you, this is quite exciting!"

"Thanks Stephen. This certainly could make life interesting at Jackson.

So that's the high level review. I haven't touched one level down. Generally we have about a 6:1 ratio of supervisor to worker ratio throughout the plant. When you read the theory, we might be able to expand that ratio – I'm making up this number, but it could go as high as 8 or 10 to one supervisor. You can do the math. This can happen by redesigning the work flow, and better..." He figuratively tipped his cap to Margaret. " ... Yes Margaret – job descriptions... task descriptions ... and feedback loops.

If we do all these things, cash flow and profits will improve, and, yes Don, I'd like to spend some money on capital improvements."

After that Segway, Don could no longer contain his enthusiasm. "JB, I appreciate your candid discussion this afternoon. I'm not writing all the numbers down as you have described them. I'm sitting here listening to an entirely new approach to running our business. We've all been working in this environment for many years, and have never explored what's outside the four walls. My gosh, have we missed opportunities. But today is a new day, and our *tomorrows* may be filled with new adventures.

We've been in this meeting for just a few hours, and I am – well, I'm just blown away by the opportunities that you've been describing. Thank you JB... Cynthia ... Margaret. Heck, thanks to all of you, because this meeting seems to be generating even more opportunity than we expected individually." Looking at Allison and Stephen, Don, with palms up, raised both hands as if levitating the table, and said, "New product development money... new products... who knows where this will take us?"

JB's next slide was a simple case study, similar to Cynthia example of T&E report processing. JB's described the production process for Machining 1, 2, 3, and polishing. The laser pointer danced around the page as if chasing a fly while JB was describing the process. First, he described how a cell configuration might reduce rework and QC efforts, since, using the new process flow, the WIP couldn't be released from the cell without meeting all specifications. This would concentrate accountability with one person, expand their career potential by increasing their marketable skills, and virtually eliminate the full time QC function. Win … win … win.

The second scenario he discussed described how to increase Company profit.

"Don, if it weren't so expensive an error, we could laugh about this. Remember last year when you approved the $200,000 machining center for Machining #2? How Cynthia and I proved that it would reduce our costs by 50%?"

"Sure thing. That was a great find, JB. Glad that we made the investment."

"Well Don, look at the right side of the page. Sure, we decreased the unit cost by 50%, if we could use that many parts. Unfortunately, this Lean Manufacturing concept helped me look at the problem in a different way. I screwed it up, Don. The 50% cost reduction doesn't help us increase profits. It just reduced one component of cost. Lean Thinking helps me understand that profits won't increase unless the number of first quality products out-the-door increases.

Check out the flow chart and you'll see that there is a bottleneck in polishing. It is really an out of balance flow when compared to – I'll call it demand.

PRODUCTION EXAMPLE

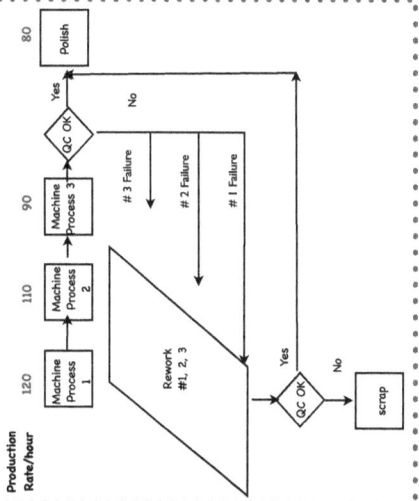

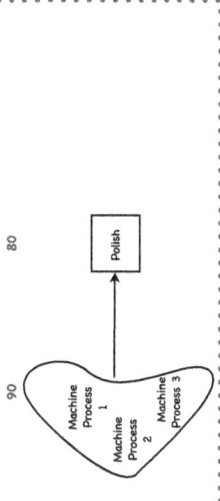

How do I make the Company more profitable?

A. Buy new equipment for Machine Process #2, to increase the throughput rate to 220/hour, resulting with a 50% per unit cost reduction for machine Process #2.

B. Buy new polishing equipment to increase throughput to 100 units per hour, reducing polishing cost by 25%.

IF WE INCREASE POLISHING CAPACITY TO 90/HOUR, THROUGHPUT WILL INCREASE AND PROFITABILITY WILL RISE

When I first saw this chart, it shocked me, but the manufacturing reality is that unless more parts go out the door, there is no need to increase capacity in any operation than Machine Process 3 or Polishing. And there is little reason to invest more in the factory, except for quality improvements that increase throughput, unless we sell more." JB's Cheshire grin aimed at Stephen caused all to laugh out loud. "Stephen, I couldn't have scripted your earlier absolutely wonderful outburst any better. We'd love to produce anything you want. On the serious side, I've discovered some things that didn't exist under the rock where I was hiding. It's a new me – 7 pounds thinner, with a gross of Nicotine patches, and a healthy diet." JB scanned the friendly faces in the room, nodded to several, and resolved to improve every day, in every way. "Thanks for your patience all. This has been an extraordinary exercise."

Satisfied with his performance, JB strolled to the refreshments, shuffled deep in the ice bath for a blueberry yogurt, peeled back the freshness seal, dropped a few fresh strawberries in the mix, winked at the observant crowd and slid into his chair.

As Joseph pushed off the back wall, he started to applaud JB's performance. "JB, you may not have the prettiest slides of the day, but what you presented included some real zingers. Absolutely awesome! Do you folks understand the treasure trove we've identified today? Sure, there are many potential dollars of savings, but think about the three presentations we've shared. We've identified *Lean* as a process that may help us improve our day-to-day management, grow the business by potentially reducing production cycle time and serving broader markets, improve the career value of those in the organization through additional training, freed-up executive time by pushing responsibility down through the organization.

This is an exceptional day, and I suspect it will only get better." Of course, Joseph knew it would get better, since he coached them about their presentation.

April 26, 2014 – Sales/Marketing: Offsite Functional Discussion

*Sales strategy
*Customer/channel/
classification & prioritization
*Pipeline management
*Resource allocation

While others arrived casually attired, Stephen was always perfectly outfitted. His custom-made Italian wool blazer with antique brass buttons, neatly pressed pants and a button-down pinpoint oxford were as if from a catalog. Since many of his presentations to clients were made with his laptop, he used a black stiletto shaped remote/laser combination to flash through his slides.

Stephen

- Inside Sales — Sue
- Western Region — Sharon
- Eastern Region — Shelly
- Central Region — Jason
- Marketing — Jacob

- First letter = Current Performance
- Second Letter = Potential

- 1st number = Years with JMI
- 2nd number = Years Experience

Sue A/C 7/11

Strengths
- Detailed oriented
- Thorough
- Self-starter
- Excellent supervisor

Weaknesses
- Limited bandwidth
- Emotional
- Short-sighted
- Executive presence
- No degree

Sharon B/B 2/5

Strengths
- Thorough
- Customer oriented
- Proactive

Weaknesses
- Hyperactive
- Organization skills
- Hates Admin Work
- Technical depth

Shelly A/A 9/16

Strengths
- Exceptional
- Intelligent
- Customer oriented
- Proactive
- Well organized

Weaknesses
- Bores easily
- Limited Mgmt exp.
- Presentatioon skills

Jacob C/B 2/3

Strengths
- Thorough
- PC nerd
- Task oriented
- Creative
- Intense

Weaknesses
- Team orientation
- Easily bored
- Intensity
- PC nerd

Jason B/B 2/2

Strengths
- Thorough
- Customer oriented
- Proactive
- Med undergrad
- PC nerd

Weaknesses
- Organization skills
- Mgmt depth
- Presentation skills
- PC nerd

Full color slides, exotic transitions among the animation filled slides kept the team's interest throughout.
Stephen was extremely thorough, assessing each sales team member's current performance and potential.
"Since this is the first time I've actually concentrated on anything other than task orientation, I've left a few with 'B' potential ratings. Suzy does a heckofajob day-in and day-out, but she has peaked in potential. We cannot - I repeat cannot – do without her experience and thorough execution. Shelly is outstanding in current performance and future potential. If I were run over by a bus, I'd recommend her as my replacement. The others on staff are just puppies. They are eager, smart, and easily bored. On the one side, if I don't challenge them, they'll be gone within 12-18 months. If I load them up too much, they may bolt, thinking that they are underpaid."

Margaret interrupted, "So what do we do with them?"

For the next 15 minutes, the team discussed the challenges of managing in a small, slow growth company. These were not just Stephen's challenges, but as they each reviewed their organizations, they identified the same personnel challenges on their staff.

Joseph interrupted to guide the conversation to clarity, and then added several notes to the parking lot. "OK, shall we say 'management experience/training' and 'challenging projects' might be solutions to some of these items?" As the team nodded in agreement, Don said, "So what are we going to do about the challenge?"

"Good questions, Don. If you don't mind, we'll leave that on the parking lot for now, and develop a solution sometime tomorrow."

"OK Stephen. Onward."

"The next segment I'd like to discuss is a change in overall process that we'd like to get going. Most folks call this the sales pipeline." He queued the color-coded chart previously reviewed with Joseph.

Sales Pipeline Management

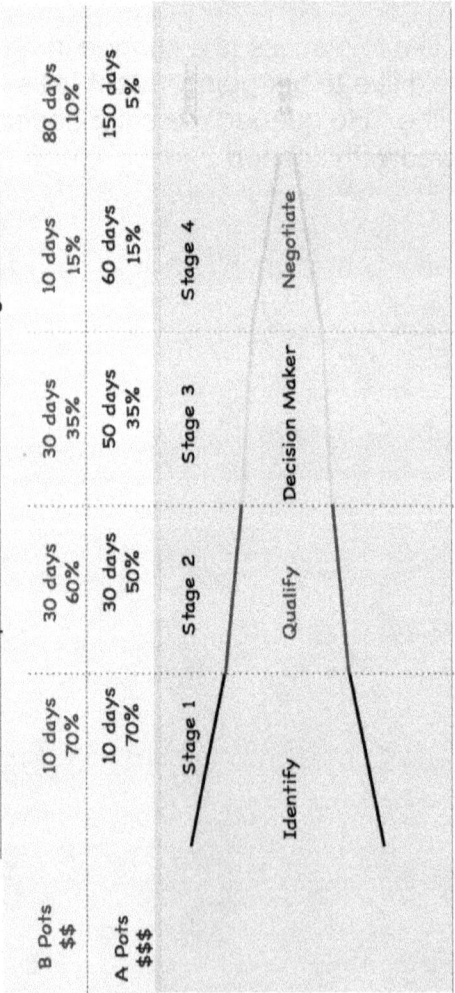

	Stage 1	Stage 2	Stage 3	Stage 4	
B Pots $$	10 days 70%	30 days 60%	30 days 50%	10 days 15%	80 days 10%
A Pots $$$	10 days 70%	30 days 50%	50 days 35%	60 days 15%	150 days 5%
	Identify	**Qualify**	**Decision Maker**	**Negotiate**	

I n t e r n e t   S e a r c h

B Pots $$
- Initial contact – Director +
- Office visit
- Follow-up mailing
- Phone contact

- Lunch
- Meet engineers
- Follow-up mailing

- Lunch – +Officer
- Meet engineers
- Follow-up mailing

- Lunch – +Officer
- Reference clients
- Proposal

A Pots $$$
- Initial contact – Director ++
- Office visit
- Follow-up mailing
- Phone contact

- Lunch – Director ++
- Meet engineers
- Follow-up mailing

He explained the pipeline concept, expected success rates, monitoring and improvement required to make the process work effectively. "Joseph and I spent some time discussing the process several weeks ago. Right now, many of the numbers are a best guess, but as we continue to manage the pipeline, we'll refine the process. Check out the 'A Pots' and 'B Pots' at the bottom of the slide. We have a different selling process and 'touch cycle' for each category. The 'A Potentials' are worth more investment to us – meaning more touches - since their volumes generate more profit. We'll spend more time with them hoping to close them within about 5 months. It is definitely a longer sale cycle.

Don, this might require a small investment in Customer Resource Management – the CRM system - software to manage this effectively. At first, we'll try to capture some of the information on simple Excel spreadsheets, concentrating exclusively on the "A" potentials."

"Sure is a pretty chart, big guy. Does it work?" Stephen expected a slight jab from JB as part of a natural tension between Sale/Marketing and Manufacturing.

"That is a great question, JB. We aren't quite sure yet, but just like in manufacturing, we're going to capture data to monitor the process. I can tell you for sure, though, that the precision of our data is nowhere near what you are able to capture in the manufacturing process. We'll do our best – and continuously improve."

Cynthia looked concerned about the discussion concentrating on new customers. "If we concentrate only on potentials, the bread and butter "A's" might abandon us. Are you concerned?"

"Absolutely. And that's a perfect Segway into the next slide. Our strategy is to have a pool of new and existing customers. Unfortunately, despite our efforts to have 1st quality products delivered complete and on time – thanks to JB - and continuously try to improve the products – thank you Allison – some customers desert us. … Could be for new & improved products, or just left us for price, or just personal relationships. Our strategy is to make every customer feel important.

If a customer calls us with a small order once a quarter, we want to make them feel important. If a major customer calls us daily with an order, we want them to know that they are important to us. We've looked at every point of contact with the customers, and have thought about how to allocate the limited resources among the actual and potential A-B-C customers."

The water drop slide transition was elegant as the next slide appeared on the screen.

Jackson Manufacturing
Sales Strategy
2015

(000's $)	A		B		C		Total
Resources	Act	Pot	Act	Pot	Act	Pot	
Direct							
Sales Reps	2,000.0	1,250.0	750.0	500.0			4,500.0
Manufacturer Rep			450.0	200.0	250.0	100.0	1,000.0
Distributor					600.0	50.0	650.0
Catalog					35.0		35.0
Direct Mail	25.0	25.0	25.0	25.0	50.0		150.0
Trade Shows	50.0	50.0	50.0	50.0			200.0
Telemarketing						75.0	75.0
Subtotal	2,075.0	1,325.0	1,275.0	775.0	935.0	225.0	6,610.0
Indirect							
Website			50.0		50.0		100.0
Advertise - Journals				50.0		50.0	100.0
Public Relations		75.0					75.0
Trade Associations		50.0					50.0
Subtotal	-	125.0	50.0	50.0	50.0	50.0	325.0
Total	2,075.0	1,450.0	1,325.0	825.0	985.0	275.0	6,935.0

"If you look at the left side of this slide, you'll see all the direct and indirect spending categories used by Sales/Marketing. Our plan is to allocate these resources among all the categories of actual and potential customers – A-B-C. Our goal is to have the right amount of contact with each group of clients. For example, we'd like to spend about 20-25% of our direct sales resource concentrating on 'A' potential customers, and one-third on existing 'A' customers.

You'll also notice that we have several new categories – Manufacturer's Rep, Telemarketing, and Website. These represent new ways for us to reach customers – most likely in more remote areas where we can't afford to staff a sales representative. We think that having a website where customers can order directly would be a great way to 'touch' the 'C' customers."

Cynthia's raised pencil caught Stephen's eye. "Our current website software can't accommodate on-line ordering."

"Right. But does that mean we won't have website ordering in the next 3 years – especially if we put a priority on the project."

"Gotcha. Good point – put that project in the queue to be evaluated with all the other IT investments."

Stephen continued, "Notice that we've allocated about 25-30% of the sales resources to Distributors and Manufacturer's reps… same concept of allocating resources. Oh, and did I mention International? Well, we won't be officially launching aggressively in the International region until late this year, so I've left it off the chart for now. I think that we all agree that within the next 3-5 years we will have considerable sales volume in International markets. A fact that I think about… there are about 320 million people in the US, and about 6 billion people in the rest of the world. I hate to miss out on 6 billion potential customers."

"But can those 6 billion afford our products?

"Good question… if only 1% can afford the product, that's still 60 million potential customers. Not a bad segment. The challenge is to figure out where that 1%

297

resides, and how to sell to them. Yes, Allison, that is a great question.

So let me summarize. We have a good lean staff in sales and marketing, but we have some challenges. We have some capable staff – some bored to death, that need a challenge; others that have reached their potential. We will identify projects to get them all excited.

We've identified a new pipeline selling process that we will monitor and continually improve to get the most out of the limited sales and marketing resources. We will jealously manage those limited resources, and allocate them across customer class and trade channels.

Things that we need? Probably software investments in CRM and Website. No doubt in the next few years, we'll have to expand the sales and marketing staff – if nothing else to provide improved service to US customers, and perhaps to expand international sales efforts to capture some of those 6 billion potential customers.

We sure could use some new products, Allison. I know you are a magician, just waiting for enough financial resource to complete our stable of products. Maybe we could even license something if not developed in house.

So let me summarize. This particular chart is not hard and fixed. I really just wanted to share with you how we will orient our resources. We'll invest a lot of direct sales force effort on the "A's", since it's the most efficient use of our resources. Overall, about 50% of all our resources will go to the "A's". About a third of all our resources will be dedicated to "B's", and the remainder to "C's". We'll expand our reach into more remote areas through Manufacturer's Reps and Distributors, primarily concentrating on "B/C" customers.   OK folks, any questions?"

Always mindful of the financial risks, Cynthia asked, "Do you have any guestimates about the costs of those expense additions? Again, limited resources... but if sales increase – well, we have more to work with, depending on Don's appetite for investment and risk."

"At this point, no, but I'd like to spend some time with you during the next week to shape out some numbers. You've got the tough duty balancing all these *needs* with available *resource*."

"Allison, it's all yours." Stephen slipped the pointer into his shirt pocket and took his seat.

April 26, 2014 – R&D: Offsite Functional Discussion

> *R&D pipeline management
> *Prioritization based on market & financial returns
> *Development, manufacturing, launch requirements

Allison started her conversation with the team while seated comfortably at the table. She distributed her slide packet so the team could jot notes on each sheet.

"Welcome to the R&D section. This will be more of a discussion about the future rather than past performance. While we refer to the department as R&D, our functions historically have been limited to quality control, minor product enhancements, labeling, consumer affairs and compliance with regulatory requirements. Said another way, our past has been to keep out of trouble with the Feds and consumers. The team is a small team that does an ok job.

After some prodding from Joseph, I decided to look at the business in a slightly different way."

With that, she slipped her iPhone from the folio, and while still seated, touched the screen several times and suddenly, the Rocky Theme blared from the inconspicuous wireless speakers that she distributed around the conference room. She arose, wielding her laser pointer and flashed her first slide - a simple yet colorful organization chart.

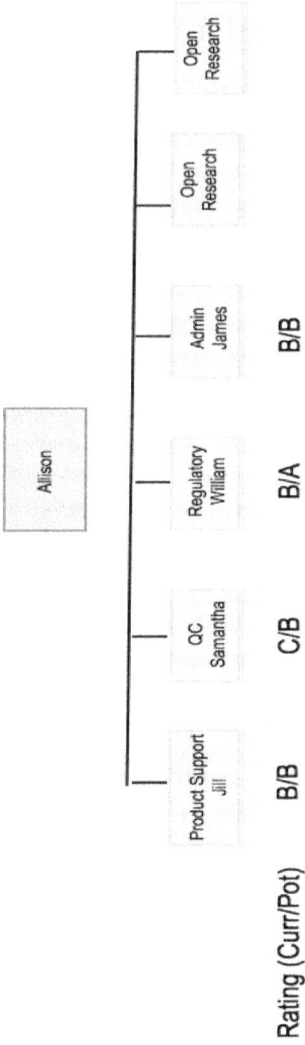

```
                              ┌──────────┐
                              │ Allison  │
                              └────┬─────┘
      ┌───────────┬───────────┬───┴───────┬───────────┬───────────┐
┌───────────┐┌──────────┐┌──────────┐┌──────────┐┌──────────┐┌──────────┐
│  Product  ││   QC     ││Regulatory││  Admin   ││   Open   ││   Open   │
│  Support  ││Samantha  ││ William  ││  James   ││ Research ││ Research │
│   Jill    ││          ││          ││          ││          ││          │
└───────────┘└──────────┘└──────────┘└──────────┘└──────────┘└──────────┘

Rating (Curr/Pot)   B/B      C/B        B/A        B/B
```

R&D Role:
Primarily manufacturing and product support,
consumer affairs and regulatory compliance.
Research responsibility dependent on available
funding. Open positions remain open due to
Budgetary constraints.

Cynthia leaned back in her chair and burst out laughing and started to applaud. "My gosh, you must be in marketing with that Rocky theme playing!"

Stephen, knocking gently on the conference table, merely smiled and boasted of her changed tempo, "Bravo mi senora!"

Margaret was speechless, while JB strode to the front of the conference room and bowed graciously as if she were the Queen of England. ""My compliments, your majesty. You have awakened your humble servant."

Although Joseph was taken aback, he knew that a latent creativity lay beneath that distracted scientist façade. His almost imperceptible nod of approval reinforced Allison's confidence.

Allison muted the volume. A nod, smile and arms slowly opening, palms up in a friendly gesture of thanks, Allison graciously acknowledged the appreciation for her radical behavior. "I thought that I might just jiggle the tempo a bit. I'll spend a short time on the past. Our job – keep the Company out of trouble."

As she was speaking, her bright laser dot continuously circled the organization chart for emphasis.

"We've done well during the past decade. No major blowouts with the FDA. No major unresolved problems with consumers, consumer advocates or organizations. Overall I grade us with an overwhelming *adequate*. I must say, every morning, my call to arms … my rallying cry is not very inspiring. 'Let's be adequate!"

"Now that does not sound like a marketing slogan to me," as Stephen jotted a few notes on his page.

"So, looking at people, organization, processes and plant - well, we are a resounding adequate." With that, she discovered eye contact with Don. As she smiled at Don, she asked Don, "Is that our call to arms? 'Let's be adequate!' Or should we say, 'Let's be average?'

She examined each face around the table, looking deeply into their eyes, as if on a quest for ancient secrets lost long ago. As she scanned the crowd, she quietly repeated, "Let's be average. Let's be adequate." Silence hung in the air like moss drooping from an ancient oak deep in Florida swamps.

"I don't want that cry any longer. I'll take a bit of a risk and talk about a future that could be. A place where our growth is based on a fully integrated effort among all of us – working as a team to make this Company not average, but stellar."

Her next slide exploded across the screen, borrowing from some of Stephen's special effects.

Cost
(Millions $)

<$3 Million

Low
Risk

9-12 Months

x 20 = I   Acquisition & JV

Modest
Risk

$3-5 Million

18-24 Months

x 50 = I   NIH; Universities & JV

High
Risk

$5+ Million

4-6 Years

x 250 = I   NIH; Universities & Corp America

"Before I launch into this next section, will you each commit to me to be radical during this phase?" As she continued, she scanned the room for a nod of approval from each participant. She looked each directly in the eye, and held their gaze until affirmed.

"And when I say radical, I want you to beat me up – that's figuratively, JB. Put that chair down willya!

Challenge my assumptions... stress me out. I refuse to work within the vacuum of my own mind, because there is just too much empty space up there. My lack of brilliance is startling." The pace of her discussion intensified as if for a cinematic climax, all the while with a smile and twinkle in her eye.

"I think that we have three avenues to accelerate the pace of this Company. First, through acquisition of existing products – here in the US or offshore. These represent the quickest means to expand the product line, and the least risk. Initial targets may be orphaned product lines from major companies that are restructuring. A fledgling product to a company like Stryker can be big business for us.

We may also want to consider a JV – perhaps for distributing a European company's products here in the US. Of course, we may have to obtain FDA approval, but if the product is already approved and sold in Europe, we should get an accelerated review."

As she continued, she shared her assessment of business risk, timeline to introduce, and estimated costs for each type of product line expansion.

Don was surprised when she explained the "x 50 = 1" section of the product development meant a 2% probability of success. "Can it really be that low in today's environment? What are you considering in the evaluation?"

"Glad that you asked. '50 x = 1' is the success rate from finding a product in a catalog to final sale and full integration into our product line. That may mean that we spend 30 minutes to evaluate a product, and drop the product from consideration. On the flipside, we may also spend 3 months, and finally decide that for many reasons – such as scarcity of raw materials – that the product isn't a good fit. One other consideration that I've seen might be the upfront costs to manufacture. For example if we need to buy a new precision molding machine that costs a half-million dollars, it simply may not be worth the investment.

You really raise a good question, Don. I've also worked briefly with Cynthia to list some of the investment considerations. Check out the list. We have more to do if this is a direction that we want to pursue.

Project Description:

	2 years historical	3-5 years future	<u>Terminal Value</u>
Cash Flows - outbound			
Capital			
Expenses			
Development			
Launch			
Maintenance			
Cash Flows - inbound			
Revenues			
Earnings			

Development Timeline

Market Potential
US
International

Competitive discussion

Launch & marketing discussion

"How do you calculate the revenues and earnings? Where have you considered cost of sales? Launch expenses?" JB was concerned that the Company may launch into a major program without enough research.

"Great questions, JB. Who has other questions?"

Stephen was feverishly listing notes on his pad, and offered, "I think that maybe all of us need to think about new products thoroughly. I've just been thinking about this for 3 minutes, and have a list of 5 items that aren't on the slide."

"Perfect." Allison stepped to the flip chart and said, "Fire away."

" Sales force training; collateral material; marketing studies; initial launch expenses; packaging costs; registration and regulatory fees; import/export research; hospital training; training videos… How can we afford market research?"

"Great questions. Market research is *we* initially. If we know enough about the market, we'll move forward. If we don't and it is a major commitment, we may have to pay for research. That's just one of the considerations before we proceed. The same is true for a discussion about competitors – who else?"

"Specialized manufacturing processes; specialty tooling; new equipment; test batches and startup inefficiency; inventory load for raw materials…"

"Working capital assumptions for inventory and accounts receivable; capital costs; registration fees…"

"This is a great start. Now you know why I had so few categories on the slide. I really hadn't considered all the details. For the parking lot, should we list a 'New Product Development' approval process?"

Joseph jumped to the 'parking lot', marker in hand. "You've got many of the details – we'll expand on them. As I listen to the discussions, I don't see any headcount allocated to the process. Do we need a new product development person?"

"Sounds like a lot of money to me," Don asserted. "I like the brainstorming ideas that are popping up, but we'll put more pencil to paper - a lot more – before I'm driving too far too soon."

He suddenly realized that he was a damper on the creative development, and quickly followed with, "But I'm amazed at the ideas that we're generating. God darn, this is magical. Onward folks… hey can we get a break for biologics?"

With that, Allison called for a 10-minute break and the team scattered to handle personal priorities.

The aroma from the mound of fresh-baked, decadent chocolate chip cookies was irresistible to Margaret. Others milled around the tray of chilled juices, Red Bull and carbonated beverages. Other than a quiet murmur

310

the only sound was chunks of ice rattling in the plastic
ice bucket just before the dull thunk into the plastic
tumblers.

April 26, 2014 – Strengths & Weaknesses: Offsite Functional Discussion

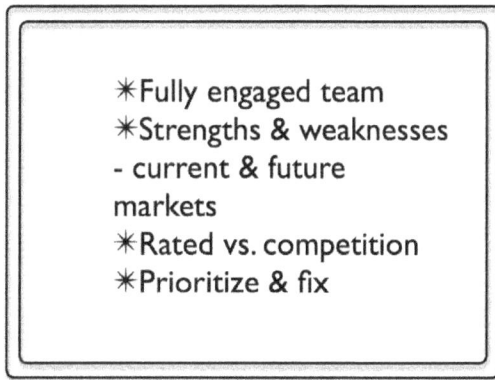

*Fully engaged team
*Strengths & weaknesses
- current & future
markets
*Rated vs. competition
*Prioritize & fix

Joseph watched the execs break into informal pods quietly discussing the morning's activities. He brought the flip charts to the front of the room, one in each corner, and aligned the multi-colored markers as if ready for battle. He tore off the flip chart page labeled "Parking Lot" and stuck it to the conference room wall.

"May I observe that we haven't discussed anything about the legal function? Who owns Legal? And, when I say owns legal, I mean every action that has legal implications – from Human Resources to Purchase Contracts?"

The silence was as if the team was waiting for the reincarnation of Abraham Lincoln to appear and recite his Gettysburg address. Several fiercely attended to massive doodles on their pads... some merely smiled agreeably while gazing absent-mindedly at Joseph. Joseph was accustomed to these dead-space interludes, and was willing to allow the gap.

After a few moments of silence, Joseph objected, "Hey, wait a minute, I thought that Cynthia owned legal."

JB rustled some papers and suggested, "I would guess that we all manage contracts and legal exposures that affect our particular areas. I know for purchasing, I review all the contracts and contract changes. If something looks like it's off the reservation, I give Keith a call."

Cynthia offered, "I deal mostly with banking matters, and anything that needs to be signed - if it's unusual, I also have Keith look at it." All nodded in agreement that Keith was the bulwark against legal gaffs.

"So is it possible that we sign a multi-year contract with a supplier without Keith's review?"

JB immediately responded, "Sure, as long as terms don't vary too much from a prior contract."

"And is it possible that we sign such a contract without Cynthia's review?"

"Sure thing. I've been around long enough to understand contract law."

"And is it possible that you sign a contract with minimum purchases?"

"Sure – I know what our historical buying trends have been, and what we should be buying in the next few years."

"And is it possible that Stephen and Allison have developed new products – perhaps with new materials – that affect the forecasted volumes?"

Cynthia smiled. "We don't do any long range forecasts, so I really couldn't tell if the volumes will go up or down."

"So let me see if I understand this. We have a progressive VP of Sales, and a talented VP of R&D who knows that new products need to be developed to remain competitive. In these roles they begin developing new products that can change the sales mix, manufacturing demand, and materials requirements, and we don't have that information fed into the CFO to understand the impact on forecasted inventories and purchases? Is that what I'm hearing?"

Cynthia took a sip of orange juice, set the bottle gently on the ceramic coaster, scanned the room and fixed her gaze on Joseph and tossed a response. "Yup."

Once again, silence equal to that experienced in the depths of the Marianas trench.

While all self-consciously fidgeted with pens, bottle caps and twirling coasters, in almost a whisper, Joseph's question, "Is that good or bad?" hung like a rotting animal carcass in a disabled refrigerator storage locker.

Joseph effectively used silence to make his point. Not one of the execs could look Joseph in the eye. After an interminable time, Joseph broke the silence in an upbeat tone, and said, "OK – can we all agree that we might want to include 'legal' as something of a weakness?"

Stephen snatched that concept, leapt to the *Parking Lot* and in bright red, bold capital letters wrote LEGAL AWARENESS. "Point made, Joseph. Let's roll."

"Great. And so now we discuss Company Strengths and Weaknesses. Will this be a short discussion, or have you folks been thinking about this at the gym while jogging on the cork track?"

Allison and Stephen were well prepared to share an extensive list of strengths and weaknesses. Their rapid-fire phrases launched Joseph into a writing frenzy that immediately covered the first two pages. Others quickly followed with a tabulation of strengths and weaknesses that startled Don. He puzzled, 'Can this be true? No one has ever mentioned these items before.'

Joseph fearlessly cheered the brainstorming by continuously repeating, "What else?" He allowed no time for critique, which might have dampened their enthusiasm and missed a critical element. After about 15 minutes, the pace slowed and Joseph summarized their efforts with a broad smile, brief applause and a congratulatory, "Well done! Absolutely outstanding effort! You folks are brilliant in brainstorming efforts – best I have ever encountered. Now, it seems that we have about 40-or-so strengths and weaknesses. We can attempt to fix all the weaknesses, and hone all the strengths. What do you think?"

JB was a bit antsy – all the while craving a long drag on one of those delicious Nicaraguans – popped a nicotine gum and said, "Pareto lives."

"Help me out JB. Exactly what does that mean."

"It's the 80/20 rule. Most of the benefits can be gained from a few items. Prioritize the list or we'll never get out of here."

"OK folks – grab a pad of those post-it notes, write the number 1 through 5 – one is most significant - and rank the top 5 strengths, and the top 5 weaknesses. Put your sticky next to the written item. No cheatin' – can't have more than one number one weakness or strength. Let's take a break – perhaps 20 minutes – and I'll have a tabulation when we return."

As always, there was some laughter, and negotiating of priorities as they individually ranked the priorities.

The tabulation summarized the top issues:

STRENGTHS

- Customer oriented
- Linkage with universities
- Market position – small hospitals
- US market penetration
- Dedicated personnel @ exec level
- Customer relationships

WEAKNESSES

- Financial resources
- Product line
- Market reach – limited to US
- Employee engagement
- Staleness/lack of creativity
- Management process
- Lack of decision information
- Depth or organizaiton

Joseph adjourned the meeting with a positive message to all, and asked Don to remain after others left. The team was abuzz with enthusiasm as they gathered their materials. Joseph overheard snippets of their comments.

"... Watch Don today? He was fairly silent... seemed to take the comments without prejudice... we were rocking ... didn't know you were so creative..."

The meeting room cleared, and Joseph questioned Don. "Well, Don, any thoughts about the first day?"

"It was difficult for me to be here, but it was important that I attend. Of course, you know that I was intentionally quiet. I was interested in their input. I have two emotions after today. First, I feel like I had the crap beat out of me, because so much imagination, commitment and concern for the business have been crushed by me for so long. Have I really been that bad a boss to annihilate their creativity? And second... wow, these folks are good. They've had all this energy trapped – unable to launch the ideas that would help the business run better. Have we unchained a monster, Joseph?"

"OK, Don. First of all, you shouldn't feel like crap. It is not at all unusual to have this scenario. I have done this exercise a few dozen times, and the general result is similar to what we experienced today. Don, let's back up a bit. You took a concept 30 years ago, started a business in your garage, and built it into a $30 million national operation that competes in a very difficult field. There are not many people who could do that. You should feel good about that. Yes, you've left some opportunity on the table, but you're attacking that problem now. Great.

As far as the team is concerned, they are pretty good at what they do, but they they've been narrowed in their focus. On the one side, if they were truly outstanding – best in class – they would not have tolerated your constraints. I think that you're recognizing that with many of the younger engineers that stay for a year and then leave – not enough personal development. Over the years, your executives have definitely become complacent... but they are ready to blossom now.

We will discover who is in the game during the next few months. As we identify programs to improve our competitiveness, we'll see who is truly engaged and is willing to execute. For now, congratulations to you for taking this first step. Congrats to the team for becoming fully engaged in the process. Let me clean up these notes for tomorrow's meeting. If you have any questions, give me a call tonight. Otherwise, see you tomorrow."

Joseph was pleased with the progress... the team's energy, and Don's concern for his past behavior. It was important for Don to recognize his shortfall before we could effectively correct the problem.

April 26, 2014 –Offsite Day 2

> *Fully engaged team
> *Strengths & weaknesses
> - current & future
> markets
> *Rated vs. competition
> *Prioritize & fix

The next morning, the team was fully assembled by 7:45 AM, despite the scheduled 8:00 start. Each seemed better organized than yesterday with yellow pads, pens and sharpies at the ready, steaming coffee at each place, accompanied by a side dish mounded with a selection of colorful fresh fruit. Joseph worked the crowd with small talk to understand their mood and noted that all were excited about the candid discussion yesterday, and about the potential for change.

Joseph smiled as he uncapped the black marker, ready to scribe. "And so we begin. I cannot compliment you enough for yesterday's candid performance. We bared our souls – observed the business as if we were an outsider – almost as if we were potential buyers. Outstanding effort! We identified some warts, and some points of greatness. Today we build on a solid foundation – one of self-less assessment. People, that is the only way we can progress.

The first thing… let's look at our accomplishments from yesterday and our agenda for today.

Today

8:30 – 9:00	Introduction
9:00 – 10:30	Vision/Mission
10:30 – 10:45	*Break*
10:45 –	Functional discussion – Organization, people, processes; strengths & weaknesses
10:45 - 11:15	- Finance & IT
11:15 – 12:00	- Manufacturing/Ops/Logistics
12:00 – 1:00	*Lunch*
1:00 – 1:30	- Legal
1:30 – 2:00	- Human Resources
2:00 - 2:30	- Sales
2:30 – 3:15	- R&D; New Product Development
3:15 - 3:30	*Break*
3:30 – 5:00	Strengths & weaknesses: prioritized

Tomorrow:

8:00 – 9:00	Discussion – macro environment; economy; globalization
9:00 – 11:00	Discussion – Competitors; mapping
11:00 – 11:15	*Break*

11:15 – 12:30	Products; substitutes; etc.
12:30 – 1:30	*Lunch*
1:30 – 3:00	Key initiatives

With that, he flashed the two-day agenda on the screen. After a few minutes of discussion, transcribing some open items from Monday on the *parking lot page*, they launched into today's discussion about the *macro* environment. The team was unusually enthusiastic, rapidly sharing ideas as if on a game show quiz. After an hour of discussion, Joseph reviewed the major points highlighted on the flip charts:

- Global economy would be in the doldrums for the next 3-5 years.
- Global demographics: People living longer; population of baby-boomers rapidly expanding in China, Japan, throughout Europe, and the US.
- China, Japan, Europe and US can afford medical care, including artificial joints.
- Major competitors will continue to expand *mass medicine*, and tend to abandon niche and orphaned products.
- Small competitors will go out of business due to regulatory pressure, depth of resources and lack of commitment by owners.
- Regulatory environment will tend to be obstructive resulting in approval delays.
- Cross-border regulatory environment will be more cooperative resulting in accelerated approvals.

"And so what do we do with this information?"

Stephen raised his pen and took the floor. "Isn't it time for us to think about our strengths and weaknesses and marry them with the prevailing macro environment?"

"Perfect Segway," As Joseph queued the next slide.

"Before we dive into strengths and weaknesses, let's think about financial goals. Cynthia provided some additional information about our sales and expenses, and Don, Cynthia and I roughed out some numbers to answer the question 'Where do we want to be in three years?" With that introduction, Joseph flashed a P&L modified slightly since the review with Don in mid-April.

000's $	2012	2013	2014	2015	2016	2017
Sales						
Baseline	19,566	19,233	18,788	18,500	20,500	22,000
Knuckles	10,041	10,779	12,226	14,955	16,055	17,476
Total Sales	29,607	30,012	31,014	33,455	36,555	39,476
Cost of sales						
Baseline	10,455	10,918	10,859	10,150	10,750	11,050
Knuckles	3,460	3,788	5,036	5,800	5,400	6,055
Total Cost of Sales	13,915	14,706	15,895	15,950	16,150	17,105
Gross Profit	15,692	15,306	15,119	17,505	20,405	22,371
Total GM %	53%	51%	49%	52%	56%	57%
Baseline %	47%	43%	42%	45%	48%	50%
Knuckles %	66%	65%	59%	61%	66%	65%
SG&A						
Sales	6,997	7,122	7,255	8,055	8,995	9,590
R&D	750	785	815	1,555	1,950	2,150
Admin	3,162	3,213	3,200	3,759	3,065	3,350
Other	1,912	2,015	2,212	2,465	2,676	3,014
Total	12,821	13,135	13,482	15,834	16,686	18,104
Pretax Profit	2,871	2,171	1,637	1,671	3,719	4,267
% of Sales	10%	7%	5%	5%	10%	11%

"We decided that the Company is in two distinctly different businesses. A commodity manufacturing operation for the baseline products, and a value added business for the knuckles. When we separate the two businesses at the gross profit line, we noticed that margins held fairly constant in the baseline business, but declined in the knuckles business. JB, we talked about some production problems in the knuckles. Cynthia thought that was about $400,000. Is that about right?" JB nodded agreement. "So without that write-off, margins held at about 63%."

The executives looked at the P&L and shuddered. The projected pretax profit increased by $2.5 million, or more than 150% compared to this years projection.

JB observed, "It's great to play with numbers on a spreadsheet, but c'mon ... pretax up by 150%? Can't be done."

Don and Joseph expected that response form a team member. Joseph smiled a broad grin. "Makes you nervous, JB? Anybody else agree with JB?" The consensus was skeptical about such growth.

"OK, let's just speculate for a few minutes. JB, are you going to throw away $400,000 of production every year?"

"No, we fixed that problem – won't happen again..."

"OK, so now we're down to a little more than a $2 million profit increase. Now, notice that we kept earnings about flat in 2015, and we did that in two ways. We increased the knuckles' sales by 15+%, cranked in the $400,000 write-off, and invested the increase margin in areas that will improve the business. Stephen, notice the $800,000 increase in selling expense? Not bad? Allison, we've nearly doubled your R&D spending. Do you think we can make some magic with that? And Cynthia, we know that there will be some increased Admin to research a new data system."

Joseph paused seemingly to sip some coffee, but was intentionally creating some space for the execs to consider the macro changes in the P&L. Eyes wide open, each executive glared at the P&L – some scratching quick calculations across their pads. Allison leaned forward as if to observe more information hidden in smaller print between the lines. Stephen quietly tapped his forefinger noiselessly on the table, while his eyes narrowed on the numbers.

JB nervously wrote the forecasted product margin numbers on the yellow pad, and complained, "An 8% cost decrease during the next three years in the Baseline is impossible. ... Can't be done." He slashed an 'x' through each year's baseline gross profit number on the page. "... Can't be done. Nope."

"JB, I'm with you in my initial reaction." Joseph continued. "Staggering change. But let's analyze this a bit. Two years ago, the baseline GM percent was 53%.

I'm gong to assume that there have been some cost increases during the past two years. Have we had any price increases during the past two years."

Stephen's response was immediate. "No, historically the customers couldn't handle an increase."

"So, for JB to assume that the only change in gross margin in the upcoming three years is cost reduction may be incorrect, since a price increase is possible. And let's go one step further. JB, are you operating at 99% effectiveness? That is, you do the right thing, exactly the right way, 99% of the time?"

"Don't be ridiculous."

"Do you do the right thing, exactly the right way, 95% of the time?"

"Hey, Joseph, we aren't perfect. If we do exactly the right thing, exactly the right way 75% of the time, I'd be surprised."

"Well, this financial model just want's you to reduce that waste by – let's say 5%. If you're operating at 75% effectiveness now, we want you to get to 80%. Of course, the model allows for increased spending to train your folks in business process improvement. We also have some capital equipment to improve your process throughput as well. If you're in agreement, we'd like to proceed with that as an assumption, knowing that we need to spend some money to get you there. As a concept, can you buy in for now, knowing that you have control over the type and extent of training you get to reduce your waste from 25% to only 20%?

And, team, we all know that it's not just JB that needs to improve from – let's say – 75% effectiveness – to 80%. I think that if we examine all the things that we do – day in and day out – we can improve. Anybody disagree with the concept that we can improve our business performance by a mere 5%?

Somewhat apprehensively, they agreed.

"JB, if we increase sales by $8.5 million, or 27%, will you increase your overhead spending by 27%?"

"No way. We're talking about more production, but I don't have to add 27% more overhead. We can leverage the existing infrastructure." As he spoke, he suddenly realized that some of the improved margin was simply volume related. " But Stephen needs to get those sales. If he does, yeah, I think I may be able to pull those numbers off." Joseph smiled and thought, 'Sandbagger. If we increase volume by 27%, you gain buying efficiencies, as well as leverage all fixed costs – from machine time to overhead spending.'

"So Stephen, you're on the hot seat. Think you can pull off a 27% increase in sales?" Joseph jabbed at Stephen.

329

"OK- let's diagnose this challenge. It's a 40% increase in knuckles, and a 17% increase in baseline. I'm going to think out loud for a minute… a few percent in price increase during the next three years… maybe beat up on some additional geography, but to do that I'll need more sales reps… damn, a $5 million increase in Knuckles… I'm going to need some new products for that. Allison, can you get me any new products in the next year or so?"

"Well, I can only say with those kind of R&D spending increases, if I can't get you some new products, I should be fired."

Joseph interrupted. "OK, we don't need to solve all the issues right now. We have the rest of the day to sort things out. But at this point, can we all agree that these numbers are not out-of-the-park stupid?"

Somewhat in dismay, all agreed that it certainly seemed possible, but they couldn't understand why they hadn't seen this possibility before.

"Now let me observe. We all know about Mergers and Acquisitions, and company value. Quite often, people think of the value of a company as a multiple of earnings before interest, taxes, depreciation and amortization – commonly referred to as EBITDA. Sometimes valuation is considered to be a multiple of cash flow. Sometimes, valuation is a multiple of Book Value. In fact, an investor looks at many different measures, compares the values to other transactions to determine if their

assessment is reasonable. Let's look at this next slide.
Cynthia, and JB, I think this is your game, but let me
know if I'm off."

	2012	2013	2014	2015	2016	2017
Accounts Receivable	8,522	12,122	10,989	9,895	8,778	8,500
Inventory Balance	-	-	-	-	-	-
DSO	96	135	119	99	80	72
Invnetory Turns	2.5	2.7	3.5	4	4.5	4.5
DSO Cash flow improvementfrom 135			1,347	2,979	4,662	5,791
DSO Cash flow improvementfrom 135			928	1,593	2,384	2,393

Cumulative Benefit 2014-2017

Cynthia immediately objected to the Days Sales Outstanding (DSO) targets. "Certainly desirable, Joseph, but not very practical. You want me to improve by 40%? What happened to the 5%improvement we were discussing a few minutes ago?"

"Ah yes. Good catch, Cynthia. Not your basic improvement. But that was before we installed the new data system. Didn't you mention that with the electronic abacus that we now use, there are many errors that require manual research, and because of pricing errors, we chase money for – in some cases – months. And let me ask another rhetorical question. What would competitive DSO be if terms were consistent with ours of Net 30?"

"Well, your right, competitive conditions would probably be in the 60 range, but the kind of improvement that you're projecting almost looks impossible."

"OK, here' my challenge to you, JB – the big silent guy over there – and everyone else. Don has an unlimited pot of money that he is ready to invest in the Company. If you ask for ANYTHING that is financially justified, he'll spend the bucks. So our role is to develop a list of all those things that make this Company better. Are you in?"

On cue, Don played along, stared at the heavens, rolled his eyes and groaned. Of course, Joseph cleared the script with Don before such an announcement. Joseph learned long ago that by removing all constraints to

333

improvement, executives focus on solutions and not reasons why something can't be done. Once the brainstorming of solutions is complete, prioritization concentrates the energy on tasks that can be done.

Again, reluctant agreement from all. Inventory turns and DSO could be achieved, with the right improvements.

"OK, so here we have a P&L and some operating improvements that increase cash flow. Any guesses about how these changes impact the Company performance?" A silent pause to allow some consideration, and after a few minutes, Joseph continued.

"Let's assume that this Company trades at a multiple of 5 times EBITDA – in this case for simplicity, rather than develop an EBITDA, we'll use Pretax Profit. The value of this Company will increase from about $8 million today, to about $21 million in three years. Not bad for that 5% improvement, plus some investment.

And Cash Flow, just from managing DSO and Inventory? Well, cash flow will increase by $20 million in the next 3 years. Don, if those values are in any way reasonable, do you think that you have any investment capital around to make those things happen?"

"Watch me write checks, folks. And by the way, if we can achieve these numbers – well, you know that I'm not afraid to share with executives that make things happen. You've seen me do that for quite a few years, and I'm not stopping now. Joseph, let me talk for a minute." Joseph was concerned by the interruption and the risk of going off-script. Although this was Don's Company, ad hoc comments may disrupt the flow of energy and commitment by participants.

"Team, I really don't know what the future holds for me... or the Company. You know that the kids - Jenny and Jerrod - won't be part of this Company. They have their own careers outside of Jackson Manufacturing Inc. I'm not getting younger, and as you know, I've lost some of the fire. I can tell you - this exercise has reignited some of my enthusiasm, but I'm not going to be here forever. One thing that I've got to do is figure out tomorrows. You are part of the team... you will be part of the tomorrows if you like, but I don't know how yet. We will develop *tomorrow* from this strategic script.

So, Joseph, I'm off the reservation for a minute, but I thought it was the right time to jump in. ... Not unusual for me to go off script..."

"This seems like a perfect time to take a ten minute break folks. I'll pass copies of the proposed P&L to you and we'll reconvene in 20 minutes." Joseph timed this interlude perfectly. Each member took the copy of the P&L and started jotting some notes on the page.

Minutes after Joseph announced the break, two women rolled polished stainless steel confectioner carts into the room. Each blue-eyed blond donned white chef's garb that included a double-breasted chef's coat, white linen apron secured with a bright red sash, a white chimney hat, and an inviting smile. Jennifer and Adele acknowledged Joseph with a subtle nod, and announced that there would be a cookie-decorating contest. The prize for the best decoration would be an iPad mini, with a consolation prize of an iPod. The stainless steel carts were covered with several dozen large sugar cookies the size of a mini-crepe pan, aligned in rows, ready for creative minds and steady hands.

Jenny and Adele, pastry chefs trained at Le Cordon Bleu Culinary Institute, assembled an elaborate array of sparkles, a rainbow of frostings, and plates overflowing with crushed pecans, walnuts and M&M's. Jenny and Adele wrapped white linen aprons around the surprised executives as they were escorted to their workstations. Jenny announced that the artists would have 10 minutes to create their designs – followed by a wink and smile, "… and you cannot consume the creation until after the judging…"

Don and Joseph enjoyed the team's visible camaraderie. Most aprons were ultimately decorated with dots and splashes of bright colored frosting when the competition finished. The break and judging lasted 30 minutes.

"OK team, let's do some competitive analysis. You may recognize some of these issues. This first slide – well, it is empty, except for the captions "Customer Service", and "Customer Relationships. Our job now is to take Jackson's top strengths and weaknesses, and plot them in relation to our competitors. I'm going to assign a colored bubble to each of the competitors that you identify. A bubble's size is a relative size versus Jackson. So for example, if a bubble is twice as large as Jackson, the company is twice our size. Its position on the chart depicts relative performance compared to Jackson. So for example, if the bubble for J&J is twice as big as Jackson, that means the competitor is twice as large as Jackson in the market – e.g. knuckles. The further from the bottom left corner, the stronger their relative performance. Questions?"

Allison tried to clarify. "And if we don't know the annual revenue of a competitor, I suppose that we just estimate the revenue, unless we don't have a clue. And if we don't have a clue, do we create a placeholder?"

"Exactly. Great observation. I think that if we don't have a clue, we would use an empty bubble of the same color to indicate the specific company and the need to know more about it."

"And who is responsible to discover more information?"

"That will turn into an assignment for one of us. You decide who is best at the research." During the next hour, they identified primary competitors, and discussed strategies that would make Jackson more successful in the global competitive environment. Joseph encouraged full participation, and when a team member was silent for too long, Joseph prodded them for their insight.

"As we review these strengths and weaknesses and competitive conditions, think about the P&L we'd like to achieve. What should we do differently to make those sales, earnings, DSO and Inventory Turns happen? And who is responsible? Just as earlier, don't be shy. There are no bad answers. Questions?"

One hour later, plots were complete and assignments noted on the page bottom.

To summarize the meeting, and get final agreement, he flashed the slides across the screen one more time, saying, "If you don't agree with anything on these slides, shout it out."

338

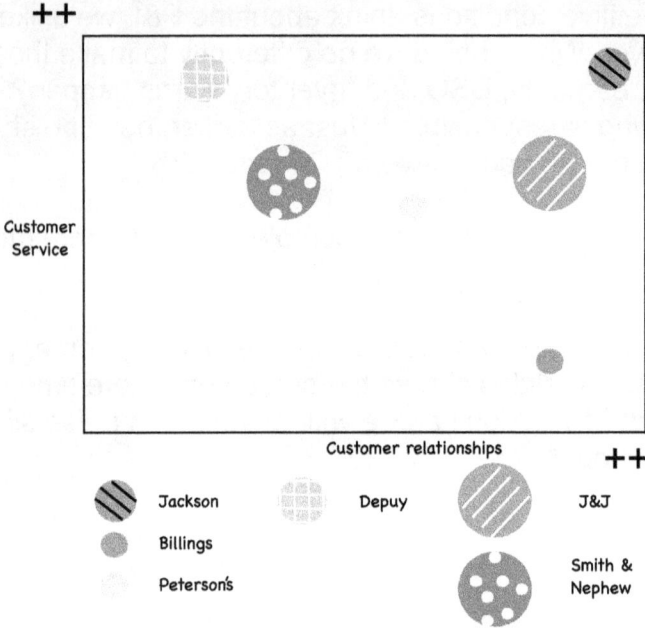

Description	Due Date	Resp	Financial Impact *(000' $)*		Profit Improvement
			Spending		
			Expense	Capital	
Define Customer Service success measures that can be used daily/weekly/monthly.	Q1 - 2015	JB	0	0	0
Establish A-B-C classifications for Actual and Prospective customers.	Q1 - 2015	Stephen	0	0	0
Evaluate and identify CRM software.	Q2 - 2015	Stephen	0	0	0
Select & install CRM software	Q3 - 2015	Stephen	5	25	

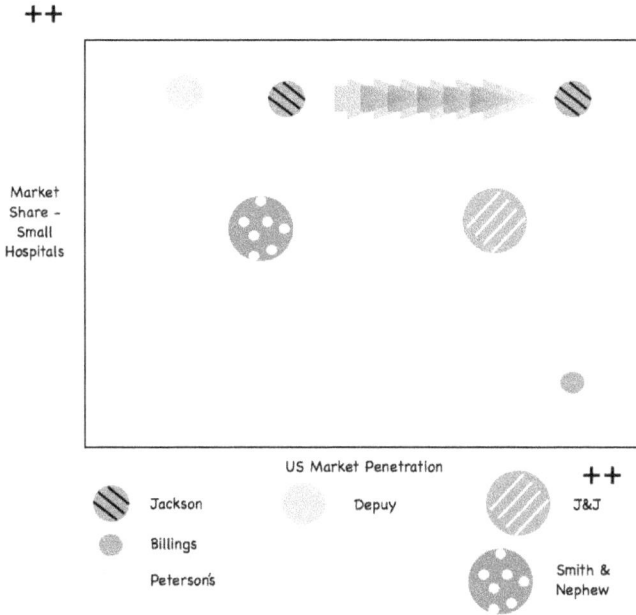

Description	Due Date	Resp	Financial Impact (000' $)		
			Spending		Profit Improvement
			Expense	Capital	
Develop marketing program for freestanding surgical centers.	Q1 - 2015	Stephen	25		Potential of Millions of Incrementl Revenue.
Develop marketing program for middle-market hospitals.	Q4 - 2015	Stephen	50		Potential of Millions of Incrementl Revenue.
Expand sales of subassemblies for non-Jackson proprietary products.	2016	Stephen			Potential of Millions of Incrementl Revenue.

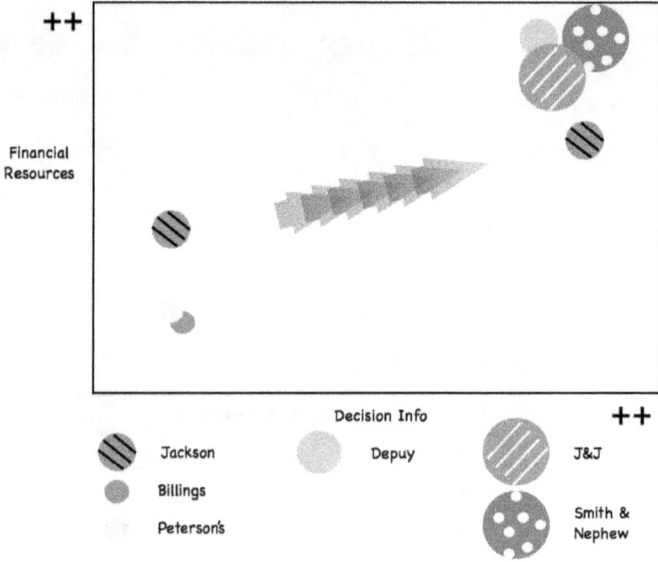

Description	Due Date	Resp	Financial Impact *(000' $)*		
			Spending		Profit Improvement
			Expense	Capital	
Implement improved periodic reporting (daily; weekly; monthly)	Q1 - 2015	Cynthia			
Implement improved quarterly forecasting process.	Q1 - 2015	Cynthia			
Implement improved annual budget process.	Q4 - 2015	Cynthia			
Investigate and select potential ERP data systems.	Q3 2015	Cynthia	50		
Install improved ERP system.	2016	Cynthia	100	500	
Explore financing alternatives with financial institutions. Summarize options and present to owners.	Q4 - 2015	Cynthia	10		

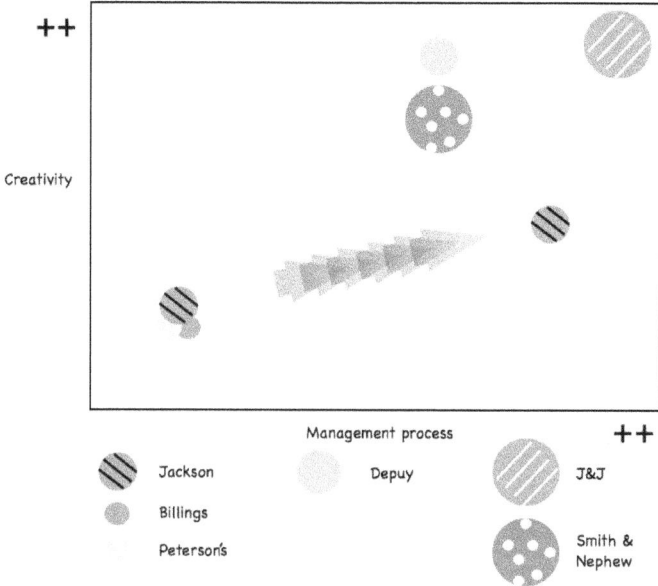

Description	Due Date	Resp	Financial Impact (000' $)		
			Spending		Profit Improvement
			Expense	Capital	
Explore and select process to assist Company in R&D creativity and management	Q2 - 2015	Allison	40		
Develop and begin implementation of improved overall management process (strategy/goal setting/responsibility & accountability).	Q2 - 2015	Margaret	50		
Complete implementation of management improvement process.	Q4 - 2016	Margaret	50		

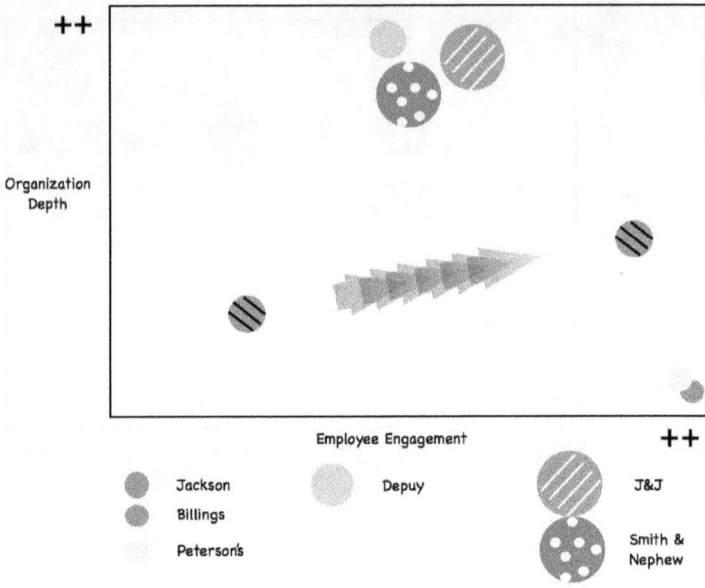

Description	Due Date	Resp	Financial Impact (000' $)		
			Spending		Profit Improvement
			Expense	Capital	
Assess organization depth, in relation to expected growth and priorities.	Q2 - 2015	Don	25		
Investigate and select programs to improve employee engagement (such as town hall meetings; newsletters; websites etc.)	Q2 - 2015	Margaret	10		
Investigate and select a performance management incentive system that could include salary benchmarking; employee bonus programs.	Q2 - 2015	Margaret	20		
Investigate and select an executive compensation program to better engage key executives (considering - e.g. phantom stock; stock options; long term incentive compensation etc.)	Q2 - 2015	Margaret	20		

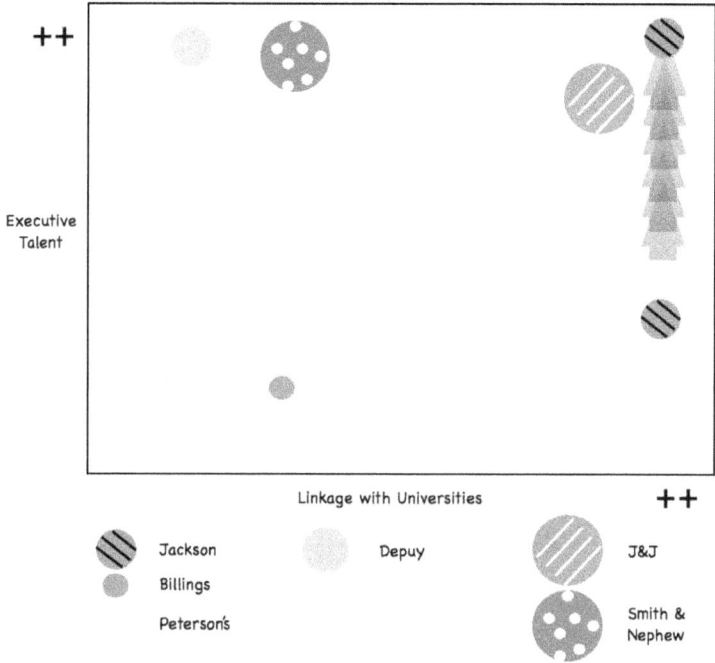

Description	Due Date	Resp	Financial Impact (000' $)		
			Spending		Profit Improvement
			Expense	Capital	
After completion of organization assessment, considering succession planning, develop a program to upgrade existing staff and/or add talent.	Q3 - 2015	Don	25		
Develop new product development liason with specialty universities.	Q4 - 2015	Allison			

344

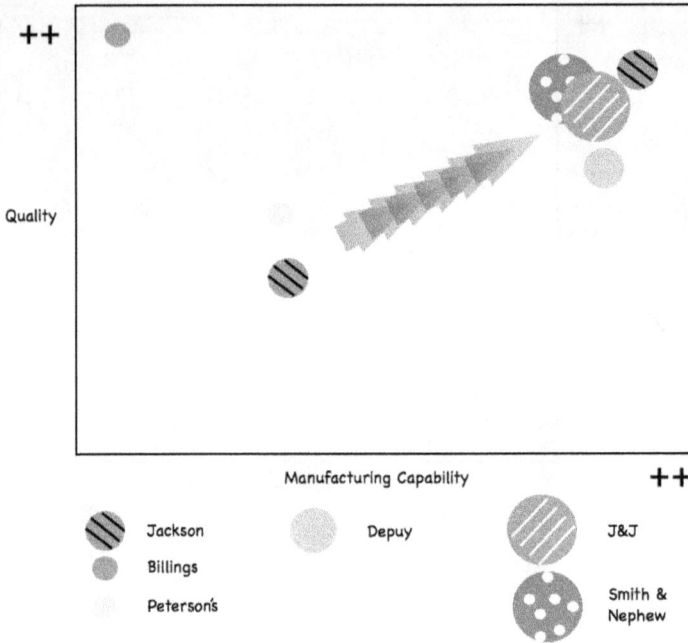

| Description | Due Date | Resp | Financial Impact *(000'$)* | | |
| | | | Spending | | Profit Improvement |
			Expense	Capital	
Identify and manage key quality metrics for manufacturing operations.	Q1 - 2015	JB			
Investigate and identify a program, such as Lean Business, to implement in the manufacturing operations.	Q2 - 2015	JB	35		
Begin implementation of the new improved operations program, such as Lean Business.	Q3 - 2015	JB	200		

Don eagerly watched these priorities develop, and nervously tabulated costs. While squirming in his seat, he circled the total cost number, and doodled numerous question marks, asterisks and stars around the total. His hands fidgeted and moved randomly from his chin, as if stroking an invisible beard, to his temple, cheek and then formed a tent with his fingertips poised against his pursed lips.

Joseph summarized the last segment. "This segment has been a rousing success – only because you folks have shed your constraints and attacked the opportunity. I know one guy in the room who is very - and I mean v-e-r-y- nervous." As he looked at Don, "Don, you've been a real trooper. We have spent – oh, maybe more than a million dollars of your money this afternoon. And you didn't object to a single dollar."

Don interrupted, "You didn't spend the money, Joseph, you put some numbers on the page. Remember your ground rules – I get to make the final decision. Right now, that is proposed spending."

"Touché Don. And you are 100% correct. The beauty of this exercise is that your team didn't let money get in the way of their creativity. So now we have a selection of alternatives that will help us eliminate our weaknesses and perhaps enhance our strengths. Worst case, the main issues are now on paper.

Now as we think about these items during the next week, you may find that while doing all these priorities, you may not be able to complete your day job. Good or bad?"

In unison, "Bad."

"That's right, because we have a business to run. But each of these priorities is designed to make us a better business. So let me pick one – Cynthia, how is it in any way possible to increase profits by installing an ERP system? That is pure overhead!"

"No way, Joseph. We have an organization of – what is it, 125 associates – that need performance information to be sure that we manage effectively. If we don't have accountability as we delegate responsibility down through the organization we'll be out of control."

JB reacted. "BS – sounds like bean-counter hocus pocus to me! All you really need is a basic P&L to manage the business."

"Hey, wait a minute, JB." Stephen was almost angry as he burst into the conversation. "If I don't know what the reps are doing for their assigned customers, how the hell am I going to get my job done. It's not hocus-pocus. Heck, until we focused on the two main product lines, I couldn't even tell you if the knuckles were doing great or poorly. And I still don't have a clue what my supply sales are. And if we don't put some targets out there, how will I know if the sales force is being effective. Definitely not BS."

"But a half-million bucks worth? C'mon."

Cynthia rebuffed, "Just because we put a number down doesn't mean we're going to spend it. It's a placeholder until we do more discovery work."

Allison chimed in, "You know this is fascinating. Until today, we would have managed the business day-in and day-out just like we have for the past few years. Now after only a few hours, we have definite programs identified – names and broad dates – about how we are going to improve the business. I'm sorry, but I don't think this is BS. My challenge is to figure out how I'm going to get all this done. But let's think about the big picture. If we actually can execute this plan, our earnings will be 2.5 times what they are today." With that, she turned silently like a gun turret on a battleship, focused on Don, smiled, and said, " …and when the business is worth 2.5 times what it is today - well, Don said we are all in it together. And, folks, Don is on the hook for an executive compensation plan. So, I'm in this game – as they say in Texas hold 'em – 'All in'.

Nods of agreement all around.

Joseph beamed. "So let's grab a cookie. By the way Allison's cookie won first place in the decorating contest. Tell us what the design represents, Allison."

"This is the maze of what is required to get a new medical device cleared by the FDA. If you look carefully, there are many ways that look like they will

348

take you through the maze – and they all have blocks. Sometimes working with the FDA means you clear every hurdle, and you still can't get to the proper answer – launching the product. Did I mention that we should license some products?"

I'll share the cookie, if anyone wants."

"Very imaginative, Allison. Ok, all let's grab some refreshments before we launch into the segment about new products... of course, we won't follow Allison's maze, but let's discover an expedited method to secure and launch new products. Let's reconvene in 15 minutes."

April 26, 2014 – Offsite Meeting - New Products

> ＊New products - develop …
> license … acquire
> ＊Corporations… universities
> are source of new products

"New products… product substitutes … JV products … subassemblies … new approvals. There are so many opportunities I almost can't count them. So what should we talk about? Make me work people. What are the key elements of the decision process?"

JB decided that he was going to take over, as he strutted to the front of the room, green marker in hand. "OK folks, let's all be sure that we understand if we're going to sell it, I'm going to have to produce it. So I think that I should drive this segment."

"Hell no, JB." Allison was angry. "What makes you think that we can't sell something unless you produce it? Ever heard of JV and distributor agreements?"

Joseph interrupted, "JB – you've got the pen. Start writin' Bubba." Although Allison was a bit upset at Joseph's direction, it was time to let JB get out on a limb.

"Sure I have heard of JV's, but we don't have the organization to make JV's and distribution agreements happen. You talking about distributing products approved in Europe? I'm guessing that it will take years to get them approved here in the US."

"Who says they're not already approved?" Stephen decided to work the argument. "You know there are some products over in Europe that may be ready to go in the US – already FDA approved – maybe grandfathered - but the European company doesn't have established relationships for distribution here in the US. I could sell something like that through my sales organization."

Joseph interrupted. "So what are some of the considerations when we think of selling new products – whether they are produced by us or not?"

JB quietly surrendered the pen to Joseph. Conversations bristled at such a pace, it was difficult for Joseph to capture all the elements that seemed to be critical in any such decision to launch new products.

Certainly cost, time to market were key considerations, but there were things like manufacturability, availability, working capital requirements, capital requirements, training, markets served and so many more issues.

After 45 minutes, Joseph scanned the numerous flipcharts scattered across the room. "So what do we do with all this information? It seems that we can identify a reason not to expand and launch any new products, yet we can also identify an equal number of reasons to launch new products. It seems that investment might be a roadblock."

"Cynthia contributed, "But remember, Don has an unlimited source of funds." Don feigned a groan, but grinned as if he had just scored the winning $450 million Powerball ticket.

"OK, well Don has unlimited funds, but our organization cannot overcome all the obstacles that we've identified."

"Wait a minute, Joseph, remember that Margaret has the job to guide an organization review. Wouldn't this be considered in that process?"

"OK – that's right, Stephen. But some of these new products – for example developing a new FDA approved product – could take years. We don't have that kind of time, do we?"

"That's why we call this a strategic plan, Joseph." Now Don was fully engaged. "Remember, Joseph, value is future cash flow and future earnings. If we lay out a plan, and begin execution, and hit all the milestones, we've got a marketable process. Maybe you can't spin that into more value, but I could. C'mon, if we develop a solid plan, with step-by-step deliverables, and we make every one of them, that's credibility!

And if we balance the new product introductions, we can have a steady stream of new products."

Joseph rebuffed, "Help me understand what your saying, Don."

"Look, we've all done this *let's pretend* thing today... pretend that Don has unlimited funds. Well, I don't, but if we can come up with enough good ideas, we'll have to pace ourselves and invest wisely. So for example, it may be a quick source of income and cash flow to increase production of the sub-assemblies. We've seen that Peterson's has worse quality than us, and their manufacturing capabilities are not very good. Why don't we target some of their customers, get some of their production volume – that may eliminate a competitor, and we increase our sales and earnings. Stephen, you up for that?"

"Sounds like a good competitive situation for us. I'll have one of the guys do some research."

"OK, Don, so let's say you can get some of Peterson's jobs. That's a small piece of growth. Where do we get the rest?"

Don's bewildered look begged for a team contribution. Margaret to the rescue. "Look, you folks are the sales – marketing – and manufacturing experts. I'm just an independent observer. But didn't we mention something called orphan products? They sounded interesting – what are they?"

"Great concept." Stephen immediately started listing some of the lesser product lines produced by Depuy, and Smith & Nephew. "These products fall directly within our wheelhouse. They don't even call on the surgical centers. Their reps call exclusively on the majors. We might be able to distribute for them."

"OK, so we may have a ready supply of orphans. How do we get them on board? And isn't a distributor margin less than a manufacturers? Can we afford to add them?"

"We'd have to run the numbers. For this kind of analysis, I've got the time to do some *what if* scenarios." Joseph acknowledged Cynthia's offer and added, "Now we're hitting the topic head on. Let's play with the numbers and balance our risk. This is just a portfolio analysis of 'what if's?' This brief brainstorming session screams of creativity. What are the issues that we have to consider?"

The team started randomly shouting phrases – "working capital requirements; capital investment; product approval risk; production risk; competitive product risk;

market size; market location – US, Europe, Latin America, Far East; regulatory risk; timing; market growth." Joseph slashed words across the flip chart, some with asterisks, and some underlined. As each page filled with ideas, he ripped the page from its backing and pasted the sheet to the wall. "C'mon – what else?" he encouraged the team. "OK – what products do you envision? Are these new knuckles or outsourced production." The pace of imagination quickened.

There was visible energy in the room. Joseph's facilitation skill orchestrated the pace of the conversation so that all contributed and the list of opportunities spanned more than 5 years. The list was prioritized by contribution, risk and timing, and if all the potential products were sold by Jackson Manufacturing, the Company would have sales over $60 million within the next 5 years.

JB puzzled over a notation on one of the pages. "OK – in the big red circle…what does 'Buy Peterson' mean?"

"Excellent question, JB. Let's go back through some of the strengths and weaknesses charts and see what we've plotted. Peterson has excellent relationships with Universities, great quality, and minimal manufacturing capability. They also have limited financial resources. The real trifecta could be that the owner is in his 70's and is ready to sell out for a reasonable price."

Said another way, their quality performance is consistent with ours, and we need closer relationships with Universities. How much of a premium over book value do we need to pay to get that linkage with the Universities? If it's a $1 million premium, will that accelerate our new product development? And what's it worth to be in the market 1-2 years earlier with new products? Remember, we show that new science will require 3-5 years to break into new product designs and materials.

Stephen leaned into the conversation, and mentioned, "…New science and new materials provide exceptional margins. Being first in the market also has a certain cachet – real market value in the medical field."

Joseph launched quickly into a series of questions. "So what is that early entry worth? How much better margins would we realize? JB, could you produce exotic materials? Yes, there are many unanswered questions. But until the last 30 minutes, these questions were never on the table. So what do we do with all this information?" He then scrawled in large letters across a flip sheet – PLAN!!!

"The opportunities are virtually endless. Our challenge is to select the most likely successful products, and begin a program to capture the value. If we properly evaluate the alternatives, develop a plan that captures the value, and actually execute, what do we have? A better business."

Cynthia nudged Allison and whispered, "Execute… a new thing for us…"

Allison nodded in agreement, and then self-consciously scanned the room to see if anyone overheard the comment.

Joseph challenged, "And just how do we propose to do that?"

Cynthia stood, unsheathed the red marker, and, also in large red block letters, carefully wrote, "EXECUTE!" She double underlined the word, and just before being seated, added three more exclamation points at the end of the word. "Any questions team?"

Joseph had unleashed a torrent of creativity. Timing was right to have the team contemplate their work for the past hour. He feigned thirst, walked to the refreshments and opened an orange juice while the team assessed their work. In an hour of brainstorming, the team identified nearly $20 million of additional business, in addition to a normal growth rate of 3-4% per year.

Millions $	Product Opportunities 1	2	3	4	5	Capital	Expense	Produced Inhouse	Outhouse
Subassemblies							.5/yr		
Peterson/Billings	1.0	2.0	2.5	3.0	3.0	1.0			
Other	1.0	1.0	1.5	2.0	2.5				
Distributor									
US									
Depuy	0.2	0.2	0.3	0.7	0.7				
Other	–	0.5	0.7	0.7	0.1				
International									
Europe									
Roche	1.0	2.0	3.0	4.0	5.0		.75/yr		
Latin Amer	–	–	0.5	1.0	1.0				
Far East	–	1.0	1.0	1.0	1.5				
New Science									
Materials	–	–	0.2	0.5	1.0		.5% sales		
Design	–	–	–	–	1.5				

Licensed
Product

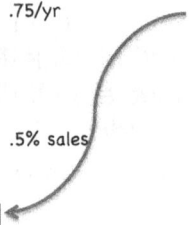

After a few sips of OJ, Joseph, invited comments. "Any thoughts?"

Don's mouth agape, hands folded quietly on the conference table, he was somewhat startled at the last hour's activity. He was unaccustomed to such a flurry of creativity and energy from his executive team. Motionless, the team awaited Don to break the awkward silence. Each team member knew they performed out of character, and were almost frightened by the energy and excitement displayed.

Margaret, the Company's unofficial culture monitor, shifted nervously in her set.

Someone cleared his throat in a deep rumble.

Don's eyes shifted apprehensively around the table, his head turned slightly as if in a neck brace. Tight lipped, he cleared his throat ready to speak. His unusually timid voice banished the silence.

"I'm not sure what to say. Several weeks ago, I was feeling like it was the end of my career. Maybe I was tired of the routine, or maybe just tired. Maybe I was seeing that the grass was greener on the other side of retirement. I had no compass to guide me for all of the tomorrows. I was complacent... but not really happy and didn't know why.

So for the past two days, we've camped out like we never have before. This team has the enthusiasm of

Big-10 football cheerleaders … there is so much energy… so many possibilities and opportunities. I feel like a 30 year old, but recognize that I'm not 30 any more. Joseph, what is the value of a Company?"

"The value is simply the future cash flow and future earnings to any potential buyer. The past is credibility, or lack of it."

"So if I understand you correctly, planning and execution according to plan will demonstrate credibility. Future plans that project increased earnings and cash flow will have more value to someone, if a management team can effectively plan and execute to plan."

"Couldn't have said it better, Don."

"So we have a management team, now it's our job to develop a credible plan and move forward. Folks, I should have done something like this year's ago. I'm not going to promise to fund everything that you've talked about, but by damn, this is just friggin' exciting. What are the next steps, Joseph?"

"Well, the majority of planning is now complete. The next steps are to assemble the plans so that we all can review and commit to deliverables outlined. Cynthia has already started to develop improved reporting, and rough forecasting using key metrics. The team needs to identify and accept the metrics, and begin execution. The normal rhythm at Jackson will change a bit. In order to manage the plan, we'll have to meet regularly to understand how the execution is going. My suggestion? A weekly staff meeting – maybe 1-1.5 hours; monthly meetings – maybe a couple of hours; quarterly meetings – maybe a half-day. The meetings would focus on near term performance, and adjustments to plans to achieve the overall goals. Some of those goals may be current sales and earnings... some of the goals may be milestones focused on longer-range activities.

This is an exciting time, for sure, but this will not be easy. We are changing how we manage to achieve goals that we never before considered achievable... heck, they were not even on the radar.

No fluff... no sugar coating. This will be work... sometimes more stressful than in the past, but when you consider what we are doing, the rewards are not just financial, but self-satisfaction like you've never before enjoyed. Are we all in?"

Joseph's piercing eyes drilled each person, and awaited acceptance of the challenge. Each executive nodded agreement. Joseph's laser-like stare now locked on Don's eyes. Silence hung in the room like a tarp smothering flames.

Don's response -"I'm in."

Joseph immediately accelerated the pace of the meeting congratulating all in a joyful refrain, "Well done... well done! Next steps will be for me to work with Cynthia and document our work. During the next week, we will assemble the plan – in draft form – so that we all get to see what the commitments will be. Then, in a final review and approval, we'll begin the process. Great job, folks. Excellent workshop."

With that, the meeting was adjourned.

Uncharacteristically, JB motioned a 'thumbs-up' to Joseph. JB and Allison huddled quietly to discuss some potential new products. Margaret picked a path among the execs as if a slalom skier, to congratulate Don on this new Company energy. Stephen and Cynthia were already scratching numbers on a page as if to validate their recent commitment to growth.

Joseph sequentially numbered the flip-chart sheets and carefully peeled them from the walls. Once neatly stacked, he rolled them into a tight tube, secured with a rubber band, and assembled them with the other meeting materials.

Joseph was pleased with the meeting results.

April 28, 2014 – Summarize & Review Strategic Plan

The meeting room at the local Hyatt was airy, well appointed, and overlooked the watershed. Midwest April afternoons were breezy and fresh with brilliant smog free azure skies. The executive team, fully assembled 15 minutes early, eagerly awaited the Strategic Plan discussion.

This meeting would be non-controversial, and would serve as the formal kickoff of the improved Jackson Manufacturing Inc. management process. Although each team member has seen the complete plan individually, this would be the first opportunity to formally accept the management challenge ahead.

Custom designed coffee mugs to commemorate the new 'Jackson' management process aligned with the stock of soft drinks and juices standing at attention like well-trained soldiers. Several small plastic trays displayed a selection of Ghirardelli Chocolate squares, granola and Snicker's bars. For the health-oriented members, a tray of fresh fruit invited attention.

Don, in a bright patterned Greg Norman golf shirt, joked with the team members as they arrived. Joseph and Don carefully reviewed the strategic plan before the meeting, and Don was prepared to share some personal thoughts with the team.

At exactly 2 PM, Don formally welcomed all as if this were a meeting of Parliament, adding to the importance of the strategic plan. "Today we'll begin to manage our tomorrow's. This is particularly important to me, since this is the first time in several years that I have been so enthusiastic about Jackson Manufacturing, Inc. In our earlier meetings, you folks demonstrated energy, commitment, and such a thorough understanding of our products, markets and competitors that I felt very foolish that I hadn't asked for your help earlier. Well, today we launch the new Jackson Manufacturing, Inc. Joseph will take us through the plan that we've all developed. Thank you for your help during the past few months, and thanks for your enthusiastic approach to our strategic plan."

"Joseph, here's the baton."

"Thanks Don. I can only say congratulations to all on our efforts during the two-day offsite meeting. One thing I mentioned at the beginning is that there are no bad ideas – but never enough ideas overall."

JB interrupted, "Do you mean that we've come up with some bad ideas?"

"Well, you've proved me wrong. The two days of planning have been one of the most candid, creative workshops that I've ever facilitated. We started with an empty page, an empty stage, and a lot of enthusiasm. So for now, we'll take an hour to review the strategy that we've crafted during the two-day offsite. First of all, the Vision/Mission."

Jackson Manufacturing, Inc.
Vision/Mission Statement

Jackson Manufacturing is the manufacturer and distributor of the highest quality, implantable artificial bones, joints and components built with the patient safety and comfort as our number one priority. Through affiliations with universities, and outstanding research organizations and companies, our mission is to develop and produce niche products for underserved global demographic segments, and produce the highest quality components for the mass-market skeletal and implantable devices. Our Company team will be treated with respect, and we will provide training and opportunity for personal development and career advancement. We will hold ourselves personally accountable for performance to the highest ethical standards, and will always act within both the spirit and letter of the law.

"Let's spend a few minutes talking about the statement. Stephen, what do you see in this statement?"

"Specifically, our customer is the patient. We want them to have the best possible solution for any of their maladies. And by targeting 'underserved global demographic segments', I envision that means we will not go head-to-head with the J&J's and Smith & Nephew who target the mass market joint replacements – like a basic hip."

"Everybody ok with that?"

JB observed, "When we talk about 'components for mass market implantable devices' does that mean we will continue to manufacture 'sub-assemblies' for the J&J's of the world?"

"That's what I read."

Anybody agree/disagree with JB?"

All agreed with that interpretation.

"What else do you see?"

Cynthia observed, "We are going to be a global Company, but we are not today. Sounds like expansion in the future."

"Great. Other comments."

"I am very happy with the commitment to the employees. They'll be treated with respect and trained for growth. That will make my job a bit easier. That may also cut back the turnover for the younger engineers that seem to flow through here."

"Excellent observation, Margaret."

Don tapped his pen on the table to be recognized, and said, "Ethics and legal – and I don't mean just within the law, but within the spirit of the law. This is my Company and my reputation. Anybody that breaks the law in my shop – well, their replacement will fix the problem."

"OK – is there anything that folks don't agree with?" Heads bobbed agreement with the vision.

Joseph pressed on. "So if a company wants us to export our products – let's say to the Middle East – and makes the customs declaration as automobile components to be charged a lower duty? What do we do, based on the vision?"

In unison, "Hell no!"

"And if someone comes to us to produce prosthetic arms?"

"Not within the vision, so no arms, but could we produce the artificial joints for the prosthetic arms?"

"Seems to fall within skeletal, but not implantable. Yes, I think so."

Joseph persisted with Q&A. "Can we distribute, here in the US, skeletal devices produced by a German Company?"

"Absolutely."

"OK, so the vision/mission can guide us for what we can do, and what we cannot do. Everybody comfortable with the Vision/Mission?

As Joseph scanned the room, he noted full agreement. The meeting continued with the projected financial statement.

000's $	2012	2013	2014	2015	2016	2017
Sales						
Baseline	19,566	19,233	18,788	18,500	20,000	21,000
Billings/Peterson					500	1,000
Knuckles	10,041	10,779	12,226	14,455	15,055	16,476
International				500	750	750
New Product				-	250	500
Total Sales	29,607	30,012	31,014	33,455	36,555	39,726
Gross Profit	15,692	15,306	15,119	17,505	20,405	20,241
Total GM %	53%	51%	49%	52%	56%	51%
Baseline %	47%	43%	42%	45%	46%	47%
Billings/Peterson %					55%	51%
Knuckles %	66%	65%	59%	60%	64%	54%
International				60%	67%	68%
New Product					60%	60%
SG&A						
Sales	6,997	7,122	7,255	7,500	7,800	8,300
R&D	750	785	815	1,555	1,950	2,150
Admin	3,162	3,213	3,200	3,759	3,065	3,350
Other	1,912	2,015	2,212	2,465	2,676	3,014
Total	12,821	13,135	13,482	15,279	15,491	16,814
Pretax Profit	2,871	2,171	1,637	2,226	4,914	3,427
% of Sales	10%	7%	5%	7%	13%	9%
After Tax Profit	1,436	1,086	819	1,113	2,457	1,714

Cash	2012	2013	2014	2015	2016	2017
Capital Spending	560	750	1,500	1,500	1,500	2,000
Accounts Receivable	8,522	12,122	10,989	9,895	8,778	8,500
Accounts Payable						
Inventory Balance	-	-	-	-	-	3
DSO	96	135	119	99	80	72
Invnetory Turns	2.5	2.7	3.5	4	4.5	4.5

Joseph thoroughly reviewed the financial statement with the team, focusing on major changes in strategy. In particular, the Company intends to obtain product line production from Billings/Peterson, expand into new products and International operations. The Company would accomplish this through expanded sales presence either through distribution relationships or expanded sales force, and a substantial increase in R&D spending.

The Company expects to realize significant leverage in the finance operation, through investment in improved data systems. These investments will also be funded by improved DSO and inventory turns, supported by improved reporting. The Company's "Other Admin" includes significant investment in training, and a Companywide bonus pool to reward employees for improved performance.

As Stephen absorbed the concepts that were a foundation of the plan, he mused, "I'd like to buy a piece of this Company – damn, look at that performance."

Don heard the whisper. "Yes, Stephen, some ownership opportunities may happen during this planning period. It is interesting as we review the potential impact of our changes. As I sit here thinking about *tomorrows*, I can only think to myself that if I ever do decide to sell, and if I were to hold the multiple constant at for example 5x, this plan would increase the selling price from $8 million to nearly $17 million. And that assumes we wouldn't sell for a higher multiple within an acceptable range. Makes me giddy... not that I'm going to sell the Company, but it is definitely an option."

Stephen's eyes rose from the page of notes. "Did you say there *might* be some ownership opportunities?"

"Absolutely. In fact, let me state that there will be ownership opportunities."

Although smiles and whispers erupted around the table, no one provoked Don with questions about details. They decided to let the details surface when timing was right.

Summary pages of the competitive analysis blinked on the screen, poised for discussion. A murmur of discussion accompanied each slide. As the last slide projected, Stephen challenged the group-thought with, "Petersons and Billings are the weak sisters in our analysis. They have limited financial resources, and limited manufacturing capability. However, Billings has decent US market penetration, outstanding quality, good relationships with customers and universities, and excellent employee engagement. Does anybody have any insight into how they get that unusual mix of attributes? How old is the Billings' owner? Maybe we should buy them and get all that good stuff right along with the rest?"

"Excellent observation, Stephen. The value of the visualization is exactly what you've done – connect the dots. Any insights team?"

All were silent. "Stephen, can you take that assignment and add it to your other commitments? Say by the end of the 1st quarter?"

"Glad to do so, Joseph."

The full tally of assignments, excluding Stephen's recent commitment, launched to the screen:

Ref	Description	Due Date	Resp	Financial Impact *(000' $)*		Profit Improvement
				Spending		
				Expense	Capital	
1	Define Customer Service success measures that can be used daily/weekly/monthly.	Q1 - 2015	JB	0	0	0
2	Establish A-B-C classifications for Actual and Prospective customers.	Q1 - 2015	Stephen	0	0	0
3	Evaluate and identify CRM software.	Q2 - 2015	Stephen	0	0	0
4	Select & install CRM software	Q3 - 2015	Stephen	5	25	
5	Develop marketing program for freestanding surgical centers.	Q1 - 2015	Stephen	25		Potential of Millions of Incrementl Revenue.
6	Develop marketing program for middle-market hospitals.	Q4 - 2015	Stephen	50		Potential of Millions of Incrementl Revenue.
7	Expand sales of subassemblies for non-Jackson proprietary products.	2016	Stephen			Potential of Millions of Incrementl Revenue.
8	Implement improved periodic reporting (daily; weekly; monthly)	Q1 - 2015	Cynthia			
9	Implement improved quarterly forecasting process.	Q1 - 2015	Cynthia			
10	Implement improved annual budget process.	Q4 - 2015	Cynthia			
11	Investigate and select potential ERP data systems.	Q3 2015	Cynthia	50		
12	Install improved ERP system.	2016	Cynthia	100	500	

Ref	Description	Due Date	Resp	Financial Impact (000' $)		Profit Improvement
				Spending		
				Expense	Capital	
13	Explore financing alternatives with financial institutions. Summarize options and present to owners.	Q4 - 2015	Cynthia	10		
14	Explore and select process to assist Company in R&D creativity and management	Q2 - 2015	Allison	40		
15	Develop and begin implementation of improved overall management process (strategy/goal setting/responsibility & accountability).	Q2 - 2015	Margaret	50		
16	Complete implementation of management improvement process.	Q4 - 2016	Margaret	50		
17	Assess organization depth, in relation to expected growth and priorities.	Q2 - 2015	Don	25		
18	Investigate and select programs to improve employee engagement (such as town hall meetings; newsletters; websites etc.)	Q2 - 2015	Margaret	10		
19	Investigate and select a performance management incentive system that could include salary benchmarking; employee bonus programs.	Q2 - 2015	Margaret	20		
20	Investigate and select an executive compensation program to better engage key executives (considering - e.g. phantom stock; stock options; long term incentive compensation etc.)	Q2 - 2015	Margaret	20		
21	After completion of organization assessment, considering succession planning, develop a program to upgrade existing staff and/or add talent.	Q3 - 2015	Don	25		
22	Develop new product development liason with specialty universities.	Q4 - 2015	Allison			
23	Identify and manage key quality metrics for manufacturing operations.	Q1 - 2015	JB			
24	Investigate and identify a program, such as Lean Business, to implement in the manufacturing operations.	Q2 - 2015	JB	35		
25	Begin implementation of the new improved operations program, such as Lean Business.	Q3 - 2015	JB	200		

Once all the plan components were reviewed with the group, Joseph completed one last step.

"I'm going to go around the room and ask each one of you 'Are you committed to delivering this plan?' If you say you're not fully committed, I'll only ask what obstacles are there to your full commitment. It's ok to say you're not committed, but you cannot do so without a reason that we have a chance to correct."

With that, he asked each participant if there were any obstacles to delivering the results in the strategic plan.

Without exception, each agreed to the plan.

The meeting was adjourned.

April 28, 2014 – Debrief: Joseph & Don

Two days after the final review meeting, Joseph met with Don at the Club. They dined on celebratory Margaritas, thick juicy burgers with melted aged cheddar oozing along the edge; and to promote health, sweet potato fries. Don's bubbly demeanor broadcast his enthusiasm for the recent planning exercise.

"One helluva job, Joseph. I'm not sure how you coaxed all that energy from this complacent group – me included – but one helluva job. You know the unfortunate part of the exercise is that I'm totally psyched. The business sounds so good now, that I'd be a fool to sell it. My god, I'm psyched."

"Don, I don't want to dampen your enthusiasm, but let's back up a bit. Our goal with the strategic plan was not to give you a roadmap to selling the place, but help you manage the business better – more professionally - so that if you chose to sell, you would get the best price for the business. Your team fully engaged with the process. They were ready for the challenge, but now you have to follow up with some things.

Let's think about a few of the open items – those actions between the lines that we really didn't spend a lot of time on, but you and I know must be done.

First of all, Chip, Janelle, and Uncle Robert. Unless you can get these folks into productive roles, you will be diluting the teams' efforts. When a leader tolerates non-performance, you've basically lowered the bar for the rest of the team. Said another way, how can you demand top performance from others when a different scale is used for relatives? If you want peak performance from the team, can you think about how you want to handle these relatives on the payroll?

And speaking of payroll, if these folks can't be prime contributors to the Company's success, you really don't want to consider them in any financial statements that may be used in the sale transaction. There may be other costs that a typical business would avoid if owned by an independent investor. Perhaps the airplane, vacation houses etc. Think about those costs."

"Got it about the relatives. But that airplane is a valuable transportation asset for this Company. It…"

"No need to defend these items to me, Don. I'll just ask you to look at the way the Company is managed as if you were an outsider looking in. What will they see? If they see a management team that plans effectively, executes according to plan, has a communication's process that keeps all informed, and pushes accountability down through the organization, that's a good thing."

A moment's pause to savor the cheeseburger, followed by a Margarita sip… "And now the delicate tissue. I told you I wouldn't be shy about this. If you were to leave – or let's say sell the business and have $10 million bucks at your ready disposal – who's in charge? Who is your successor?"

Don was visibly angry at the directness of the question. "Sip your Margarita, Joseph. We're not going to discuss that now."

"And if not now, shall we wait a year? And if we wait a year, and you decide to sell the Company, what will an outsider see? A business with a leaderless Company? Or perhaps a leader who was hired 2 months before the sale? What will they see? Dysfunction? I'd like to postpone this discussion, Don, but this is particularly sensitive, since so much of the value depends on the *future* income, and – well you tell me, what value is there in a leaderless Company? Or a Company with an unproven leader?

I'll leave that question alone for now, but you're not paying me to give you a warm and fuzzy theoretical massage. You're paying me for advice, and when I'm paid for something, I deliver.

So let's move on. Tell me about your legal representation. That also sounded like a weak spot in the organization."

"Keith has been our attorney for many years. He's helped us through real estate transactions, purchase contract negotiations, employee legal matters. He's a good guy all around that would not leave us out to dry with any legal exposures."

"OK, but has he done any M&A work for you or anyone else? When I think about the fragmented approach to the legal environment, another question: Has anyone reviewed all of your contracts and legal commitments recently? Can we be sure that there are no snakes in the woodpile? And I don't want an answer now. I just want you to think about the questions. We'll resolve open items later."

Don usually avoided these decadent cheeseburgers to better manage his cholesterol. As he savored each bite, he gazed across the fairways watching amateur golfers slash through underbrush attempting to seat their ball near the flag. At one point, he gestured to Joseph. A teenage athlete who didn't understand that pure muscle and swinging hard did not result with the best outcome. "That boy's gotta get some finesse in his game."

"Just like business, Don."

"Speaking of finesse, what kind of management process do you intend to use in this Company? Weekly or monthly meetings? Updated forecasts? Any thoughts?"

""I've got to spend more time with Cynthia, since reporting seems to drive effective action in the Company. My first thoughts are perhaps a weekly meeting, concentrating on immediate goals and requirements – maybe discussing major orders in process or key customers, manufacturing operations – and then progress on projects that are important to the Company. Maybe an hour every week – Tuesday morning after we get the prior week's performance metrics."

"Perfect and well thought out, Don."

"Monthly meetings – maybe 2 hours, updating everyone on the monthly financial performance, and progress on the longer term projects. Maybe something like a discussion of milestones or deliverables on a system implementation."

"Right on so far, Don."

"And based on your suggestion, a quarterly meeting that updates the financial forecast with everyone's input, so that we can realign actions to reach our goals. Maybe 2-3 hours, where each exec confirms that they can meet their promised objectives."

"Doesn't get any better, Don. This may sound like a lot of work, but think about the cascading effect of reconfirming objectives every time you meet with the team. And here's another question that I always like to ask after these routine meetings. 'Is there anything else that we should discuss that will help us run the business better… more successfully?' This really puts every one of them on the spot to reconfirm their goals in general."

"Some might consider that a dirty question – to reconfirm their goal at every meeting. But I do see how that keeps the accountability front and center every day. Yes, I like the approach."

"I'd like to get the executive compensation on the table. Last week we hinted at possible ownership for the team. We haven't talked much about executive compensation, but there are experts around that have a full bag of tricks ranging from phantom stock, to deferred compensation, to insurance with annuity kickers. Some are tax deferred, some taxable, some deductible and some not. I'm not an expert on Executive Compensation, but you may want to have Margaret check with such an expert. The team is fully engaged, and we'll want to keep the fire stoked and burning.

And now, tell me about your next vacation. As I recall, it seems that half your staff has taken a walk on the Camino. Did you pay them bonuses to take the trek?"

During the next hour, they enjoyed trading backpacking stories, hangar flying, sipping Margarita's and celebrating the initial success of the strategic planning.

"So, Don, how would you like to proceed?"

"Joseph, you've given us a mini-MBA. I'm not going to trouble you for weekly and monthly meetings, but would you mind spending some time coaching each team member – and me – for our first quarterly meeting? I think that it would be helpful to keep us on track, and it would pretty much load the responsibility for performance on each executive."

"Sounds good, Don." See you in a few months.

With that, Joseph waved at Janet, and signed the check.

June 22, 2014 – Update: Joseph & Don

Don invited Joseph to the Company headquarters for a tour and brief update of the Company's progress. With a fiscal April 30 year-end, the first quarter disappeared quickly and the second quarter rocketed to a quick start, considering all the process changes and new initiatives.

Joseph immediately identified the thoughtful cosmetic changes in the Company reception area. In addition to the colorful burst of fresh flowers framing the receptionist, new carpeting in muted earth tones complemented the seating area. The clean lines of Scandinavian designed furnishings boasted of efficiency and concern for guest comfort. The ginger toned overstuffed leather couch and chairs, and a work area with a modular teak desk and chair would meet any guest's needs.

Minutes after Joseph introduced himself to the receptionist, Don appeared in the doorway. Don's broad smile and quick steps foretold of good times in the business. "Great to have you join me for the afternoon, Joseph," as Don tightly squeezed Joseph's hand, one hand on Joseph's shoulder. "C'mon into the conference room and let's talk." His pace so quick that Joseph trailed several steps behind.

"So what's going on, Don? I'm not sure that I've seen you this energetic – ever."

"Well, since our last meeting, I decided to take better care of myself...sort of a reincarnation consistent with the business reincarnation. Six days a week at the gym – working out to a plan set up by the personal trainer. Changed my eating habits – I try to avoid too many of those 'heart-stoppers' at the Diner – cutting back on the martini's. Honestly – I haven't felt this good in years.

The business is going well – getting daily reports from Cynthia – she sends them to the rest of the staff as well. Monthly staff meetings – so much better than before. ... Accountability prevails. It was a bit difficult at first. Hey, wait a minute. I'm talking too much. Would you like a soda or juice?" He slid the tray of refreshments toward Joseph.

Don's enthusiasm was so infectious that Joseph declined the soda to allow Don to continue. "Onward, Don. Please continue."

"I can't tell you how different things are now. There is a different energy ... a spring in everyone's step... people are smiling more and things are getting done!"

For the next two hours, Don boasted of increased information visibility and a level of cooperation among the staff that he had never before experienced. The team created a self-check process where each monitored their performance compared to the goals established only 2 months ago. While no projects were yet completed, all were on schedule. The team reviewed a written status of all projects in the monthly meeting.

Monthly financials were expanded far beyond the basic P&L and limited balance sheet information, and each executive responsible for first quarter deliverables provided a brief status report:

Ref	Description	Due Date	Resp	Status 5/31/14	Financial Impact *(000' $)*		Profit Improvement
					Spending		
					Expense	Capital	
1	Define Customer Service success measures that can be used daily/weekly/monthly.	Q1 - 2015	JB	In process... target completion 7/15	0	0	0
2	Establish A-B-C classifications for Actual and Prospective customers.	Q1 - 2015	Stephen	In process - target completion 6/30/14	0	0	0
5	Develop marketing program for freestanding surgical centers.	Q1 - 2015	Stephen	In process - target completion 6/30/14	25		
8	Implement improved periodic reporting (daily; weekly; monthly)	Q1 - 2015	Cynthia	Monthly reports complete 5/31/14; daily/weekly in process - target completion 6/30/14			Potential of Millions of Incrementl Revenue.
9	Implement improved quarterly forecasting process.	Q1 - 2015	Cynthia	In process - target completion 6/30/14			
23	Identify and manage key quality metrics for manufacturing operations.	Q1 - 2015	JB	Templates complete 5/31; live reporting planned for May closing			

"JB slipped a bit when we looked at the quality stats. While the templates were complete, he wasn't able to capture the live data as of month end, before we had our monthly review meeting. He fessed-up and we moved on."

"Did you kill the messenger?"

"Heck no. Look, Joseph, we're in this together. I followed your advice and thanked JB for pointing out the information problem. Hey, let's take a walk around the facility. I'd like the folks to see we care about how they are performing."

As they strolled in quiet discussion to JB's office, Joseph noticed fresh paint throughout the facility. As they entered JB's office, Joseph was startled by the change from his earlier visit. The aroma of a fresh spring rain room freshener replaced the earlier scent of a stale barroom, and the nicotine encrusted ashtrays and air purifiers vanished. JB, dressed in a starched Tattersall cotton shirt and neatly pressed pants, was visibly pounds thinner, and now, as he gazed downward to see his shiny black loafers, they were visible for the first time in years. Without his paunch and smelly Nicaraguans, he almost appeared physically fit.

Shelves previously jammed with dusty manufacturing artifacts were now orderly, and neatly displayed several trophies from earlier triumphs and a limited selection of polished products, each with a display card describing the unit.

"What's up JB?"

JB bounced from his seat with a teenager's energy, hand extended to give a welcome and hearty handshake. "Good to see you Joseph. …Didn't realize you were touring today."

After a few minutes discussing the progress made during the past two months, JB rose and nudged Joseph's elbow and said, "C'mon. Let's take a walk. Don you've seen this before, but the gang likes to see you on the floor."

A quick stroll through the fire doors to the factory, and once again, Joseph was startled. JB immediately donned safety glasses, and offered a pair to Joseph. "… Can't afford to have a work-related accident. As we examined all our expenses and challenged ourselves to be better, we noticed that our Workmen's Compensation premiums were through the roof. When we discovered that a recent inspection flagged our lax safety attitudes, and raised our premiums, we made the change immediately. And yes, we also want to protect our employees from work place risks. We bought quite a few pairs of optically pure safety glasses for those folks that were having trouble viewing tolerances through the less expensive eyewear."

As the tour continued, the change from the previous tour was striking. Joseph noted that the many bins of dusty parts were removed, and shop floor inventory was limited to specially marked trays aligned neatly within floor markings near machine centers. Several of the machine centers seemed to be rearranged to improve workflow, but Joseph couldn't quite identify the changes.

As JB escorted Joseph and Don around the floor, there were whiteboards scattered throughout the factory with production numbers proudly displayed. Joseph probed, "What's up with the whiteboards, JB?"

"Well, I've read a few books about Lean Manufacturing, and decided to make some basic improvements. We're definitely not lean, but cleaning up the floor inventory, and putting up a few visual measures boards is a start. To do this right, we're going to have to spend some money, but I didn't want to wait for a few months. If it's the right thing to do, let's get at it. In the next quarterly review, we're going to schedule out the incremental spending required for Lean."

As the final stop on the tour, JB strolled past the 'spare parts warehouse' previously filled with derelict equipment in various stages of disrepair. "You know, this was a big mess for us. The original problem is that we didn't make this *machine dump* a priority... we needed to disassemble the junk that we had stored here and organize the spares. ... Spent a few bucks on the shelving, and had some university co-ops come in and label, tag and inventory the spares. The rest of the equipment – out the door for scrap."

After some socializing with floor workers and supervisors, the three executives concluded the tour at

389

the office entrance. Joseph tapped JB lightly on the shoulder, "Nice show JB. Keep up the good work."

Don and Joseph adjourned to Don's office.

"Joseph, I can't describe the energy in this facility. It seems that everyone's attitude has moved up a notch. Within the next few months, we will be pushing the culture change – one of accountability and responsibility – down through the organization. You've tipped us that a culture change requires relentless follow-up – with established performance standards and reporting. Without the follow-through, this will just be another flavor of the month, and quite simply, I don't have the time to dilly-dally with a flawed execution.

We're going to do a quarterly review and update the forecast in a few weeks. Will you join us, coach?"

"Sounds good, Don. Any thoughts about the family in the business? Was it Chip and Janelle... and maybe Uncle Robert? As I recall from the strategy session, folks were a bit sensitive about the family disrupting the basic flow of business."

"Yes, Joseph. That has been and is an unresolved problem. To keep peace at home, I've had to shelve any real actions. I've asked the staff to let me know of any disruptions so that I can resolve the conflicts."

"OK – but we both know that if you allow the family to disrupt value added activity, you will be diluting the efforts of the rest of the staff. Said another way, if you tolerate the family's poor performance, why should the unrelated staff bust their butts to get results."

"Yeah, I get it – but I have to live with Janice, and for now, we'll just have to deal with the disruption."

"And succession planning, so that if you were to sell the business…"

"Not ready to discuss that yet, Joseph, but I have some ideas. And – well, I'm not as sensitive as I was a few months ago. Time doesn't stop just because I don't want to discuss a topic."

With that, they deferred to discussing golf and upcoming vacations. The quarterly review meeting was scheduled for August 12.

August 12, 2014 – Quarterly Forecast Review

The team assembled for the forecast review about 20 minutes early. The team, visibly different than at the strategy meeting, resembled a team ready for a national championship contest. While there was some tension in the air, displayed by some nervous fidgeting with files, the upbeat tempo and readiness to share information was conspicuous.

At 8:20, Don invited the team to top-off their coffee, grab a juice and collect their fruit and muffins for a prompt 8:30 start.

Joseph scanned the attendees and noticed the lively attitudes and intermittent smiles. Stephen, as usual, dressed perfectly from the highly polished Ferragamo shoes to the John Varvatos shirt wrapped in a Dolce & Gabbano tie – always ready for a magazine cover photo shoot.

The ladies' look, consistent with earlier appearances, ranged from Margaret's *Nordstrom's finest* to the middle-of-the road business casual worn by Cynthia and Allison.

The most startling change was that of JB's appearance... perhaps 15 pounds lighter, wearing conservative button-down blue oxford shirt, pressed pants, and polished penny loafers.

Don launched the meeting promptly at 8:30, smiling and playing a segment of the theme song from "Top Gun". Self-consciously he admitted, "Allison, your start with the Rocky theme was off the charts. I just couldn't resist. Now let's get on with this."

He clicked the agenda alive on the screen.

8:30	Open	Don
8:45	Financial Results	Cynthia
9:15	Sales Operations	Stephen
9:45	R&D	Allison
10:45	Break	
11:00	Manufacturing/Ops	JB
12:00	Lunch	
1:00	Human Resources	Margaret
1:45	Summary	Don

Don opened the meeting congratulating the team on the quarter's performance. He complimented them on their ability to adapt to the changing culture and the increased accountability, noting that there were some transgressions from expected behavior – a wink and a subtle nod to JB who self-consciously turned his eyes downward.

As the owner, Don also confessed to his delays at resolving executive compensation, family member participation in Jackson, and stock ownership. With renewed commitment, he asked them to hold him personally accountable at the next meeting to demonstrate progress on these most important topics.

Don nervously twirled the marker pen in his hand as he paced floor. He looked each team member in the eye as if he were a lion guarding his cubs and said, "Folks, the past few months have been fantastic. I've seen an incredible commitment by you to improve this business. The results of your efforts – measurable as we will see in the next few hours.

I've thought a lot about the future, and want to share with you that I think we should approach the business as if I were going to sell the Company. I haven't made any such decision yet, but it seems that there is little downside to moving along that path. This Company has great potential, and I recognize your contribution to its success. We need to continue to build our processes, improve the business and make sure that our organization has the capability to succeed without me around. That is why I need to resolve compensation, family distractions, and stock ownership. So, let's get on with the review."

Cynthia took charge and discussed the business using the new financial statements. Her dashboard highlighted all the critical metrics, without infringing on the detailed analysis to be provided by each of the other executives. Throughout the discussion she discussed macro information about performance metrics that could be easily compared to other companies. Her information demonstrated how Jackson differentiates itself from competitors and similar sized companies.

The difference from a mere 10 months ago was inspiring. The Company had moved from an accounting shop to a financially managed, highly competitive business. In addition to the financial review, she updated all about her progress on the strategic objectives, and focused on the Information Technology upgrade.

If the Company expected to be acquired by a strategic buyer, major investment in new data systems would provide little benefit, since a strategic buyer would likely abandon Jackson Manufacturing's system and install the buyer's system. After some spirited debate among the team, they turned like a gun turret on a ship toward Joseph, looking for his advice.

"It's a judgment call, and no matter what you do you will be taking a risk. If you don't upgrade your systems, you will not have adequate information to manage successfully. If you do a major upgrade, you may be spending money that could be better invested in something like new product development or improved manufacturing equipment. Let's spend some time understanding our competitive strengths and weaknesses, and who the potential buyers might be. Once we identify potential buyers, let's rank them from high to low probability, and see what the list looks like. An immediate answer may surface from the initial assessment. If so, that's great. If not, we move into higher risk areas."

Cynthia took responsibility for setting up another meeting to discuss the possibilities, and relinquished the floor to JB.

A trim JB queued the first slide with manufacturing and operations metrics. His dashboard covered everything from customer satisfaction to the ratio of orders shipped complete and on-time. In addition to the non-financial metrics, graphs indicating departmental costs and variances, profit improvement success stories, and inventory turn statistics. He punctuated each segment with a discussion of the business trends and expectations for the next month.

"Don, these are the early metrics that we've identified, and as you know, we have just started to focus on Lean Manufacturing techniques. Lean should improve all our operating metrics, and within 6 months be completely cash flow positive. And while we haven't launched lean officially, we have started to cross-train some of the associates to give them a broader career base. I've been surprised at their enthusiasm. Some have started taking outside training classes. Of course we're paying for the courses, but not their time. Considering the flexibility we gain in manufacturing, I can only wish we had done this years ago. The consultant expects that we can reduce operating cycle times – perhaps by as much as 30% - which would cut inventories – and also give us the resources to expand throughput.

... Quick update on some of the new subassemblies that we've picked up from the majors. J&J recently gave us 3 new components used in their new artificial hip. This should add about $.5 million to sales, and we have no incremental expenses to manufacture the product. All labor and materials are standard issue... just a case of some new designs. The beauty of these additions is no increase in overhead to slide these units into production. After initial startup costs of about $50,000, we'll have a contribution margin from this $500,000 annual volume of more than 60%. Said another way, the Company's pretax earnings will increase by about 10% from this single addition. There will be more to come.

So Allison, how about some new products? Any questions?"

"Thanks JB." Allison distributed some pages to the team. "We'll hold the Rocky theme for today, since I have a lot to cover during the next hour. I've distributed these pages so that you can write notes on them. We'll also look at the pages on the screen. This is an expanded summary of an R&D project plan."

New Product Development

Project Description:

	2014	2015	2016	2017	2018	2019	Terminal Value
Incremental Headcount							
Units Sold							
Comp Units							
Avg Selling Price							
Avg Cost							
000's $							
Sales							
Cost of Sales							
Units							
Comp Units							
Total Cost of Sales							
Gross Profit							
GP%							
SG&A							
Direct Selling							
Base Compensation							
Spifs							
Advertising							
Trade Shows							
Sales Materials							
Research & Development							
Labor							
Overhead							
Materials							
Subcontract							
Other							
Total Research							
Other SG&A							
Total SG&A							
% of Sales							
Contribution Margin							
% of Sales							
Capital Required							
Development Capital							
Production							
Machines							
Tooling							
Other							
Other							
Total Capital							
Cash Flow							

New Product Development

Project Description:

Competitive Conditions:

Marketing Process:

Net Present Value
Internal Rate of Return
Cash Flow Breakeven

	Signed	Date:
Project Champion		
Approved By:		
CFO		
Manufacturing VP		
Marketing VP		
CEO		

"I know that it looks ominous, but after a few minutes, you'll see that I've tried to capture all the criteria we need to make a decision, on a couple of pages."

With that, Allison invited comments, and explained each element of the new product development proposal. Don had seen an earlier draft and liked the detail required before he had to fund a project. In particular, he liked the idea of the executives 'approving' the assumptions.

Cynthia, eyes narrowed consuming each line of the document, jotted some notes on her copy while Allison explained the content. Stephen was pleased with the thought behind the document, and complimented Allison on her thorough analysis. He quipped, "Seems like we will have a steady flow of products coming once we look at the population of what's available. Well done, Allison."

While JB was pleased with the overall summary, especially because it included a section for Machinery & Equipment investment if required, he also said, "I think that we need more information about the product manufacturing cost. I'll get you some notes describing some items."

After 15 minutes, Allison jumped to the next topic. "I'd like to give you a quick update on some of the university research projects." She spent about 15 minutes discussing the various projects that included new metallurgy, dramatic new designs, and the prototype agreements that she is negotiating. "Of course, since these are new products, I'll have a more complete report available for JB, and Stephen to review before we proceed. Don, one last thing... Since we are involved in some unusual legal negotiations, I've been *checking around for an Intellectual Property attorney*. After I discussed the projects with Keith, he recommended that we get a specialist."

Don interrupted. "Say Cynthia, since we're talking about legal, have we done anything about the legal function? Have we changed any processes so that all contracts are reviewed by an attorney – guess I prefer Keith – but what's happening in legal?"

"Great question, Don. I should have mentioned this during the finance review. We've started a project to centralize and review all existing contracts from each functional area. Keith is responsible for maintaining an up-to-date schedule of contract requirements – terms, performance criteria, extensions and modifications. I've also charged him with the personal responsibility for proper legal review. In some ways, I shattered his ego by suggesting that if he didn't have enough expertise to get the job done, he should find someone who could *best* represent us. He was initially angry, but eventually understood that the client interest was most important.

Well, we discovered that we have been operating with several expired contracts, have missed the opportunity in several of our supply contracts to increase price, and we've not complied with terms of several other contracts. Overall, it was a bit of a mess, but in the long run, we'll be better off because of the review. Keith is also the point person for all of us whenever anything *legal* arises. Our initial out-of-pocket will increase, but the investment will reduce our risk."

Don challenged the team, "So if an outsider came in to *audit* our legal process, how would we score?"

Cynthia volunteered, "…a B now, on the way to an A. Don't forget, a few months ago we were at best a C-.

Don was visibly pleased at the progress achieved during the past 10 months. The team has focused on growing the business and cooperating among themselves. Internal energy was now focused outside the Company – customers and vendors - rather than in counterproductive discussions within the Company. Don declared, "Let's break for 20 minutes." He signaled Joseph to join him in his office.

"Any comments Joseph?"

Joseph pulled a sheet with some handwritten notes from his inside jacket pocket. He opened the page, which was folded in quarters. Headings in each quadrant were underlined: "Yesterday; Today; Tomorrow; To Do." Joseph tabulated his ratings while listening to the team discuss their performance.

"Don, you've got a lot to be proud of during the past few months. Up until late last year, you had little concern for tomorrows. Every month you collected a paycheck, you had money left in the bank, and your business was slowly digesting itself. You were somewhat dictatorial – defining business as the current year plus 3-5%.

You swallowed your pride and opened the management process to the team. You discovered aggressive business professionals who were stunted in their imaginations and virtually unable to think creatively given their constraints.

One word, Don – BRAVO!

Today's meeting demonstrated that you are getting ready for a competitive sale process. The team is proactive, focused on critical issues, not wandering around backbiting each other, and they are dealing well with the increased responsibility… maybe even enjoying the change. Given the numbers, you have increased your personal wealth by – what can it be - $3-5 million based on average multiples and the increased earnings? And you really haven't captured all the growth prospects yet. Not a bad year, Don. Definitely not a bad year for you."

Quarterly Forecast Review – 8/26/14

Yesterday

Logistics	C	• Company far too informal
Operations	D+	• Visible measures not available
Sales	C	• No proactive performance
Marketing	C+	• Little executive engagement
Service	C	
Human Resources	C+	• Too much control by owner... not enough management
R&D	C+	
IT	D	
Finance	D+	• IT & Operations desperate need for improvement
Legal	D	

Today

Logistics	C+	• Engaged executives
Operations	C	• Progress in all functions
Sales	B	• Owner adapting to delegation of authority
Marketing	B	
Service	C+	
Human Resources	C+	• Team accepting accountability
R&D	B+	
IT	D+	
Finance	B	
Legal	C	

Tomorrow (within 12 months...)

Logistics	B	• Keep momentum going
Operations	B	• Family matters add risk due to eroding standards
Sales	B+	
Marketing	B+	• Exec compensation & stock ownership = big hole
Service	B	
Human Resources	B	• IT needs help
R&D	B+	
IT	C+	
Finance	B+	
Legal	B	

To Do

- Family in the business needs resolution
- Exec compensation
- Stock ownership
- IT – must invest to anticipate buyer
- Start shopping the business?
- Audited statements

"So let's spend a few minutes on the 'To Do' section of these notes. ... Anything particularly bothersome?"

Don and Joseph continued the discussion for 15 minutes. Joseph probed Don's understanding of the Company's progress by asking questions, since executives that develop their own solutions, implement the solutions.

Joseph posed a final question. "Are you committed to sell the business? If yes, let's put a process in place and get moving. Your value is big this year, when compared to last year, and the value will only increase."

Don gazed at the still water in the pond, the cluster of cattails protecting the surface from the gentle breeze. After only a year, the Company's outlook has changed completely. A year ago, he felt that the Company was reasonably well managed, but with Joseph's independent vision – that of a prospective buyer – Don realized that something was missing. The gap? There was no effective business process that allowed responsibility and authority to be pushed down through the organization.

Don discovered that by pushing responsibility down through the organization, he actually had more control, since his judgment and skill could be multiplied through the team. Cynthia proved her dormant skills by developing reporting that provided the right information to the right people at the right time. While developing standard daily, weekly and monthly reporting would have been anathema a year ago, the reports implemented allowed each member of the team to thrive.

Cynthia's challenge was compounded when the Company completed their *first* year-end audit. While the audit consumed weeks of the finance department resources, the credibility gained related to the Company's potential sale was significant.

Before the culture change, the team itself was being crushed by Don's micromanagement. The creativity and skills in each functional area were stunted by Don's dominance and control. Once unleashed, their creativity expanded the Company's opportunity well beyond that previously seen by Don. Previously he squandered the true value of their technical and managerial skill.

The team used the same process within their organizations… raised the performance bar for their entire staff. By delegating more responsibility down through their organizations, the quality people within the organization rose to the challenge. The best people thrived in the new management paradigm, and improved their career value. Supervisors learned to delegate and effectively manage. Some employees were taking evening training to improve their technical skills and were prepared for increased responsibility.

The Lean Business concept was being adopted – although still in the early stages. The Lean experts described a business that 'could be'… a business that would achieve above average sales growth and profitability. The Company has already seen both sales and profitability growth during the past year, and the strategic plan outlines continued improved performance. A year ago, the Company was a business growing at 3-4% annually, and now they expect to grow at a compounded growth rate of nearly 8% during the strategic planning period. The strategic growth – unimaginable a year ago – was the result of excellent near-term planning. During the past year, the Company opened new markets, added new products, improved return on assets through inventory and accounts receivable controls. Scrap and rework costs – never effectively measured before – are now reduced by hundreds-of-thousands of dollars annually. Manufacturing improvements allowed more throughput with no incremental workforce.

New product development has been a priority, and the development cycle time has been reduced by 40% from historical trends.

Don evaluated his future and understood that without his replacement in place, or nearly so, Company value would be diminished. The entire staff respected Stephen's professionalism, product knowledge and relationships with key customers. Don started to relinquish authority to Stephen, grooming him to be his replacement within a year.

And yes, the family issue was – and is - a difficult one to deal with. But when Don looked out a year or more, he clearly understood that if Chip, Janelle, and Robert weren't contributing meaningfully to the success of the Company, they were diluting the efforts of the key executives. While he had not yet executed his decision, the decision was made. He would give each of them meaningful responsibilities, discuss the need for performance, and within 6 months, review their performance. If they weren't performing at a proper level, they would leave the Company. He explained that it was unfair to Chip, Janelle and Robert to allow their non-competitive performance to continue. If the Company were sold, new owners would not tolerate lax performance, and the family members would be eliminated.

It was best to raise their standard of performance well in advance of any sale to ensure that they understood the requirements of an independent, competitive business.

The employee bonus plan and stock ownership program is ready to roll out, thanks to Margaret's diligent efforts. Before thoroughly discussing ownership and growth with Joseph, Don thought owning 100% of the Company was the best way to proceed. Now, once the plan is implemented, Don will dilute his ownership by 10-15%. He discovered that it is better to have 85% of a $15 million sale value, than 100% of $7 million. There are just so many creative ways to reward and incentivize employees that create wealth for everyone. It is not a zero sum game.

Just then a small flock of geese swooped onto the pond
and landed with a great flutter of wings. The ripples
from their three-point landing rolled quickly across the
surface.

Don extended his hand to Joseph and said, "Thank you,
Joseph. It's been one-helluva year."

July 5, 2015 – Epilogue

The sale transaction was finalized at noon.

The private equity (PE) firm that acquired Jackson Machinery, Inc. was pleased to own a new platform company that would be the basis of their implantable medical device operations. While broad valuations may suggest that they paid a premium for Jackson, the PE firm understood the value of the management processes at the firm. They were impressed with both the product pipeline planned, the established relationships with research universities and development ventures with other for-profit companies. The allocation of manufacturing resources between subassemblies produced for other companies, and the proprietary work for Company devices provided a steady cash flow stream, and opportunity for growth in higher margin proprietary products.

The basic pricing premium for the acquisition did not include the 3-year earn-out expected from the near term, new product pipeline and the European expansion.

The PE firm considered this an ideal platform since they could leverage the executive management team's skills and the business processes already established.

Don received his $15 million… the executive team shared an additional $5 million of proceeds, and the entire team would enjoy the earn-out once the near term strategy was completed.

Don left for a 6-week tour of the Camino de Santiago.

About the Author

Mike Gendron is the founding partner of CFO Insight LLC. He has extensive global experience throughout Europe, Latin America and the Far East at companies ranging in size from public "Business Week's Hottest Growth Companies in America" to billion dollar global organizations. Industry experience includes high-tech electronics, telecom equipment, FDA regulated operations, and industrial instruments. In addition to this book, he has written 4 other books on topics including international business, mergers & acquisitions, and E-business.

During his career, he has been the CFO of global corporations – both public & private - and has extensive executive experience in Fortune 500 corporations. He has led or participated in M&A buy/sell transactions in France, Germany, China,

Mexico, Canada and the US in industries such as high-tech electronics, telecom equipment, FDA regulated industry and industrial instruments.

He frequently speaks and writes about topics such as mergers & acquisitions, strategy, and E-business, and he maintains a website (http://www.cfoinsight.net) dedicated to financial management, and mergers & acquisitions.

In addition to flying high-performance airplanes as an instrument rated pilot, Mike enjoys backpacking, skiing, and golf.

Mike is Vice-chairman of the Management & Entrepreneurship Advisory Board at Xavier University, and a member of numerous private company advisory boards.

Education & Credentials:

BS (Accounting); MBA (Finance)– – Rochester Institute of Technology
Executive Professor – Strategy – 2010: Xavier University
CPA – New York State (Inactive)

www.ingramcontent.com/pod-product-compliance
Lightning Source LLC
Chambersburg PA
CBHW022050210326
41519CB00054B/294